The Nordic States and European Unity

CHRISTINE INGEBRITSEN

CORNELL UNIVERSITY PRESS

Ithaca and London

Publication of this book was made possible, in part, by a grant from the University of Washington.

Frontispiece: Danish agriculture, Finnish forestry, Swedish mining, Icelandic and Norwegian fisheries. Woodcuts in O. Magnus's *Historia* (1555), reprinted in the Nordic Council, *The Source of Liberty: The Nordic Contribution to Europe*, p. 194. Reprinted by permission of Uppsala universitetsbibliotek, Sweden.

Copyright © 1998 by Cornell University

First published 1998 by Cornell University Press

Printed in the United States of America

Library of Congress Cataloging-in-Publication Data

Ingebritsen, Christine.
    The Nordic states and European unity / Christine Ingebritsen.
      p. cm.
    Includes index.
    ISBN 0-8014-3484-X (cloth : alk. paper)
      1. European Union—Scandinavia.   2. Europe—Economic integration.
    I. Title. II. Series.
    HC240.25.S34I54   1998
    337.1'42—dc21   97-48658

Cornell University Press strives to use environmentally responsible suppliers and materials to the fullest extent possible in the publishing of its books. Such materials include vegetable-based, low-VOC inks and acid-free papers that are recycled, totally chlorine-free, or partly composed of nonwood fibers.

Cloth printing   10 9 8 7 6 5 4 3 2 1

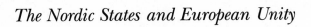

The Nordic States and European Unity

A volume in the series

Cornell Studies in Political Economy

EDITED BY PETER J. KATZENSTEIN

A full list of titles in the series appears at the end of the book.

To my parents,
Karl and Shirley Ingebritsen

Contents

CONTENTS

viii

Preface

This book is about Nordic economic and security policies. How did a group of exceptional states that have been a model to other societies adapt to the rapid and irreversible transformation of international politics between 1985 and 1995? The responses of Nordic governments were novel, and in many ways defied the expectations of experts in international relations and comparative politics. European unity—not the threat of a great power war—has become the foremost concern of these states. Although *all* Nordic governments pursued closer ties with the European Community (EC) after 1985, some faced far more formidable domestic political obstacles than others.

This book contributes to a wider debate on the sources of state capacity. The capacity to resist deepening political cooperation with the EC varies *within* northern Europe, in ways unanticipated by scholars who focus on the position of the state or economy in the international system, or the role of international institutions, or the relative power of labor and business in domestic politics. Instead, the capacity of the state to pursue an integrationist strategy varies according to the political influence of leading sectors. Economic sectors are not uniformly affected by European policy coordination, and the experience of the Nordic states demonstrates these differences. The book shifts the focus away from institutions that are enduring and domestic to an understanding of institutions as sectoral and transnational.

Sweden, Denmark, Norway, Iceland, and Finland have historically resisted the idea of European unity. How are the northern European states, so skeptical in the past, responding to the creation of a regional system of governance? How are these states seeking to protect their borders against new security threats? These questions led me to Europe's northernmost corner for extensive interviews with representatives from the trade unions, government ministries, parliamentary committees, social movements, industry, interest organizations, and the military.

I was guided in collecting data by the "most similar" case design: here was a group of small, export-dependent states, all confronting changes in international politics. Because of the compatibility of Danish, Finnish, Icelandic, Norwegian, and Swedish political systems, the Nordic subregion provides an ideal context for testing alternative hypotheses. I posed similar research questions in each state, and made seven separate visits to the area between 1989 and 1996.

I have discussed the historic and contemporary relationship between each of the Nordic states and the European Community with numerous academic colleagues and policymakers in northern Europe. I have conducted more then one hundred interviews with experts in the five states and maintained contacts with foreign ministry representatives during the EC negotiations. As a recipient of a Norwegian Marshall Fund Grant, I observed Norway's EC referendum in November 1994 and conducted interviews in Oslo before and after the vote.

While in residence at the Norwegian Institute of International Affairs in Oslo (1990–91), I interviewed Johan Jørgen Holst, former defense and foreign minister. Holst was particularly helpful in outlining the history of Norway's relationship to the Atlantic alliance and the reasons why Norway should no longer resist European unity. That interview was critical in developing my understanding of the security situation in the Nordic area, and I am grateful to have had the opportunity to discuss these issues with him.

Ambassador Ulf Dinkelspiel, the chief negotiator for Sweden with the EC, and Lars Nyberg, EC adviser at the Swedish trade union movement (LO), provided detailed information about changes in foreign and economic policies in Sweden. Dinkelspiel documented Sweden's negotiating position in the formation of the EEA (European Economic Area) and as an applicant to the EC. Nyberg offered insights into changes in Swedish policy and the preferences of the trade union movement.

Finnish defense experts Pauli Järvenpää and Tomas Ries described the eastern Nordic response to the post-1989 security environment and the revival of European integration. They provided helpful materials; they referred me to other knowledgeable people; and they introduced me to policy debates published in the Swedo-Finnish language daily *Hufvudstadsbladet.*

The Danish International Studies Program (DIS) and the Center for Security and Disarmament (SNU) provided institutional support during my visit to Copenhagen. At the recommendation of Robert Rinehart, senior foreign policy adviser on Nordic affairs at the U.S. Foreign Service Institute, I contacted foreign policy experts Mary Dau and Svend Aage Christensen, who arranged meetings with prominent Danish policymakers and observers. Anders Urshkov introduced me to the Danish political science community and provided me with an office and computer facilities at the Danish International Studies Program. For this assistance and support I am extremely grateful.

In Iceland, the foreign ministry accommodated many requests for information on government policy. I am also grateful to the embassy in Washington, D.C., for being so forthcoming with documents that outline official policy and Icelandic attitudes toward European integration.

At the University of Washington, visiting Norwegian political scientist Henry Valen was one of the first to weigh in on the manuscript: "Remember geography, Ingebritsen!" were his words. We have continued to discuss the book on subsequent visits to Norway, and I am grateful to him for his input and encouragement. To Joel Migdal, the founder of the International Political Economy Program at the Henry Jackson School of International Studies and my mentor, I owe special thanks.

I also acknowledge a group of scholars who have provided me with helpful advice: James Caporaso, Maria Green Cowles, Eric Einhorn, Miriam Golden, Ron Jepperson, Lauri Karvonen, Peter Katzenstein, Audie Klotz, Stein Kuhnle, Paulette Kurzer, Ulf Lindström, Jonathon Moses, T. J. Pempel, Jonas Pontusson, Bo Rothstein, Herman Schwartz, Michael Shafer, Lars Svåsand, Sidney Tarrow, and John Zysman. I also appreciate helpful insights from discussions with Arne Olav Brundtland, Ulf Dinkelspiel, Jonas Hafstrom, Johan Jørgen Holst, John Keeler, Janne Haaland Matlary, Lars Mjøset, Brent Nelsen, Iver Neumann, Martin Sæter, Sven Steinmo, Bengt Sundelius, Henry Valen, and Wayne Sandholtz. I thank Beate Kohler-Koch, Ulf Sverdrup, and the other participants in the 1996 workshop, Transformation of Governance, at the European Consortium for Political Research (ECPR) in Oslo, for their comments. In the preparation of the appendix, I received assistance from the Delegation of European Communities in Washington, D.C. Many thanks are due Bill Burros and Jonathan Davidson for providing summaries of official documents and references to European publications.

For personal support and encouragement essential to completing the project, I owe special thanks to my colleagues, Ia Dubois, Katherine Hanson, Terje Leiren, Tiina Nunnally and Marianne Stecher-Hansen; to my friend Barbara Lysholt Petersen, who is the director of the Fulbright Exchange Program in Norway; to my parents, Karl and Shirley Ingebritsen; and to my husband, Jim Rogers.

The interviews, research, and writing would not have been possible without generous support from Cornell University's European Studies Center and Peace Research Program, the Fulbright Exchange Program, the Norwegian Marshall Fund, the European Free Trade Area Association Scholarship Fund, the American-Scandinavian Foundation's King Olav Scholarship, and the University of Washington–University of Bergen Exchange Program. Institutional support was also provided by the Henry Jackson School of International Studies, the Department of Scandinavian Studies, and the Center for West European Studies at the University of Washington; the Norwegian Institute of International Affairs in Oslo; the Norwegian Social Science Data Services in Bergen; Denmark's International Studies Program; the Center for Security and Disarmament in Copenhagen; and the Institute for Comparative Politics in Bergen.

For editorial assistance in the final preparation of the manuscript, I owe special thanks to Steven T. Murray, editor of Fjord Press in Seattle.

Several friends provided lodgings during my research visits. Kari and Bill Anderson graciously provided hospitality during my year-long stay in Oslo and fed me numerous fish dinners on subsequent visits. Kjell and Ann Sjöberg welcomed me to their home in suburban Stockholm.

To my other colleagues, friends, and associates in the United States and northern Europe, I express my thanks for all their support, intellectual capital, and enthusiasm. Without you, this book would not have been possible.

CHRISTINE INGEBRITSEN

Seattle, Washington

Abbreviations

CAP	Common Agricultural Policy
CSCE	Conference on Security Cooperation in Europe
EC	European Community
ECU	European Currency Unit
EEA	European Economic Area
EEC	European Economic Community
EFTA	European Free Trade Area
EMS	European Monetary System
EPC	European Political Cooperation
ERM	European Exchange Rate
ERT	European Round Table of Industrialists
EU	European Union
LO	Landsorganisationen, Trade Union Organization
NACC	North Atlantic Cooperation Council
NATO	North Atlantic Treaty Organization
NDU	Nordic Defense Union
NHO	Norwegian Federation of Industries
SAF	Swedish Federation of Industries
SEA	Single European Act
TFCMA	Treaty of Friendship, Cooperation and Mutual Assistance
WEU	Western European Union

PART I

Overview

CHAPTER ONE

The Nordics and European Integration

In a finance bill presented to the Swedish Parliament in 1990, Social Democratic prime minister Ingvar Carlsson indicated that the government intended to join the European Community.[1] This event marked an unprecedented reversal of foreign economic and security policy for northern Europe's model social democracy and neutral power. At a speed uncharacteristic of Swedish politics, the government readily abandoned its cherished principles of freedom from alliances and nationally determined economic policies. Instead, the Swedish government accepted EC-mandated economic reforms and agreed to provisions for security cooperation with EC member states in the Western European Union, both planks that directly contradicted Sweden's long-held policies. A dramatic reversal in foreign policy also occurred in Finland as the government renounced its defense agreement with the Soviet Union and joined the European Community, accepting all of the conditions for economic and political union negotiated by the twelve member states at Maastricht. In ways less surprising than Sweden's and Finland's about-face, the other Nordic states—Norway, Denmark, and Iceland—also took important strides away from their previous paths. Why did the Nordic states change from a shared resistance to

[1] Political and economic cooperation among Western European states has evolved from the original six members of the European Economic Community (EEC) in 1957 to the twelve members of the European Community (EC) in 1990. Since the approval of the Treaty on European Union in November 1993, the European Community has been known as the European Union (EU). I refer to the European Community, or EC, throughout.

European institutions to the pursuit of political cooperation with the European Community?

Among the Nordic states important differences did appear within this general movement toward political cooperation with the EC. The Norwegians have been much more reluctant to abandon national economic policies and Atlanticist security policies. The Conservative-led coalition government resigned in October 1990 when the Center Party contested negotiations to form a limited partnership with the EC, the European Economic Area (EEA).[2] For the second time in twenty-two years, a majority of Norwegians voted against EC membership in a national referendum, forcing the government to withdraw its application. The Danish, Icelandic, and Norwegian governments have been much less willing to relinquish their commitment to the North Atlantic Treaty Organization (NATO), and they view the Western European Union (WEU) as an organization without an adequate security guarantee. In Iceland, the issue of membership in the EC is more controversial than the decision to place a NATO base at Keflavik just after the Second World War. Following a lengthy debate, the Icelandic Parliament approved the EEA agreement by a margin of ten votes in January 1993. In Denmark, the government endorsed the provisions of political and economic union embodied in the Maastricht Treaty, yet on June 2, 1992, the Danish people voted by a narrow margin to reject the treaty.

Why have Norway, Denmark, and Iceland been more resistant to European policy coordination than Sweden and Finland?

NORDIC SIMILARITIES

Located in Europe's northernmost corner, the five Nordic states share common characteristics.[3] The Nordic states have small populations; they are dependent on export trade; and they sustain a relatively high standard of living measured in GDP per capita (Table 1.1). As political systems, all five are parliamentary democracies with strong, centralized interest groups, and labor parties (Social Democrats) are

[2] The European Economic Area was formed in 1994 and extended the EC's internal market to Sweden, Finland, Iceland, Norway, and Austria.

[3] See Arend Lijphart, "Comparative Politics and the Comparative Method," *American Political Science Review* 65 (September 1971), 682–693.

4

Table 1.1. Comparison of economic data: Denmark, Finland, Iceland, Norway, and Sweden

	Denmark	Finland	Iceland	Norway	Sweden
Area (1000 sq. km)	43	338	103	324	450
Population (million)	5.2	5	.26	4.3	8.8
GDP per capita (US$)	28,048	19,174	23,292	28,429	22,499
Currency (per US$)	5.6	5.7	70	7.0	7.7
Exports (%GDP)	35	33	37	43	31

Sources: OECD Economic Surveys, Denmark, Finland, Iceland, Norway and Sweden (1994–95) and *The Nordic Countries in Figures,* 1996, Copenhagen.

prominent in national politics. These states have not only earned a reputation internationally for innovative social welfare systems; they have also charted a distinct path in international relations.

The Nordic states have historically resisted regional political cooperation and were among the last to seek to join the EC. Sweden, Finland, Norway, Denmark, and Iceland were absent at the creation of the Treaty of Rome and eventually joined the European Free Trade Association (EFTA), a more limited trade partnership that was less threatening to national control over policy than EC membership would have been. At the time the European Community was created in the 1950s, and again in the 1970s, Sweden rejected membership precisely because of the supranational ambitions of European political cooperation and the anticipated infringements on national policies.

In formulating security policy, the Nordic states have also sought the greatest possible freedom from supranational authority. Alliance membership became acceptable to Nordic governments as a last resort, when neutrality was no longer a viable option. Even in 1949, Norway, Denmark, and Iceland joined NATO with reservations and sought to retain national priorities within the alliance.[4] During the cold war, security policy considerations prevented Sweden and Finland from applying to join the European Community. After 1985, however, northern European governments became more willing to pursue binding forms of collaboration with the European Community in both economic and security policy matters.

[4] Nordic security analysts refer to Denmark and Norway as the "footnote" members of the Atlantic Alliance.

Explaining Nordic Strategies

Regional integration among European Community member states and the end of the cold war led Nordic governments to pursue a strategy of integration instead of autonomy.[5] Integration occurs when governments perceive that certain economic or security problems cannot be solved by national means alone and they agree to joint policymaking in supranational institutions.[6] Autonomy, on the other hand, is the pursuit of the greatest possible freedom from other states, as a means of resisting dependence.[7] The decision to pursue autonomy or integration is a political strategy, not a property that can be quantified in economic terms. As Mark Zacher points out, "States are concerned about protecting their political autonomy from military incursions, from major economic and social incursions by foreign organizations, and from excessive dependence on foreign states."[8] In contrast to the liberal interdependence literature of the 1970s that predicted the erosion of state control, or sovereignty, my analysis focuses on how and why states willingly transfer political authority to nonstate actors.[9]

Small trading nations never have the luxury of autonomously pursuing policies incompatible with the interests of more powerful states. Indeed, for the Nordic states, economic interdependence is not new, nor have they ever been truly independent of global markets or continental politics.[10] Nordic countries have depended on European trade since the turn of the century, and economic cooperation has been a

---

[5] Autonomy is a core concept in international relations theory. In Kenneth Waltz, *Theory of International Politics* (Reading, Mass.: Addison-Wesley, 1979), the greatest possible freedom from other states is deduced from the structure of the anarchic, self-help system where "states strive to maintain autonomy" (p. 204). For a discussion of important distinctions between neorealist and neoliberal conceptions of state autonomy, see Mark Zacher, *Governing Global Networks* (Cambridge: Cambridge University Press, 1996), pp. 19–24.

[6] Wayne Sandholtz and John Zysman, "1992: Recasting the European Bargain," *World Politics*, 41, no. 1 (October 1989), 98.

[7] Dependence is the "net reliance on others," in James Caporaso, "Dependence, Dependency, and Power in the Global System," *International Organization* 32, no. 1 (1978), 22; and is the polar opposite of independence in James Rosenau, *The Adaptation of Small States* (London: Frances Pinter, 1981), p. 109.

[8] Zacher, *Governing Global Networks*, p. 29.

[9] Janice Thomson refers to state sovereignty as "meta-political authority" in "State Sovereignty in International Relations: Bridging the Gap between Theory and Empirical Research," *International Studies Quarterly* 39 (1995), 214.

[10] Discussions with James Caporaso, International Political Economy Colloquium, University of Washington, 1993–97.

Table 1.2. Economic interdependence: Nordic trade
with the EC as a percentage of total foreign trade

	1960	1970	1980	1990
Sweden				
imports	38	31	50	56
exports	30	26	49	55
Denmark				
imports	58	47	49	52
exports	54	41	51	52
Finland				
imports	52	45	35	46
exports	58	48	40	47

Source: Official Statistics, Sweden (Stockholm, 1991); *Danish Statistical Yearbook* (Copenhagen, 1991); *Economic Survey, Finland* (Helsinki, 1991).
Note: The EC market expanded from six members in 1960 (Germany, France, Italy, Belgium, the Netherlands, and Luxembourg) to nine members in 1980 (Britain, Ireland, and Denmark joined in 1973) and twelve members in 1990 (Greece joined in 1981, Spain and Portugal in 1986).

way of life.[11] Trade with the EC has accounted for approximately 50 percent of the total for Sweden, Denmark, and Finland from the signing of the Treaty of Rome in 1957 to the recent applications for accession in 1990 (Table 1.2). When measured according to the total value of trade, the extent of Nordic reliance on European markets is even more pronounced, as indicated in Table 1.3.

Although the degree of economic interdependence between the Nordic states and the European Community has historically been high, the level of political integration has been remarkably low.[12] Nordic governments long viewed political integration with the European Community and other entangling alliances such as NATO as options of last resort, and instead, these states have maintained the greatest possible distance from supranational forms of cooperation. To trade without

[11] See Ulf Olsson, "The Nordic Countries and Europe in the Twentieth Century," Olsson, "Sweden and Europe in the Twentieth Century: Economics and Politics," Hans Chr. Johansen, "The Danish Economy at the Crossroads between Scandinavia and Europe," and Riita Hjerppe, "Finland's Foreign Trade and Trade Policy in the Twentieth Century," all in *Scandinavian Journal of History* 18, no. 1 (1993).

[12] Denmark joined the EC in 1973, and the other Nordic states signed bilateral trade agreements with the European Free Trade Association as an alternative to EC membership.

Table 1.3. Nordic trade with the European
Community as a proportion of foreign trade, 1990

Country	Trade with the EC (in %)
Norway	66
Sweden	63
Finland	60
Denmark	67
Iceland	60

Source: International Trade Statistics Yearbook (New
York: United Nations, 1994), pp. 764, 991, 350,
275, 470.

entering into binding treaties with other states has been the Nordic
tradition.

Since the mid-1980s, however, the appropriate means of managing
change has shifted from the national level to the European level. The
Nordic states have willingly relinquished control over national policymaking and pursued closer cooperation with the European Community.

A qualitative shift has occurred in the way Nordic governments seek
to provide security and economic welfare for their citizens.[13] From the
1930s to the international oil crisis of the 1970s, Nordic governments
demonstrated considerable success in combining export dependence
and independent national policies.[14] With the increasing mobility of
capital in the 1980s, however, and new challenges to domestic institutions and policies, the period of Nordic exceptionalism has ended.[15]
The Nordic states have sought to negotiate claims on national autonomy at another level of governance: the region. In an age of growing
dissatisfaction with national policy instruments, this type of collaboration has emerged as the appropriate way to cope with change in the
international political economy.[16] As in previous periods of regional in-

[13] Discussions with members of the European Consortium for Political Research group,
"Transformation of Governance in the European Union," conference held in Oslo, Norway, March 28–April 3, 1996.
[14] See Peter J. Katzenstein, Small States in World Markets (Ithaca: Cornell University
Press, 1985).
[15] Ton Notermans, "The Abdication from National Policy Autonomy: Why the Macroeconomic Policy Regime Has Become So Unfavorable to Labor," Politics and Society 21
(June 1993), 133–167; and Jonathon Moses, "Abdication from National Policy Autonomy: What's Left to Leave?" Politics and Society 22 (June 1994), 125–148.
[16] Alan Milward makes a similar point in his discussion of the changing capacity of

tegration, however, societal groups constrain or enable the capacity of Nordic governments to trade national solutions for European collaboration.

This book documents the depth and substance of changes in northern European institutions and policies after the introduction of the Single European Act (SEA) in 1985 and the rapprochement between U.S. and Soviet leaders. Between 1985 and 1995, the Nordic states substantially altered the nature of their collaboration with the European Community. The political process of choosing Europe, aligning with distinct models of European unity, and the domestic political effects of European integration are notably absent from analyses that rely solely on broad changes in capitalism.[17] As in other European states, integration committed Nordic governments to adopt policies that otherwise might not have been chosen and created another form of political commitment outside the state.[18]

What is exceptional about Nordic political integration with the European Community since 1985 is a shift in governance structures. In contrast to the 1970s and early 1980s, European integration did not require Nordic governments to transfer authority or competencies to European Community institutions.[19] Once Europe developed extensive common legal, monetary, and regulatory policies, however, the Nordics were presented with new requirements for membership. By the time northern European governments pursued European integration, fewer decisions were left in the hands of domestic authorities. And none of the five Nordic states was able to resist closer collaboration with the European Community. Even Iceland and Norway, as signatories of the European Economic Area agreement, have been compelled to accept the *aquis communitaire* (the body of EC law and regulations) and have implemented hundreds of changes in national laws and regulations.

---

nation-states in the modern economy. See "The Frontier of National Sovereignty," *The Future of the Nation-State*, ed. Sverker Gustavsson and Leif Lewin (London: Routledge, 1996), pp. 149–167.

[17] I reject the inevitability hypothesis: broad structural changes in capitalism, or in the transition from one metaregime to another, do not compel states to adjust.

[18] David Cameron discusses the effects of European integration on France in "France and European Union: Dilemmas of Integration in the Chirac Era," paper presented at the Conference on French Public Policy, Center for Western European Studies, University of Washington, April 12, 1996. Parallels between the dilemmas facing French and Scandinavian policymakers are more visible in the 1990s than in earlier periods.

[19] Beate Kohler-Koch, "The Strength of Weakness: The Transformation of Governance in the EU," *The Future of the Nation-State*, p. 175.

For a group of states that has been very skeptical about the creation of a regional polity, this shift marks a growing recognition that regions, not states, are the appropriate level of governance.

The shift in government strategies has not been simply a result of broad changes in the world economy, forcing Nordic countries to fall into line. Rather, those forces took effect only when the opening provided by the disintegration of the cold war system of East-West alliances made it possible for neutral states, Finland and Sweden, to conceive of joining the European Community. The traditional obstacle to joining the EC—"What will leaders in Moscow think?"—was no longer significant. The changes in international politics after 1989 inverted the relative importance of defense and economic policy within national polities and enabled the Nordic states to develop their relationship to the European Community.

Even when an opening is achieved, broad systemic changes do not affect all countries similarly. How can we explain Sweden's rapid and surefooted change and Norway's foot-dragging? A sectoral approach will illustrate how and why European integration mattered differently to each of the Nordic states. Sectors, defined as complexes of activities that produce related products, may vary according to organization, techniques of production, and relationship to the state.[20] In northern Europe, particular sectors have an important role in each state's political economy. A leading sector is the largest single contributor to national revenue—for example, manufacturing in Sweden, fishing in Iceland. Secondary sectors may be politically important in ways that defy a strict economic logic.[21] My analysis focuses on the role of leading sectors and the political coalitions that organized for or against accession in each state.

Leading sectors in northern Europe vary: Sweden is a capital-intensive, manufacturing exporter; Denmark, Norway, and Iceland are ex-

[20] See Peter Evans, *Embedded Autonomy: States and Industrial Transformation* (Princeton: Princeton University Press, 1995), pp. 81–82, 259; Philippe Schmitter, "Sectors in Modern Capitalism: Modes of Governance and Variations in Performance," in R. Brunetta and C. Dell'Aringa, eds., *Labor Relations and Economic Performance* (New York: Macmillan Press, 1990); and Michael Shafer, *Winners and Losers: How Sectors Shape the Developmental Prospects of States* (Ithaca: Cornell University Press, 1994).

[21] The political power of agriculture in France is an example of a sector whose role in national politics far exceeds its economic contribution to the finance ministry. See John Keeler, "Agricultural Power in the European Community," *Comparative Politics* 28, no. 2 (January 1996), 127–149.

porters of raw materials. Finland relies on both types of producers in its export structure. In Sweden, manufacturing accounted for 80 percent of total exports of goods and services in 1993.[22] Denmark's leading sector has traditionally been agriculture, although the economy has diversified in recent years. Norway relies heavily on its petroleum industry, while Iceland's economy is dependent on the resources of the sea. In Finland, manufacturing and forestry each accounted for approximately 40 percent of total exports when the state sought to join the EC.[23]

How did these sectors matter in the accession process? These five states have strong, centralized economic interest organizations. Employers, industry, and agriculture are represented nationally and consulted directly in the formation of government policy.[24] Organized interests, however, are not affected equally by European policy coordination, nor do they share the same degree of political influence within the Nordic states. States dependent on manufacturing felt more pressure to join the EC from industrial leaders and trade union officials than did states that export raw materials, because of patterns of foreign direct investment from the Nordic states to the EC after 1985.

The leading sector argument can also explain the structural conditions underlying the policy choices of Nordic governments. Social coalitions prevented Norway from following Great Britain's lead into the EC in the early 1970s. Denmark's entry into the EC was viewed as an economic necessity for the agricultural nation. In Denmark a majority of the public endorsed EC membership in the fall 1972 referendum, while a majority of Norwegians feared the consequences of joining the EC and the government withdrew its application. The Danes anticipated economic benefits because of long-term agricultural trade arrangements with Great Britain and the guarantee to farmers participating in the EC's Common Agricultural Policy (CAP). "When the Danes

[22] Ministry of Industry and Commerce, *Economic Restructuring and Industrial Policy in Sweden* (Stockholm: Norstedts, 1996), p. 12.

[23] Juhani Kuusi, *Invest in Finland* (Helsinki, Finland: Technology Development Center, 1993), p. 1.

[24] See Niels Chr. Sidenius, "Organized Interests, Governance, and the European Union: The Case of Denmark," paper presented in the ECPR workshop "The Transformation of Governance in the European Union," Oslo, March 29–April 3, 1996; Nils Elvander, "Interest Groups in Sweden," *Annals of the American Academy* 413 (1974), 27–43; and James Alt, "Crude Politics: Oil and the Political Economy of Unemployment in Britain and Norway, 1970–1985," mimeo, Harvard University, 1986.

joined the European Community," Eric Einhorn comments, "they did so with their purses—not their hearts."[25]

NEW POLITICAL CHOICES

Between 1985 and 1995, northern European governments confronted two profound changes in international relations: the breakdown of the East-West alliance system and the revival of integration among the twelve member states of the European Community. The international system was no longer defined by a tight bipolar configuration of power between the United States and the Soviet Union, and the United States was no longer capable of acting as a hegemonic stabilizer in the international political economy. The emergence of three regional trading blocs (North America, Asia-Pacific, European Community) and the increase in the number of states with nuclear capabilities are indicators of the transition to a multipolar system. For the northern European states, the growing interdependence of European political economies and the changing distribution of military power required a reassessment of economic and security policies.

The principal military challenge faced by the Nordic states during the cold war period no longer exists. The risk of a great-power war in Europe engaging Nordic territory, airspace, and surrounding seas was the primary threat to security under conditions of bipolarity. One diplomat aptly described the view from Finland: "In the history of our nation we have never felt so at peace with our neighbors."[26] This calm has not, however, led to complacency among Nordic defense planners. Instead, the priorities have shifted from conventional or nuclear threats to soft security threats. Regional security threats have been more broadly defined as nationalist movements which could escalate into armed conflict, terrorism, and threats to the environment. NATO's mission may seem to have been rendered obsolete, but the institution has been remarkably resilient. It has redefined its objectives, and for many Europeans the central pillar of the new European security architecture is still provided by NATO. It is inconceivable for them to give up the Atlantic Alliance when no comparable security institu-

[25] Discussions with Eric Einhorn, at the annual meeting of the Society for the Advancement of Scandinavian Study, Augustana College, Rock Island, Illinois, May 1994.

[26] Briefing by Aapo Polho, deputy chief of mission, Embassy of Finland, at the University of Washington, Seattle, July 31, 1995.

tion exists.[27] The Conference on Security Cooperation in Europe (CSCE), initiated by the Nordic states, has offered an alternative multilateral forum to NATO for conflict resolution. Thus, alternative strategies, such as bandwagoning (a systemic response to conditions of multipolarity in international relations) and the prospect of joining with other European states to forge alliances, evolved into new options as the system's structure changed.[28] Simultaneously, the Europeans decided among themselves to deepen political, economic, and security ties in novel ways.

Institutional and policy innovations in the EC affected Nordic outsiders (European Free Trade Area member states Iceland, Norway, Sweden, and Finland) and Nordic participants (EC member state Denmark). The most profound changes that have occurred within the EC are the extension of the internal market to incorporate new participants, the deepening of integration to include political and monetary union, the expanded decision-making capability of the EC's institutions, and the capacity of an individual state to maintain its own policies within a common legal or regulatory framework. With the adoption of the Single European Act (1987), policy coordination extends to the free movement of capital, goods, services, and persons. The Maastricht Treaty negotiated by the EC twelve is a commitment to the creation of a political and economic union with common foreign, economic, and security policies. Policy areas once considered the domain of national governments have been increasingly viewed as areas of EC competence. As Paul Pierson and Stephan Leibfried argue, "The EC is no longer simply a multilateral instrument, limited in scope and firmly under the control of individual member states. Instead, the EC possesses characteristics of a supranational entity, including extensive bureaucratic competencies, unified judicial control, and significant capacities to develop or modify policies."[29] As an international institution, the EC is an anomaly, with substantial and intricate connections to the domestic political institutions of its member states and with extensive capacities for

---

[27] Emilio Columbo, "European Security at a Time of Radical Change," *NATO Review* 40 (June 1992), 5.

[28] The differences between bandwagoning and balancing in international relations are discussed in Stephen Walt, *The Origin of Alliances* (Ithaca: Cornell University Press, 1987).

[29] Paul Pierson and Stephan Leibfried, "Multitiered Institutions and the Making of Social Policy," in *European Social Policy* (Washington, D.C.: Brookings Institution, 1995), p. 1.

monitoring and enforcement.[30] It was neither predicted nor inevitable that the most skeptical of Europeans would pursue tighter forms of policy coordination with the European Community.

In response to changes in European institutions, all Nordic governments had important political choices before them. As one possible strategy, they could have exported the middle way between capitalism and socialism, or the "security community," by advocating social democratic solutions in European institutions.[31] For example, the inclusion of organized labor in economic planning and the political regulation of capital are legacies of traditional social democratic politics, more solidaristic than the ambitions of the Treaty of Rome. The absence of military rivalries among the Nordic states is another example of political experience that these governments share, consistent with the aims of European economic and political cooperation.

Nordic governments could have restructured economic and security policies to correspond with policies of other European states. Sweden, for example, could have remained outside the European Community and encouraged other Nordic states to do so. Alternatively, Sweden, Finland, Iceland, and Norway could have retained their membership in EFTA and either maintained bilateral free trade agreements or formed a new, expanded trade partnership with the EC. Norway, Denmark, and Iceland could have reevaluated their defense agreements with the United States and pursued cooperation with the European defense pillar (WEU). Sweden and Finland might have opted for a new form of cooperation with NATO or maintained a policy of neutrality and improved the quality of their independent military forces. As the international political system was transformed, northern Europe faced new choices. The European option was not the only one available—nor was it inevitable.

How did these profound changes in international relations play out in the domestic political systems of the North? All Nordic states reassessed their relationship to the European Community. While the controversiality of "project Europe" varied from the most hostile to political integration (Iceland) to the most supportive of political integra-

[30] Miles Kahler, *International Institutions and the Political Economy of Integration* (Washington, D.C.: Brookings Institution, 1995), pp. 86–87.
[31] See Marquis Child, *Sweden: The Middle Way* (New Haven: Yale University Press, 1936). A "security community" is a group of states for whom the prospect of waging war against each other has become unthinkable. See Karl Deutsch et al., *Political Community and the North Atlantic Area* (Princeton: Princeton University Press, 1957).

tion (Finland), the battle lines were drawn between pro- and anti-EC coalitions within each state.

COMPETING CONCEPTIONS OF EUROPE

In 1990, when Swedish Conservative Party leader Carl Bildt warned that "the European train is leaving the station and we're not on it," he expressed the fears of the pro-EC political coalition throughout northern Europe. Across the Nordic states, federations of industry, employers' associations, industries that produced for export markets, urban intellectuals, the young "interrail generation," and leaders of the Conservative and Social Democratic Parties typically endorsed European integration. For these internationalists, rejecting a partnership with Europe risked marginalizing the society and economy from developments on the continent. Many northern Europeans viewed economic growth, employment and education opportunities in the EC, lower prices on consumer goods, and the rationalization of noncompetitive industries as some of the benefits associated with European integration. Security motivations provided a further incentive to cooperate with the EC, it was argued, in order to stabilize the political and military situation in the Baltics and Russia and to facilitate the peaceful transition to democracy in Central Europe.

The pro-EC coalition throughout northern Europe appealed to the rationality of market forces and the desire to reform the welfare state (which, it was widely believed, was too expensive to maintain) and emphasized the importance of having a voice in European institutions in order to affect the direction of political change. In the 1991 national election campaign, the Swedish Social Democrats promoted the image of a Social Democratic Europe where Swedes could enjoy the amenities of Europe and EC member states could learn from the the Swedish model. In a brilliant public-relations move, a restaurant in Gamla Stan (Stockholm's historic district) featured "EG priser" (EC prices) on its menu to give Swedes an indication of how life would improve once they became more continental. The employer's federation, SAF, launched a media campaign with full-page ads in the Swedish daily *Dagens Nyheter*, praising the health of Denmark's economy and attributing it to EC membership. "If Denmark is in, and its economy is performing better than ever, why not join?" Some Finns, when polled about Europe, responded, "Aren't we already in?" The Finns viewed European integration as a means of securing their lengthy border with Russia and reviving the ailing economy. Norwegian prime minister Gro Harlem Brundtland pointed to the risks of higher trade barriers with the EC if Norway remained aloof from European collaboration. She emphasized the positive effects of integration for national welfare, employment, and industry.[32] According to Danish trade union leaders, there was no better way to counter the growing political and economic power of France and Germany than to participate in the creation of common institutions and policies. Even Danish Socialists favored deepening integration as a means of influencing the development of EC social policy.

Anti-EC leader Kristen Nygaard called the Rome Treaty "a threat to the Scandinavian model and the Norwegian way of life."[33] Nygaard expressed the deeply held sentiments of a political coalition that actively resists the European project and seeks to bring back "the good old days" of Social Democratic Scandinavia. The anti-EC coalition in northern Europe has typically comprised residents of rural areas who work in traditional sectors (small farmers, fishermen), religious fundamentalists, urban leftists, older members of each society, workers in industries sheltered from international competition, and those employed in the public sector. Women, to a greater extent than men, have feared the consequences of aligning with European states that lack a commitment to egalitarianism in the workplace and do not share a universal welfare system.[34]

The anti-EC coalition appealed to the ideological legacy of decades of Social Democratic leadership. Skeptical voices warned that markets require regulation, national policies are "better" than what Europe has to offer, jobs will be lost to foreigners, outside investors "just don't understand our way of doing business," and "we will have no influence in a Europe dominated by larger powers." The implications of political

---

[32] See Gro Harlem Brundtland's position on Norway's relationship to the EC, in UD-Informasjon, "EØS-Debatt i Stortinget," December 12, 1990, pp. 44–50.

[33] See *Fakta og Meninger om Norge og EF*, ed. Per Lund, Kristen Nygaard, and Birgit Wiig (Oslo: Hilt and Hansteen, 1989).

[34] In the Nordic states, all citizens are entitled to social welfare benefits. See the Nordic Council, *Social Security in the Nordic Countries: Scope, Expenditure, and Financing* (Copenhagen: 1993); and Jon Eivind Kolberg, ed., *The Study of Welfare Regimes* (Armonk, N.Y.: M. E. Sharpe, 1992).

integration were viewed critically—as sacrificing a particular way of life and affecting "who has the power to make national decisions."[35]

The battle between these two opposing coalitions has waxed and waned in Nordic domestic politics. The debate intensified after the fall 1990 announcement of the Swedish intent to join the EC and was keen throughout 1992 as the Finnish and Norwegian governments sought EC membership, until the referenda were held in the fall of 1994.[36] Public disapproval of European integration increased across the Nordic area following Denmark's rejection of the Maastricht Treaty on June 2, 1992. The skeptics asked, "If Denmark is a member, and *they* have problems with Europe, why should we be more European than the Danes?"[37] Sweden joined the EC by a slim majority; then the tide turned the other way, and public opinion polls registered disillusionment with the European Community. In Icelandic politics, only one major party has endorsed closer ties to the EC, and opposition there remains the strongest in northern Europe. While the people had the opportunity to choose sides in this political debate and to approve or reject the treaty with the European Community, the process of integration has been well under way.[38]

As Nordic societies contemplate their relationship to Europe, the choices have been structured by national governments. That choice is which Europe to join. It is not fruitful to debate whether or not the other northern European states will join the EC. I believe it is only a matter of time. More interesting are the questions that remain. What is being traded off? Why do the leaders feel compelled to make this choice? Who stands to win or to lose in the integration process? What role will these states play in European politics?

[35] See, for example, Center party leader Anne Anger Lahnstein's position in the Norwegian parliamentary debate, UD-Informasjon, "EØS-Debatt i Stortinget," December 12, 1990, pp. 38–43.

[36] See Centre for European Policy Studies, *The Fourth Enlargement: Public Opinion on Membership in the Nordic Candidate Countries*, CEPS Paper No. 56 (Brussels, 1994); Ulf Lindström, "Scandinavia and the European Union: The Referenda in Denmark, Finland, Norway, and Sweden, 1992–94" (Bergen: Institute of Comparative Politics, 1995); and Katherine Moen et al., *The 1994 Nordic Referendums Study* (Trondheim: Department of Sociology and Political Science, 1995).

[37] Interview with representative from the Swedish foreign ministry, Stockholm, fall 1992.

[38] In order to transfer sovereignty to supranational institutions, it is customary in the Nordic states to seek approval from both the national parliament and a majority of voters.

THE BRITISH AND GERMAN MODELS OF EUROPEAN UNITY

The debate in northern Europe identifies competing visions of European unity, alternative conceptions of the relationship to European institutions. The states of the European core also disagree among themselves over the appropriate balance of power between regional and national institutions. The rule guiding decisions about the locus of decision-making is known as the principle of subsidiarity.[39] The British conception of subsidiarity "stops at the borders," whereas the German understanding consistently seeks to deepen and strengthen a multilateral Europe.[40]

Within the European Community, there are varying degrees of commitment to the form and substance of integration. Germany and the Benelux states are the most committed to moving ahead and forging common European policies in areas previously considered the domain of national governments. For these states, policymaking authority should be transferred to European institutions, and national authorities should carry out only what cannot be coordinated at the European level. Improving the efficiency of European Community institutions and moving rapidly ahead to achieve the aims set out by EC members at Maastricht are the ambitions of this group of Europeanists.

Britain and Denmark, and to a lesser extent Italy, Spain, Greece, Portugal, and Ireland, are more resistant to the pace and depth of European unity initiated by the other members. The governments of these states prefer limits on the supranational character of the EC and seek to retain substantial authority for national governments. EC institutions, it is argued, are antidemocratic, and progress toward European unity should proceed at a pace acceptable to *all* member states.

These competing models of European unity differ in three aspects, which are outlined in Table 1.4. Although other visions of European unification have been articulated *within* British and German politics,

[39] The concept of subsidiarity originates in Catholic social doctrine. See William Wallace, *Regional Integration: The West European Experience* (Washington, D.C.: Brookings Institution, 1995), pp. 77–80; and Andrew Duff, John Pinder, and Roy Pryce, *Maastricht and Beyond: Building the European Union* (London: Routledge, 1994), pp. 27–29.
[40] See "A Wider Europe: Britain's Vision," British Information Service, May 6, 1996; Simon Bulmer, "Britain and Germany in the European Union: British Realism and German Institutionalism?" paper presented at the Conference of Europeanists, Chicago, March 14–16, 1996; and Gary Marks, paper presented to the conference "The Challenges of EU Enlargement," Center for European Studies, University of Washington, Seattle, May 10, 1996.

Table 1.4. Models of European unity

	The German Model	The British Model
Attributes	Authority centralized in EC institutions	Authority vested in national institutions
Speed	Rapid (variable geometry)	Slowly (consensus of all)
Motivations	Improve national and EC economies; obtain greater freedom from the United States	Resist subordinating national economy to EC; retain partnership with the United States

the two governments pursue distinct foreign policy strategies, with important consequences.[41] Britain is the most powerful and vocal representative of the slow road to integration, while Germany represents the desire to proceed ahead and institutionalize cooperation at the regional level.

Under the leadership of Chancellor Kohl, Germany has sought to pool its sovereignty and consistently advocated closer economic and political cooperation with the EC.[42] In Britain, the Conservatives have actively resisted the transfer of authority to a European level of governance and have opposed efforts to deepen political integration. In the negotiation of the Maastricht Treaty, Britain received an opt-out on social policy and has actively opposed the efforts of the EC to forge common foreign and monetary policies. Even under Tony Blair's Labor government, the opposition to the EC and the desire for veto power over policies remain strong in Britain.[43]

Britain has been an awkward, semi-detached partner ever since it joined the EC in January 1973.[44] Britain was, after all, the leader of the

[41] See David Cameron, "British Exit, German Voice, French Loyalty: Defection, Domination, and Cooperation in the 1992–93 ERM Crisis," paper prepared for the Project on Transnational Relations, Domestic Structures, and International Institutions presented at Cornell University, Ithaca, November 1992, for a discussion of differences between German and British visions of Europe; and Gunther Hellmann, "Goodbye Bismarck? The Foreign Policy of Contemporary Germany," *Mershon International Studies Review*, 40 (April 1996), 1–39, on differences among German foreign-policy makers on the pursuit of multilateralism.

[42] Pooled sovereignty is a concept from Peter J. Katzenstein, ed., *Tamed Power* (Ithaca: Cornell University Press, 1997).

[43] See Michael Calingaert, *European Integration Revisited* (Boulder: Westview Press, 1996), pp. 102–103, for British resistance to European unity.

[44] See Stephen George, *An Awkward Partner: Britain in the European Community* (Oxford: Oxford University Press, 1990); and Stephen George, ed., *Britain and the European Community: The Politics of Semi-Detachment* (Oxford: Clarendon Press, 1992).

EFTA group, an anti-EC institution which sought an alternative to the supranational ambitions embodied in the Treaty of Rome.[45] Charles de Gaulle's assessment that Britain lacked a "European vocation" seems as relevant in today's Europe as it was in the 1960s.

The British government's response to the transformation of the cold war security system and to the proposals for European-level cooperation in foreign and defense policy has much in common with the reaction of Norway, Denmark, and Iceland. As NATO members, these countries share concerns about giving up a partnership with the United States. British Foreign Secretary Douglas Hurd reminded Parliament that NATO "offers a sure link between Europe and North America. . . . It offers the cheapest insurance policy against the uncertainties and possible turbulence of the 1990s."[46] The Western European Union, or European defense pillar, is not considered a viable alternative to NATO. Critics point to the Gulf War and the crisis in Yugoslavia to argue that Europe lacks the resolve or the military capability to create a common defense program.

Britain's special relationship to the United States and its Atlanticist orientation are impediments to common security policy in Europe. "For the British, any non-NATO defense option is unpalatable."[47] Although Britain has long supported proposals for the integration of political and economic dimensions of security or EPC (European Political Cooperation), this process was never intended to encompass defense policy, which in Britain's view was NATO's responsibility.[48] "All the member states have experienced problems in their transition to multilateral decision-making in an open, interdependent system," Geoffrey Edwards observes. "Britain, in some ways, is no different except insofar as it retains the perspective of an offshore island with a powerful imperial past."[49]

In terms of European monetary cooperation, the British government has become much more hesitant to sacrifice national economic priorities than have other EC member states. Britain was the last to join the Exchange Rate Mechanism (ERM) and the first to exit during the

[45] David Calleo, *Britain's Future* (New York: Horizon Press, 1968); and Mariam Camps, *European Unification in the Sixties: From the Veto to the Crisis* (New York: McGraw-Hill, 1966).

[46] House of Commons, Hansard, February 22, 1990, col. 1094, cited in Dan Keohane, "The Approach of the British Political Parties to a Defence Role for the European Community," *Government and Opposition* 27 (Summer 1992), 303.

[47] Alan W. Cafruny and Glenda G. Rosenthal, eds., *The State of the European Community* (Boulder: Lynne Reinner, 1993), p. 277.

[48] Jonathan Story, *The New Europe* (Oxford: Blackwell, 1993), p. 225.

[49] Quoted in ibid., p. 226.

1992–93 currency crisis.[50] Thus, the British vision of Europe endorses a particular interpretation of the principle of subsidiarity, where supranational activities are restricted.[51] "For London," as Desmond Dinan argues, "subsidiarity was a vital safeguard of national sovereignty and a way to prevent the Community from involving itself unduly in member states' affairs; for Brussels, subsidiarity was a central tenet of Euro-federalism."[52]

The centralization of economic and security policymaking in common European institutions is an alternative vision of Europe promoted by Germany, which is much more willing to embed its political economy and security policy in common European institutions. Since the signing of the Treaty of Rome in 1957, Germany has been described as "the most communitaire of the European countries, receiving markets for its goods and, as a bonus, respectability."[53] While Britain has resisted supranationalism, Germany promotes the strengthening of EC institutions to temper its own power.[54]

The German government and its main opposition party also promoted the creation of common European policies as a means to restore national competitiveness in world markets.[55] For the German Social Democratic Party, "a United States of Europe" with common institutions guarantees peace and economic prosperity to the region. Adopting ideas about distancing Germany and Europe from American hegemony that were prominent in the Social Democratic Party, the CDU, Germany's governing party, pursued a common European security policy after 1986.[56] According to Oskar Lafontaine, "the transfer of state functions to Brussels was to prepare EC members for the future in a world society."[57] While Germany promotes a continuing presence in NATO, the foreign ministry (particularly under Hans Dietrich

[50] The ERM was established in 1979 and consists of parameters for exchange rates and common intervention rules among participating national currencies. For an analysis of Britain's decision to abandon the ERM, see Cameron, "British Exit, German Voice, and French Loyalty."

[51] See Cafruny and Rosenthal, *The State of the European Community*, pp. 23–24; and Desmond Dinan, *Ever Closer Union?* (Boulder: Lynne Reinner, 1994), p. 4.

[52] Dinan, *Ever Closer Union?*, pp. 188–189.

[53] "Germany's Europe," *Economist*, June 11, 1994, p. 45.

[54] Werner Weidenfeld and Josef Janning, eds., *Europe in Global Change: Strategies and Options* (Gutersich: Bertelsmann Foundation Publishers, 1993); and Hellmann, "Goodbye Bismarck?"

[55] Lothar Gutjahr, *German Foreign and Defence Policy after Unification* (London: Pinter, 1994), p. 125.

[56] Ibid., p. 177.

[57] Quoted in ibid., p. 125.

Genscher's leadership) endorsed the Conference on Security Cooperation in Europe, or "CSCE process."[58] The CSCE (or Organization for
Security and Cooperation in Europe, OSCE) combines NATO members, neutral states, and former members of the Warsaw Pact and is
considered by many Europeans to be a more democratic institution
than NATO.

German unification has not altered the commitment of political
leaders to supranationalism. Instead, Helmut Kohl sought to embed a
united Germany into the EC's institutions.[59] As further evidence of Germany's preference to move ahead with European integration plans, in
September 1994 leaders of the CDU put forward a proposal calling for
a two-speed Europe. The idea of "variable geometry," or "European
integration at different speeds," is not new, but previously governments
had agreed to move forward with integration plans at a speed agreed
upon by all member states. The plan envisions a European core (Germany, Belgium, the Netherlands, Luxembourg, and France) that moves
ahead with integration plans at a more rapid pace than do the remaining member states. This risks creating a Europe of first- and second-
class members, according to some critics.[60] Nonetheless, important alternatives coexist as Europe unifies.

These two contradictory visions of European unity are also replicated
in Nordic efforts to integrate economic and security policy after 1985.
When the Nordic nations all pursued closer ties to the European core,
Sweden and Finland followed a German model, while Denmark, Norway, and Iceland aligned more closely with a British model of European unity. Neutral Sweden and Finland no longer confronted a security dilemma by forging an alliance with EC member states. Instead, the
new security threat became the prospect of economic exclusion from
their most important trading partner. Embedding the Finnish and
Swedish political economies within the European project has imposed
necessary liberalizations on each domestic economy, yet it has also provided them with some assurance against economic marginalization and
new security vulnerabilities.

For Norway, Iceland, and Denmark, on the other hand, the centralization of authority in European institutions has transferred too much

[58] Story, *The New Europe*, p. 179.
[59] "Model Vision, A Survey of Germany," *Economist*, May 21, 1994, p. 34.
[60] See Stephen Kinzer, "German Plan for European Union Brings Protests," *New York Times*, September 4, 1994, p. 4.

power away from national governments. Instead, they prefer power to be vested at the state level, with governments determining the appropriate national economic and security policies. This view of federalism was expressed by a representative from Norway's Social Democratic government: "During the negotiations with the EC, we will place decisive emphasis on Norwegian control over the country's natural resources and the formulation of satisfactory arrangements for the primary industries and the rural districts."[61] Consistent with this view, Icelandic political leaders have maintained that they are unable to pursue membership in the EC since it requires the state to abide by the Common Fisheries Agreement and thereby subordinates vital national resources to regulation by supranational authorities. Danes have expressed concern about the "democratic deficit" in European policymaking and won praise from Margaret Thatcher for refusing to approve the Maastricht Treaty.

THE NORDIC MODELS AND EUROPEAN INTEGRATION

Observers of Nordic politics have witnessed a dramatic change in northern Europe as these states accepted the imperatives of the internal market program (the EEA agreement) and, in the case of Sweden, Finland, and Norway, prepared to join the European Community. Despite the claims of northern European diplomats that "we have always been European," this marks a historic moment in Nordic political history. In comparison to other European states, the Nordics have more to give up, they have weaker traditions of multilateralism, and their institutions and ideologies seem incompatible with the EC.

Although Nordic societies have suffered internal crises of economic viability and legitimacy since the 1970s, the process of choosing Europe has meant abandoning some successful practices and programs. In pursuit of regional integration they have also relinquished their role as model societies. The Nordic states have been drawn into European affairs in ways that alter their unique policies and institutions.

The democratization of Eastern Europe, disintegration of the Warsaw Pact, the breakup of the Soviet Union, and the unification of Germany have necessitated a reassessment of standoffish policies held dur-

---

[61] "Norway Applies for EC Membership," *Norinform* 35 (Oslo: Norwegian Information Service), November 10, 1992, p. 1.

ing the cold war period. A. the same time, changes within the EC have created pressures on the governments of these small, open economies to reduce tariffs and other barriers to trade and to reform economic policies to correspond to EC regimes. Nordic leaders preferred the strategy of multilateralism as the system's structure changed.

The willingness of Nordic governments to subordinate national policies to supranational policy regimes is a significant change from their historic role in international relations. In the aftermath of the cold war, the small European states no longer position themselves in relation to East or West but rather in relation to the regional core: the European Community. Yet this shift represents a fundamental redirection in state strategy. As members of EFTA, the Nordic states traditionally objected to the supranational, free market-oriented EC because of the implications for political autonomy. Cold war Nordic defense policies were also designed to preserve state autonomy by limiting involvement in entangling alliances. By combining strategies of reassurance and deterrence, the five Nordic states had sought to reduce conflict between the two alliance blocs. According to the security policy logic of Nordic defense planners, neutral or militarily weak states could be unwillingly drawn into the foreign policy activism of larger powers if they were to agree to join a political union. Iceland maintained the only NATO base in northern Europe yet did not establish an independent military. Norway and Denmark did join NATO, but Nordic security analyst Arne Olav Brundtland calls them "footnote" members because they restricted their participation in NATO activities. Sweden's defense policy, which dates from the Napoleonic wars, combined a national defense force with a policy of avoiding alliance in peacetime in order to remain neutral in times of war. Swedish neutrality, the Finnish policy of neutrality and treaty with the Soviet Union, and Norwegian, Danish, and Icelandic membership in NATO defined the "Nordic balance" between East and West.[62] Northern European governments traditionally maintained that economic and security policies should be determined by national authorities, not by Eurocrats in Brussels.

The redirection in Nordic foreign policy has not only deviated from

[62] Arne Olav Brundtland and Johan Jørgen Holst introduced the concept of the "Nordic balance." The Nordic states have, to a varying degree, been embedded in the Eastern and Western security systems during the cold war period and have sought to adjust the balance according to changes in great power relations. See Arne Olav Brundtland, "The Nordic Balance—Relevant for Europe?" in *Sicherheit durch Gleichgewicht* (Zurich: Schultheiss Polygraphischer Verlag AG, 1982).

the desire to keep critical distance from more powerful European nations, but it also runs counter to the ideological and institutional traditions of northern European social democracy. In northern Europe, the legacy of the trade union movement is visible in legislation, institutions, and traditions. While the relative power of labor in politics varies within the EC, the Nordic states have a longstanding tradition of strong labor parties and active trade unions. The social democratic institutions of the north are a poor fit with the business-led initiatives of the EC's integration project.[63] The EC is a reregulation project, embedding institutional authority in a social partnership in which business enjoys more relative power than labor does. Its economic priorities are distinct from the traditional Nordic pursuit of solidarity, equality, and full employment. When the Swedish government embraced the Maastricht criteria, for example, it sought to adjust the budget deficit to meet the 3 percent of GDP required for monetary union and implemented a new EC menu of austerity solutions.[64]

Few scholars anticipated the national patterns of accession or the speed and depth of the changes in Nordic policies. One prominent Swedish political scientist maintained that the ideological commitment to social democracy and neutrality policy precluded Sweden's entry into the EC. Other analysts predicted that because Sweden was joining the EC, the others would follow suit: "With the Nordic countries [Finland and Sweden] to join, it is hard to imagine Norway failing to follow them."[65] The extent of changes throughout the north and the distinct reception of European integration in domestic politics from Swedo-Finnish acquiescence to Norwegian-Icelandic resistance defied the expectations of many scholars of comparative politics and international relations.

[63] Christine Ingebritsen, "As Europe Changes, Will Scandinavia Remain the Same?" *Scandinavian Studies* 64, no. 4 (1992), 641–651.

[64] Sweden's Social Democratic finance minister Erik Aasbrink announced a more restrictive fiscal policy in April 1996, including spending cuts and increases in taxation in order to meet the imperatives of monetary union (*Economist*, April 20, 1996, p. 44).

[65] Mike Artis and Nick Weaver, "The European Economy," in M. J. Artis and N. Lee, eds., *The Economics of the European Union* (Oxford: Oxford University Press, 1994), p. 52.

CHAPTER TWO

Explaining Policy Choices

From Thucydides' account of the conflict between the city-states of Athens and Sparta to contemporary debates over structure and agency, students of international relations have analyzed the interaction of systemic and domestic politics.[1] The recent history of northern Europe is an excellent opportunity to study how governments respond to international constraints on policy that they have tried hard to resist.

INTERNATIONAL POLITICS

Systemic theorists are better at characterizing macropolitical and economic conditions than they are at differentiating between the relative capacities of small states or explaining why some states in a similar structural configuration of power may choose alternative paths in international relations.[2] Instead, these scholars offer insights and predictions based on general patterns in global politics. State behavior varies according to the particular distribution of capabilities in the system, by

[1] Peter Gourevitch introduced the concept of "the second image reversed," which refers to the constraining effects of the international system on domestic politics, in "The Second Image Reversed: The International Sources of Domestic Politics," *International Organization* 32 (Autumn 1978).

[2] The works of Kenneth Waltz, Robert Keohane, and Immanuel Wallerstein offer three distinct ways of conceiving of the Nordic states in the global political system. The specific characteristics of units are defined by the system itself in Waltz's anarchic market economy of states, while institutions merely condition the behavior of the units in the Keohane conception of international structures. In Wallerstein's world-systems perspective, on the other hand, the internal and external relations of the Nordic states are defined by their semiperipheral position in the international division of labor.

participation in international institutions, or according to the position of the state in the international economy. These systemic theories can account for why it has been so difficult for the Nordic states to resist integration after 1985 yet are insufficient to account for intra-Nordic differences in the politics of accession.

For Kenneth Waltz, the structural setting places constraints on the actions of the state. The strength of Waltz's framework, outlined in *Theory of International Politics*, lies in its parsimonious characterization of the relationship between structure and agent. For example, a bipolar distribution of military power brings greater stability, while multi-polarity is less stable and leads states to bandwagon.[3] Waltz's structural framework captures the external forces of change that drove all Nordic states to align more closely with the European core after 1985. As Robert Powell argues, however, there are limits to Waltz's spare definition of structures. When units in similar systems do not act in similar ways, we have to look elsewhere for the sources of variation.[4]

From another theoretical perspective, the neoliberal account of how international institutions structure the alternatives available to states, we gain an insight into how small states respond to international change.[5] As Robert Keohane argues, international institutions modify the Hobbesian or Darwinian tendencies of the international system. The "stickiness" of institutions can explain why states remain loyal to historic policy choices. Yet if we apply Keohane's approach to northern European politics, some institutions (NATO) appear stickier than others (EFTA). EFTA member states (Finland, Sweden, Norway, Iceland) initially pursued a less binding alliance with Europe—the EEA. By 1990, Sweden and Finland had adjusted their policies to position themselves to join the European Community; yet Norway and Iceland had retained national policies, and societal resistance to the European project had increased. NATO member states (Norway, Iceland, Denmark) held divergent views about the appropriateness of cooperating with the European project in the 1970s yet shared similar views concerning their relationship to the WEU. Although the Danish state has had longer experience in the EC, Sweden and Finland have been more committed to the European project than the Danes have

[3] See Kenneth Waltz, *Theory of International Politics* (New York: Random House, 1979), p. 126.

[4] Robert Powell, "Anarchy in International Relations Theory: The Neorealist-Neoliberal Debate," *International Organization* 48, no. 2 (1994), 317.

[5] Robert Keohane, *After Hegemony* (Princeton: Princeton University Press, 1984).

been.[6] Thus, when and how institutions matter varies in the Nordic context, yet changes within the EC and NATO structure the incentives for or against integration.

An analysis of the system as a whole enables us to see changes in one part of the world as interdependent with other regions. Immanuel Wallerstein describes the capitalist world economy as a hierarchic system in which social class is linked to the position of producers or workers in the international political economy. "Particular regions of the world may change their structural role in the world-economy, to their advantage," Wallerstein says, "even though the disparity of reward between different sectors of the world-economy as a whole may be simultaneously widening."[7] As the core capitalist states integrate, we can predict from the logic of Wallerstein's analysis that the northern European states will be drawn into this process with subsequent changes in the internal balance of social and political classes. Yet just how those changes occur, or why and how Nordic states move from the semi-periphery to the core, requires more intricate knowledge of subsystemic factors.

According to structural theorists (Waltz, Keohane, and Wallerstein), the Nordic states should have relatively few options given their position in the international system. In this situation, however, the commonly held view that the strong do as they wish and the weak do as they must attributes too much weight to systemic forces. Iceland has been the most resistant to joining the European Community; yet as the smallest of the Nordic states, it should have the least freedom from international pressures. Instead, Sweden, the largest and most powerful, has experienced far greater pressure because of the political and economic effects of capital flight.

It is through the insights provided by international structural theorists that we can account for why all Nordic states were compelled, in a parallel manner, to confront the consequences of structural change. Systemic changes in the distribution of capabilities and in the institutions of the European core pulled these states in the same direction; and as predicted by the structural theorists, the Nordic states sought to

[6] When Sweden and Finland joined the European Community on January 1, 1995, they agreed to all the terms for political and economic union outlined in the Maastricht Treaty. Denmark, on the other hand, rejected the conditions outlined at Maastricht and negotiated a separate protocol with the EC.

[7] Immanuel Wallerstein, *The Modern World-System*, vol. 1 (Orlando, Fla.: Academic Press, 1974), p. 350.

bandwagon with the European Community.[8] In the transition from economic interdependence to political integration, however, we have witnessed a more complex pattern of Nordic responses than theories of international politics would suggest. Thus, the specific patterns of Nordic accession and the roles these states will play in European politics remain elusive at the systemic level of analysis.

Comparative Political Economy, Domestic Politics, and Corporatism

Peter Katzenstein encourages theorists to focus on the domestic level of analysis to account for why states pursue distinct strategies in response to international change. Yet many of our previous assumptions about how small corporatist states react to international change are challenged by the responses of Nordic governments between 1985 and 1995. Some of the major theoretical explanations in comparative political economy, domestic politics, and corporatism have difficulty explaining why some states resist European integration and others actively participate. While all Nordic states are compelled to adapt to changes in European politics, they do so in ways contrary to the expectation of theory.

Sweden, the state that traditionally has sought the greatest possible freedom from supranational institutions and seemed to have the most at stake, pursued a more integrationist strategy. According to Gøsta Esping-Andersen's assessment of the relative power of social democracy in *Politics Against Markets,* Sweden should have been the *least* interested in signing on to the neoliberal European project. Esping-Andersen praises the success of Sweden's social democratic movement in implementing parliamentary reforms and in decommodifying labor.[9] In contrast to what we might expect, the Swedes have been more willing to cooperate in the creation of common European institutions and poli-

[8] Stephen Walt relies on the concept of bandwagoning to explain why weaker states enter into binding partnerships with more powerful states: "Only when a state is weak, allies are unavailable, and its leaders believe that potentially threatening states can be successfully appeased—does bandwagoning take place." Walt's approach, relying on power disparities between states, accounts for patterns of alliance formation in international politics. See Stephen Walt, *The Origins of Alliances* (Ithaca: Cornell University Press, 1987).

[9] Gøsta Esping-Andersen, *Politics Against Markets* (Princeton: Princeton University Press, 1985).

cies than have the Norwegians, and they have more readily abandoned social democratic solutions.

Jonas Pontusson's assessment of the relative power of labor and capital in Sweden provides a better predictor of how the Swedish state will respond to the imperative of European integration than does Esping-Andersen's labor power theory.[10] Pontusson documents how the successes of Swedish social democracy depended on cooperation with the business sector. The power of capital and its international orientation are as integral to the Swedish model as the strength and organization of the labor movement. Pontusson joins Peter Swenson in "bringing capital back in" to theoretical discussions of state capacity.[11] Within northern Europe, however, governments face varying types of business pressure, depending on the nature of each state's leading sector.

Scholars who focus on enduring patterns of politics in individual Nordic states often understate or omit the profound effects of systemic change or regional integration on the political economy, and they lose the benefits of comparative analysis. For example, Tim Knudsen provides a rich account of Danish state building to explain why Danes are such ambivalent members of the European Community.[12] Yet for Danes, the accession decision was influenced by the agricultural dependence of the state on the British market. Norway, with even greater distances (geographically and politically) between center and periphery, faced separate market pressures, and European integration has been, and remains, less of an imperative for the political economy.[13] Examining the distinct features of one Nordic state risks the exceptionalism fallacy, where all institutions, policies, and values appear unique.

Comparative political scientists are the micropolitical experts with the tools to account for national differences and relative state capacities. For example, Bo Rothstein argues that the success or failure of

[10] Jonas Pontusson, *The Limits of Social Democracy* (Ithaca: Cornell University Press, 1992).
[11] See Peter Swenson, "Bringing Capital Back In, or Social Democracy Reconsidered: Employer Power, Cross-Class Alliances, and Centralization of Industrial Relations in Denmark and Sweden," *World Politics* 43, no. 4 (1991), 513–545; and Jonas Pontusson and Peter Swenson, "Labor Markets, Production Strategies, and Wage Bargaining Institutions," *Comparative Political Studies* 29 (1996), 223–250.
[12] See Tim Knudsen, "A Portrait of Danish State-Culture: Why Denmark Needs Two National Anthems," in *European Integration and Denmark's Participation,* ed. Morten Kelstrup (Copenhagen: Copenhagen Political Studies, 1992), pp. 262–296.
[13] See, for example, Brent Nelsen, *Norway and the European Community: The Political Economy of Integration* (London: Praeger, 1994).

policy reforms in Sweden depends on the structure of the administrative apparatus responsible for implementation. In a detailed study of policy reform in two agencies with separate institutional structures, Rothstein refines our understanding of the Swedish model and asserts the importance of "underlying power structures" in society.[14] For Rothstein, institutional variance across policy-issue areas is critical to understanding the politics of Swedish reform.

Henry Valen relies on a conflict model developed by Stein Rokkan to account for why EC membership is so problematic for Norway.[15] In his analysis, the controversy over European political cooperation aggravates deep divisions within the society that have existed since the founding of the nation. He maintains that attitudes toward the European Community have remained remarkably stable since 1972, when Norway first rejected membership. In my discussions with Henry Valen, however, he agrees that his analysis is contingent on economic conditions unique to Norway.[16] Oil revenue has enabled the state to support peripheral districts that have the most to lose by joining the EC. As a petrol-subsidized economy, Norway can afford to stay outside the community, in contrast to neighboring Sweden or Finland. In the absence of oil, the capacity of the Norwegian state to resist European integration fundamentally changes.

Theories of corporatism have, until recently, understated the effect of international variables on domestic political structures and processes. As Michael Huelshoff argues, systemic factors such as meeting the expectations and demands of international regimes and responding to the internationalization of markets and capital are treated as exogenous by theories of corporatism. "Beyond responding to domestic interests, states must also respond to other, international interests and expectations, as embodied in international regimes. On the economic side, the internationalization of markets and capital has accelerated over the past few decades. Many industries can no longer be said to be 'national' in orientation."[17] As a consequence of internationaliza-

---

[14] Bo Rothstein, *The Social Democratic State: The Swedish Model and the Bureaucratic Problem of Social Reforms* (Pittsburgh: University of Pittsburgh Press, 1996), p. 5.

[15] Henry Valen, *Konflikt og opinion* (Oslo: NKS, 1995).

[16] Discussion with Henry Valen, University of Bergen, Bergen, Norway, spring 1995.

[17] Michael Huelshoff, "Corporatist Bargaining and International Politics: Regimes, Multinational Corporations, and Adjustment Policy in the Federal Republic of Germany," *Comparative Political Studies* 25 (April 1992), 5.

tion, important changes are occurring in domestic political systems and in the structure of the state.[18]

In Peter Katzenstein's *Small States in World Markets,* small export-dependent states adopt "flexible adjustment strategies" to cope with the forces of internationalization. Internationalization is external to the institutions of "democratic corporatism," and market imperatives are assumed to be uniform. Nevertheless, the differences between Katzenstein's two variants of democratic corporatism become less distinct when capital has greater mobility.[19] As Paulette Kurzer argues in her comparative analysis of the breakdown of corporatism in the smaller European democracies (Belgium, the Netherlands, Austria, and Sweden), European integration fundamentally changes the relationship between corporatist actors in ways unanticipated by Katzenstein.[20] As Kurzer says, "the most persistent dilemma for labor is that increased mobility of capital has also increased the power resources of capital."[21] Her analysis is particularly important for understanding the political economy of integration in Sweden. Capital's relative power changed as Swedish businesses relocated to European markets, thereby altering the very institutions of democratic corporatism. In my analysis, the source of state capacity is less a function of differences among Norwegian, Finnish, Swedish, Icelandic, or Danish corporatism and more a function of each state's dependence on international markets.[22]

---

[18] Herman Schwartz argues that, in response to declining competitiveness in international markets, new domestic political coalitions are reforming the nature of politics and the structure of the state, in "Small States in Big Trouble: State Reorganization in Australia, Denmark, New Zealand and Sweden," *World Politics* 46 (July 1994), 527–555.

[19] Democratic corporatism has two variants in Katzenstein's analysis. Belgium, the Netherlands, and Switzerland conform to the liberal variant of democratic corporatism with strong, centrally organized business interests and weaker labor unions. Norway, Denmark, and Austria conform to the social variant of democratic corporatism, characterized by stronger labor unions and a less centralized business sector. Sweden shares characteristics of social corporatism (strong centralized unions) and liberal corporatism (strong centralized business).

[20] Paulette Kurzer, *Business and Banking: Political Change and Economic Integration in Western Europe* (Ithaca: Cornell University Press, 1993).

[21] Ibid., p. 12.

[22] See Lars Mjøset, ed., *Norden Dagen Derpå* (Oslo: Norwegian University Press, 1986); Lars Mjøset, "Nordic Economic Policies in the 1970s and 1980s," *International Organization* 41, no. 3 (1987), 403–456; Atle Midttun, "Norway in the 1980s: Competitive Adaptation or Structural Crisis? A Comment on Katzenstein's Small-State/Flexible-Adjustment Thesis," *Scandinavian Political Studies* 12 (1989), 307–326; Klaus Nielsen and Ove K. Pedersen, "Is Small Still Flexible? An Evaluation of Recent Trends in Danish Politics," *Scandinavian Political Studies* 12, no. 4 (1989), 343–371.

BRINGING SECTORS BACK IN

Systemic approaches to the study of international politics predict Nordic willingness to bandwagon with emerging power blocs (the EC). Yet when all Nordic governments, no longer bound up in the East-West security system, contemplate European integration, and some choose to do so while others do not, it becomes appropriate to turn to differences in each state's political economy.

The power to resist Europeanization varied *within* northern Europe in ways unanticipated by scholars who focus on the position of the state or economy in the international system, or the role of international institutions, or the relative power of labor and business. Instead, the capacity of the state to pursue an integrationist strategy varied according to the political influence of leading sectors.[23]

The innovation of sectoral analysis is to bring the logic of institutional economics to the political sphere by demonstrating that not all states face similar structural constraints. To account for how and why sectors matter, we need to understand what markets countries participate in and the structure and hierarchy within those markets. Sectoral analysis, when combined with the importance of political variables, can get us where we want to go.

Sectoral analysis has its origins in the study of economic systems. By examining the structure of markets, the work of Ronald Coase and Oliver Williamson reveals political choices.[24] According to the logic of sectoral dependence, the characteristics of industry favor certain groups or classes over others and structure the choices available to actors.[25] By differentiating economic interests within the state, the sectoral approach rejects the conception of nations as unitary, rational actors.

A prominent example of the sectoral approach is found in the work

---

[23] In the literature, the political importance of sectors varies among the position of the sector in the international economy (Kurth, Gourevitch, Ferguson), the institutional relationship between the sector and the state (Katzenstein, Kurzer), and the specific attributes of the export sector (Pontusson, Mjøset, Kitschelt, Shafer). The sectoral approach applied in this analysis combines insights from these three schools.

[24] Ronald Coase, "The Nature of the Firm," *Economica* 4 (1937), 386–405; Oliver Williamson, *Markets and Hierarchies: Analysis and Anti-Trust Implications* (New York: Free Press, 1975); and Oliver Williamson, *The Economic Institutions of Capitalism* (New York: Free Press, 1985).

[25] Bradford Barham, Stephen Bunker, and Denis O'Hearn, eds., *States, Firms and Raw Materials* (Madison: University of Wisconsin Press, 1994), p. 9.

of Bela Belassa. Integration is a process of creating and distorting equilibrium, and every step affects prices, costs, and patterns of resource allocation. As Belassa noted, "the sectoral approach is bound to bring about a conflict between producer and user interests in individual countries. In countries with relatively high production costs, for example, users will welcome integration because of its price-reducing effect; high-cost producers, however, will object to it. Experience suggests that producer interests have greater influence on government decision-making."[26]

James Kurth, Ronald Rogowski, Jeffry Frieden, and Michael Shafer further differentiate the effects of economic dependence on political outcomes in their applications of sectoral analysis. They differentiate the preferences of producers within particular states and reject the notion of a unified rational actor. The sectoral school shares the logic articulated by Frieden: "Government actions are the response of policy makers to sociopolitical pressures brought to bear upon them by interest groups."[27]

When one specifies when and how sectors matter to the state, this relationship of economics to politics is a particularly good fit for the study of export dependent Nordic states confronting a more integrated European market. By combining the insights of these scholars, it is possible to understand why prominent economic interest groups in some Nordic states align in favor of integration, while prominent economic interest groups in other Nordic states fight tooth and nail against integration.

James Kurth applies the logic of sectoral analysis to account for the political tendencies of the textile, steel, and automobile industries in Europe and the United States.[28] In "The Political Consequences of the Product Cycle," Kurth traces the political preferences for free trade or protection of leading industrial sectors.[29] He finds that the timing of the emergence of leading sectors and their position in the interna-

---

[26] Bela Belassa, *The Theory of Economic Integration,* excerpted in Brent Nelsen and Alexander Stubb, *The European Union: Readings on the Theory and Practice of European Integration* (Boulder: Lynne Rienner, 1994), p. 135.

[27] Jeffry Frieden, *Debt, Development and Democracy: Modern Political Economy and Latin America, 1965–1985* (Princeton: Princeton University Press, 1991), pp. 5–6.

[28] Kurth's approach is informed by Barrington Moore's contrast between the economic basis of political development in Britain and Prussia and Alexander Gerschenkron's distinction between early and late industrialization.

[29] James Kurth, "The Political Consequences of the Product Cycle: Industrial History and Political Outcomes," *International Organization* 33 (Winter 1979), 1–34.

tional market created particular types of policies and institutions. The approach is generalizable to northern European political economies, as some leading sectors resist integration while others promote integration.

Another application of sectoral analysis by Ronald Rogowski examines how changes in the international trading system affect the distribution of power among three groups (landowners, capitalists, and labor) within the state.[30] Rogowski demonstrates how state preferences tend to reflect the preferences of those groups that benefit the most from international trade. By disaggregating the state into separate units and acknowledging when and how the relative power of these groups changes, Rogowski advances the sectoral approach by linking changes in international markets with domestic politics. An application of Rogowski's analysis suggests that changes within northern Europe's largest trading partner (the EC) create domestic political cleavages within each state. Thus, sectoral analysis reveals both the domestic political conflicts between societal groups *and* the implications of changes in the European trading regime.

The sectoral approach is distinct from class-based approaches.[31] Politics is primarily competition among various sectors of the economy rather than between members of the capitalist and working classes. As Jeffry Frieden argues, "In the sectoral approach, steelworkers have cross-cutting interests. On the one hand, they are workers, and their interests in the long run are similar to those of other workers. On the other hand, they produce steel, and their interests in the short run are similar to those of managers and shareholders in the steel industry."[32]

One of the innovations of Frieden's analysis is his reliance on a specific-factors model to account for how and why capital mobility affects national politics. In Frieden's view, changes in the international political economy affect producers in specific sectors in a uniform manner, as opposed to groups of workers or capitalists.[33] Frieden's analysis is particularly helpful when we apply the logic of his argument to Euro-

---

[30] Ronald Rogowski, *Commerce and Coalitions* (Princeton: Princeton University Press, 1989).

[31] See also Herbert Kitschelt's work on redefining industrial structures, in "Industrial Governance Structures, Innovation Strategies, and the Case of Japan: Sectoral or Cross-National Comparative Analysis," *International Organization* 45 (Autumn 1991), 453–493.

[32] Jeffry Frieden, "Invested Interests: The Politics of National Economic Policies in a World of Global Finance," *International Organization* 45 (Autumn 1991), 438.

[33] Ibid., p. 436.

35

pean integration and examine the fundamentally different constraints faced by producers in separate markets (from Norwegian oil to Swedish manufacturers) with a high degree of variance in the degree of factor mobility.

In a further elaboration of the sectoral approach, Michael Shafer, in *Winners and Losers,* introduces a theory of economic development contingent on the sectoral dependence of states. Although Shafer seeks to explain restructuring and the capacity of the state to pursue a particular developmental strategy, my analysis focuses on the implementation of European-led reforms and the capacity of the state to pursue an integrationist strategy. Sectoral attributes structure the alternatives available to the state and the relative capacity of the state to implement strategies—whether these are developmental or integrationist.

Where my project differs from Shafer's analysis is in the relationship between sectors and the state. The instrumental logic of reading state preferences based upon the structure of dependence on international markets is not how sectors matter in the Nordic context. The capacity of some sectors to mobilize even when they are less important economically to the state differentiates European states from the developing world. With long traditions of political parties, interest group representation, and social movements, sectors in the Nordic states were important politically *and* economically.

SECTORS AND THE STATE

In Nordic political economies, sectors vary in economic importance to the state, in mobility, and in political representation. Some sectors account for a disproportionate share of export revenue and hold the attention of national finance ministries, regardless of which party is in political power. These economic producers are *leading sectors,* defined as the most important contributors to national wealth. Some economic producers may be more mobile than others and therefore capable of relocating productive activities outside the territorial boundaries of the state. There are separate political consequences for governments depending heavily on manufacturing, in contrast to agriculture, fishing, or the petroleum sectors. In the Nordic states, sectoral preferences are well represented in national politics through the political party system, interest groups, and social movements.

Leading Sectors

Leading sectors are strategically important to the state. Norwegian petroleum and Swedish manufacturing account for such a significant share of gross national product that the preferences of economic producers in these sectors matter.[34] Because of the macroeconomic importance of these sectors, Nordic governments are attentive to the preferences of peak associations representing their interests. As one Swede argues, "if Volvo accounts for 10 percent of your GDP, the preferences of the corporation are not insignificant."[35]

Sector Mobility

Sectors vary in mobility and the power to influence national governments. For example, Sweden's internationally oriented manufacturing sector responded rapidly to the Single European Act and invested heavily in the European market between 1985 and 1990, pressuring the government to adopt a pro-EC policy to stem the tide of foreign direct investment (see Appendix). In Norway, companies threatened to leave, but the effect on the political economy was not as profound as in Sweden.

Political Representation

Economic producers are represented in political parties, interest groups, and social movements. The export-oriented businesses typically support parties to the right of center, and domestic industries tend to favor center/left parties. Farmers typically support the Center Party, which was founded to represent agricultural producers in national politics.

In northern European political systems, economic interest organizations are the insiders in the formation of government policy.[36] Through participation in interest organizations, representatives of sectors are in-

[34] Crude petroleum, for example (80 percent oil, 20 percent natural gas), accounted for 42 percent of Norway's merchandise exports in 1991, and Swedish machinery accounted for 29 percent of total exports in the same year.
[35] Author's interview with a representative from Sweden's Export Council, Stockholm, 1990.
[36] See Jacob Buksti and Lars Norby Johansen, "Variations in Organizational Participation in Government," *Scandinavian Political Studies* 2, no. 3 (1979), 208.

volved in the formation of policy.[37] Enduring patterns of politics such as the Nordic remiss system (invitations by the government to the interest organizations to submit their position on legislation at the proposal stage) frame the way in which sectoral interests can interact with the state.[38] In economic policy formation, interest groups are regularly consulted, as in the negotiations to create a new free trade area between the six members of EFTA and the twelve members of the EC.

In the EFTA-EC negotiations, a small group of officials from the government ministries was responsible for submitting guidelines for policy coordination. This group reported directly to the Parliament. Access to the decision-making process was informal and behind the scenes. In Sweden, an advisory committee on the EC was formed that included the prime minister and representatives from industry, trade unions, the central bank, and the ministries. In Norway, a similar advisory committee for European matters was composed of the prime minister; the ministers of foreign affairs and of trade and shipping; as well as representatives from industry and services, agriculture, fisheries, and trade unions.[39] In Denmark, interest organizations met formally and informally with representatives of the Folketing's EC market committee and with government officials.

Some interest groups representing particular sectors of the economy participate in social movements to promote or protest government cooperation with the EC. In 1991, the Norwegian coastal fisheries union organized a blockade of the Oslo harbor to protest the Social Democratic government's negotiating position with the EC. Prime Minister Gro Harlem Brundtland confronted anti-EC agricultural interests, dressing in national costumes and waving Norwegian flags imprinted with the word "no" when she toured the country in 1992. In Sweden, a "Yes to Europe" organization funded by the Conservative Party and endorsed by business interests launched a high-visibility campaign to inform the public about the benefits of European integration. The politi-

---

[37] See Bo Strath's study of the role of Nordic federations of industry and the failure of the Nordic customs union, *Nordic Industry and Nordic Economic Cooperation* (Stockholm: Almqvist and Wiksell, 1978).

[38] See Robert Kvavik, "Interest Groups in a Cooptative Political System: The Case of Norway," in *Politics in Europe: Structures and Processes in Some Postindustrialized Societies,* ed. Martin Heisler (New York: McKay, 1974), pp. 93–116.

[39] See *Trade Policy Review: Norway* (Geneva: GATT, December 1991), p. 41.

cal influence of sectors in the accession debates will be discussed at length in Chapter 6.

Some sectors are not as essential to the economy yet enjoy a privileged position in domestic politics. By allying with social movements, cultivating close ties to political parties, or including themselves in decision-making as an interest group, some sectors have considerably more influence than a reading of national preferences from the nature of leading sectors would suggest.[40] Sectors vary in the capacity to influence the state depending on strategic importance, mobility, and political representation.

The strength of sectoral analysis lies in the implicit interaction of both the domestic and international polity. The small Nordic states are particularly appropriate for the application of sectoral analysis because of their high degree of dependence on a limited number of exports. For their economic survival, small states depend on economic openness and foreign trade. Sectoral analysis can also enhance our understanding of how and why European integration is more problematic for some states than others.

EUROPEAN INTEGRATION THEORY AND SECTORAL ANALYSIS

The sectoral approach is particularly well suited to the study of European integration. European integration has proceeded according to a sectoral logic—from coal and steel to agriculture, capital, goods, and services. European policy regimes may reward some sectoral participants and impose costs on others. A small fisherman may be threatened by the greater competition required by the terms of the EC's Common Fisheries Policy; an export-oriented fish farmer may favor European integration in order to have greater access to the European market; a small farmer may be threatened by the loss of subsidies associated with liberalizing national agricultural policies to the EC's agricultural policy regime; a large farmer may anticipate benefits from the CAP; a multinational firm producing manufactured goods may prefer to operate within the EC's territorial boundaries; and an energy-

[40] John Keeler has shown how agriculture is overrepresented in French politics, even though the relative economic importance of farming has declined. See "Agricultural Power in the European Community: Explaining the Fate of CAP and GATT Negotiations," *Comparative Politics* 28 (January 1996), 127–149.

producing company may "free ride" on the absence of barriers to the European energy market. Depending on whether a particular producer anticipates costs or benefits from European integration, preferences are relational.[41] In small export-dependent states, governments typically defend leading sectors in foreign economic policy. For example, when a state enters the EC, it usually requests exemptions or special treatment for particular sectors of the economy.

Two prominent approaches to the study of European integration (neofunctionalism and intergovernmentalism) offer alternative ways of analyzing Nordic accession. Ernst Haas offers a neofunctionalist explanation for how and why states willingly give up national sovereignty to a regional entity relying on the concept of spillover.[42] As Haas argues, national leaders seek transnational cooperation in order to obtain common objectives.[43] Precisely because integration in one policy area leads to further integration in another, his analysis suggests that the Nordics should have difficulty resisting the pull of Europe. The shift from national policymaking to supranational policymaking, however, has been much more contested in the Nordic states than neofunctionalist integration theory would suggest. Haas's approach has difficulty explaining why the Nordics waited so long to join the European Community and why some states staunchly refuse to join.

The most compelling argument for the deepening of European cooperation in the mid-1980s is made by Andrew Moravcsik, who offers an explanation relying on intergovernmental bargaining and a state-centered account of how integration deepens.[44] His approach attributes state behavior to the pursuit of the national interest.[45] If we apply the logic of Moravcsik's analysis to the Nordic states, we interpret accession

[41] The conception of interests as relational is derived from Isaac Balbus, "The Concept of Interest in Pluralist and Marxian Analysis," *Politics and Society* 1 (February 1971), 151–177.

[42] For an excellent analysis of neofunctionalism and the importance of the concept of spillover (one area of policy coordination automatically leading to another), see James Caporaso and John Keeler, "The European Union and Regional Integration Theory," in *The State of the European Union: Building a European Polity?* vol. 3, ed. Carolyn Rhodes and Sonia Mazey (Boulder: Lynne Rienner/Longman, 1995).

[43] See Ernst Haas, *The Uniting of Europe* (Stanford: Stanford University Press, 1958); and Ernst Haas, *Beyond the Nation State* (Stanford: Stanford University Press, 1964).

[44] See, for example, Andrew Moravcsik, "Preferences and Power in the European Community: A Liberal Intergovernmentalist Approach," *Journal of Common Market Studies* 31 (December 1993), 473–524.

[45] See Andrew Moravcsik, "Negotiating the Single European Act: National Interests and Conventional Statecraft in the European Community," *International Organization* 45 (Winter 1991), 19–56.

as an interactive process of national governments pursuing their interests. The intergovernmentalist approach rejects the inevitability of integration posited by earlier waves of theorizing and seeks to explain choices from the perspective of national governments responding to international or externally driven change.

Moravcsik's approach, however, assumes that the national interest can be determined exogenously according to the position of states in the international system. Differentiating between interests of the Nordic states and tracing where interests come from become problematic for the intergovernmentalist approach. My analysis modifies the intergovernmental approach and concurs with those theorists who view preferences as endogenous.[46] When cold war security concerns no longer divided northern Europe between East and West, the national interest was redefined. Yet this process was political: governments confronted different political coalitions within each state—some favoring European accession, and others opposed.

Intergovernmentalists miss important variations in the political influence of societal actors, as Maria Green Cowles argues. Some economic groups have more political power than others in the European integration process. For example, a well-coordinated group of business leaders organized by Swedish industrialist Pehr Gyllenhammar formed the European Roundtable of Industrialists (ERT) and independently mobilized support for the Single European Act (SEA) at the EC level and within European states.[47] Cowles's analysis challenges the intergovernmentalist approach to European integration and emphasizes the role of nonstate actors in the implementation of the Single European Act. She reveals how manufacturers are better able to mobilize outside the state than other actors are.

Thus, in order to understand Nordic state preferences in European politics, we need to know more about which economic interests are expected to win and which economic groups are expected to lose in the EC. Interests were contested by societal groups with different stakes in the process. In European politics, some policy regimes impose greater transaction costs than others.

---

[46] See, for example, Wayne Sandholtz, "Choosing Union: Monetary Politics and Maastricht," *International Organization* 47 (Winter 1993), 1–39.

[47] Maria Green Cowles, "Setting the Agenda for a New Europe: The ERT and EC, 1992," *Journal of Common Market Studies* 33 (December 1995), 501–526.

ALTERNATIVE EXPLANATIONS:
CONSTRUCTIVISTS AND ECONOMISTS

A rival approach in international relations theory is an emerging
school of constructivism.[48] These scholars discuss the boundaries of
community and analyze why some states are European and others are
not.[49] Among the scholars examining how ideas are constructed and
national identities are defined (and redefined) in European politics
are two prominent Nordic scholars, Iver Neumann and Ole Wæver.[50]
By interpreting how the idea of Europe takes hold and the nature and
substance of the discourse about European integration, these scholars
offer a promising alternative to interest-centered approaches to international relations. From this perspective, how the Swedes constructed
their image of Europe and how that differed from the Norwegian, Danish, Finnish, and Icelandic idea of "the other" is critical to understanding the Nordic accession process.

The strength of the constructivist framework lies in rich, detailed
accounts of identity formation and change. As Nordic governments
pursued closer cooperation with the EC, citizens expressed grave concerns about how to retain national languages, cultural traditions, and
policies. "Won't the intensified communication present new and dan-
gerous ideas to us? Un-Danish, un-Swedish, or particularly un-Nor-
wegian ideas! Can we preserve our languages, each of which is spoken
by four to eight million people? Will our children begin to see German
or French television instead of Danish? . . . Will Danish women be
chased back to the kitchens? Can the social welfare state survive?"[51]
These questions were a part of the domestic discourse over EC accession but were not uniformly heard by Nordic governments.

How and why certain ideas take hold and which groups within each

---

[48] See Audie Klotz, *Norms in International Relations* (Ithaca: Cornell University Press,
1995).

[49] Identity is relational and is a process of defining boundaries between self and other.
Defining where the European Community begins and ends is a process of identity formation.

[50] See Iver Neumann, *Russia and the Idea of Europe* (London: Routledge, 1996); Iver
Neumann, "The Forging of European Identity: EU Expansion and the Integration/Ex-
clusion Nexus," paper presented to the International Political Economy Colloquium,
University of Washington, Seattle, April 15, 1996; and Ole Wæver, Ulla Holm, and
Henrik Larsen, *The Struggle for Europe: French and German Concepts of State, Nation and
European Union* (Cambridge: Cambridge University Press, 1997).

[51] Bent Rold Andersen, "The Nordic Welfare State under Pressure: The Danish Experience," *Policy and Politics* 21, no. 2 (1993), 114.

state have political influence are outside the scope of the constructi-vist's narrative, descriptive approach to international relations. In my view, the political influence of leading sectors (Norwegian oil, Swedish manufacturing, Finnish manufacturing and forestry, Danish agriculture and industry, and Icelandic fisheries) is a systematic way to understand the politics (and economics) underlying the discourse about European integration. My analysis reveals how constructions of Europe in na-tional politics are more favorable in those states where leading eco-nomic sectors anticipate benefits accruing from closer political cooper-ation with the European Community. Nordic constructions of the EC are not just a discourse but also reflect the preferences of prominent, well-organized groups within each society. European unity is not just an idea, but it has political and economic consequences for societies.

Another alternative to the sectoral approach focuses on broad changes in economic conditions that pull some states into Europe, while others remain more aloof. Since the Swedish economy was suffering a serious downturn in 1994, with a public deficit of approximately 12 percent of GDP and unemployment at 13 percent, it could be argued that Swedes felt compelled to join the EC for economic reasons. Norwegians, on the other hand, had a much more favorable economic situation in 1994 and decided not to join the EC. Although the economic crisis in Sweden made EC membership more attractive, it did not determine the political outcome. Entry into the EC had to be negotiated by politi-cal actors, who at each stage of the negotiations had to engage the particular concerns of societal groups affected by the integration pro-cess. The accession process was not merely an optimizing choice based on a rational assessment of costs and benefits but a domestic battle within each state over political cooperation with the EC. Changing eco-nomic conditions made the European option more attractive for a group of states that have historically been better off than the rest of Europe. European integration was a political choice, however, affected by the profound changes in international security and the depth of European policy coordination.

Economists isolate the costs and benefits of integration but often give too little attention to the political dimension. For economists, en-try into the EC was logical for *all* of the Nordic states to improve com-petitiveness, profits, and the overall health of national economies: "In-dustrial firms in Norway, Finland, or Sweden have their major markets and major competitors in the (expanded) EC. They need to be able to compete on equal terms in that area."[52] The transformation of the cold war system of military blocs, however, created possibilities for Sweden and Finland that were inconceivable: the prospect of joining a bloc of predominantly NATO member states. Nor did industry play a similar role in each of the Nordic states. Corporate Sweden had much more influence in pressuring the government toward its desired outcome; and as in Finland, industrialists were important actors in the domestic accession debates. In Norway, on the other hand, the government favored accession yet confronted a well-organized, anti-EC coalition of fishermen and farmers that sought to block Norwegian entry into the EC. Thus, the push and pull of European integration was distinct for each of the Nordic states, and my task is to spell out how, when, and why those differences became politicized within each state.

Constructivists portray Nordic integration with the EC as an impressionistic, subjective process of changing identities. Economists focus on macroeconomic conditions as a predictor of accession and obscure the intense political struggles that raged within each state as some societal groups pushed for accession and others actively resisted. Neither the combined Nordic pursuit of political integration nor the divergent roles these governments will play in European politics can be captured by relying on these two alternative approaches.

WHEN SECTORS MATTER

In an effort to address what some scholars refer to as the absence of politics in sectoral analysis, the sectoral approach applied in this book offers two important qualifications.[53] First, sectors do not always define the choices available to the state. Security interests may override the political and economic influence of sectors. When security imperatives prevail, states may resist integration with the European core, and no amount of sectoral pressure will convince state authorities to trade off autonomy for integration. Second, sectors are caught in a two-level game because by their very nature they bridge the international and domestic political spheres. In each state, economic sectors define their interests in relation to European policy regimes. The process is politi-

[52] Per Magnus Wijkman, "To Be or Not to Be a Member," working paper no. 8 (Stockholm: Industriförbundet, 1995), p. 9.
[53] Discussions with Michael Shafer, University of Washington, Seattle, 1995.

cal and depends on who is expected to win or lose in the integration process, in contrast to an optimal economic choice made by a rational, unitary actor. While parsimony may be sacrificed in an effort to trace the interaction of sectors and the capacity of the state to act, it is possible to predict, based on a comparative analysis of differences in sectoral dependence, that some states will face greater societal resistance to European integration than others will.

As Chapter 6 demonstrates, politically influential and economically important manufacturers in Sweden exerted pressure on the government to pursue accession. In Norway, on the other hand, the leading sector (petroleum producers) was not compelled to deepen integration. Other sectors actively resisted integration (agriculture and fisheries) and put the government on the defensive from the beginning of the EC campaign. Farmers in Norway view the Common Agricultural Policy as a threat to lavish subsidies that exceed the EC average, and one of Norway's three most important political parties (the Center Party) vehemently defends the interests of farmers in the Norwegian Parliament. Iceland, where fishing *is* the national interest, has viewed the European fishing regime as a liberal market regime promoting competitive market forces as opposed to social regulation. Iceland remains protective of its vital national resource and is likely to be the last of the Nordic states to join the EC. My comparison reveals how economic sectors in northern Europe become politically important in the integration process once international security threats are no longer the primary concern of states. Thus, understanding the relevance of security policy considerations in foreign economic policymaking is also important to this analysis.

In international relations, security and political economy are frequently treated as separate spheres of study.[54] Because of the development of the field, theorists often analyze either the military balance or the dynamics of international trade. I examine the combined effects of changes in the balance of power and the regionalization of trade on a particular group of states. In the process of adjusting to international political and economic change, northern European states confronted a "crisis" where "system creating choices are made."[55] Not since the 1930s

[54] See James Caporaso, "False Divisions: Security Studies and Global Political Economy," *Mershon International Studies Review* 39 (April 1995), 117–122.
[55] Systemic change reveals the importance of competing societal interests as argued by Peter Gourevitch, *Politics in Hard Times* (Ithaca: Cornell University Press, 1985).

45

have these states faced a simultaneous transformation of the security and economic system. To account for variation in Nordic responses to international political change, this book offers an explanation that combines systemic and domestic-level attributes and relaxes traditional borders between the study of international security and political economy.

The subsequent chapters go beyond mere assertions of a transformation in Nordic politics to provide evidence of how and why these changes have occurred. Nordic governments have collectively adopted a regional strategy to cope with the inability to resolve problems at home through reliance on traditional policy instruments, which marks a sharp redirection from earlier periods of European integration. By joining the EC, Nordic governments have begun a process of Europeanization that is difficult, if not impossible, to reverse.[56] The change reflects the inability of northern European states to resist the web of European integration; and in contrast to the 1970s, it is no longer possible to sign a free-trade agreement and retain independent policies. My analysis demonstrates the Nordic evolution from an era of economic interdependence to an era of political integration.

While systemic changes initiated the process of political change, Nordic governments differed in how they responded to the idea of European unity. These differences reflect core divisions within the European Community itself over how to reconcile national and supranational competencies.

Nordic political choices in the 1990s will affect the distinctiveness of this subregion and influence the development of common European economic and security policies. As these policies change, some of the innovations of Nordic social democracy are lost. Thus, the decision to participate in the European project is distinct from what Peter Katzenstein refers to as a "flexible adjustment strategy" that is intended to meet the challenges of the world economy yet leaves the domestic polity unscathed.[57] It is also a decision about the future of politics and state-society relations in the Nordic states. As Ulf Lindström argues, in

[56] Christine Ingebritsen, "Pulling in Different Directions: The Europeanization of Scandinavian Political Economies," paper presented to the American Political Science Association, Chicago, September 1995, and revised for publication in Peter J. Katzenstein, *Tamed Power* (1997).

[57] The "flexible adjustment strategies" of small European states is a concept developed by Peter J. Katzenstein in *Small States in World Markets* (Ithaca: Cornell University Press, 1985).

a Europe where business is free to establish itself in any market yet politics is restricted by national borders, Nordic social democracy is left to preside over its own sunset years.[58]

International market forces and changes in the balance of power have led all five of the Nordic states to redefine their relationship to the European center or risk missing out on the most important revolution of our time. For some Nordic states more than others, there was more to be gained in creating a unified Europe. The alternative visions of Europe represented in Nordic responses to international change will, in turn, affect the political coalitions within the EC in the years to come. For all Nordic states, the stakes of giving up national policies and accepting European collaboration are high. Once Nordic governments trade off national governance for political integration, their role in international politics fundamentally changes, with important implications for how we study northern European political systems and how Nordic citizens view their relationship to the rest of Europe.

[58] Ulf Lindström, *Euro-Consent, Euro-Contract, or Euro-Coercion? Scandinavian Social Democracy, the European Impasse, and the Abolition of Things Political* (Oslo: Scandinavian University Press, 1993), p. 12.

PART II

Changes in the Nordic Models

CHAPTER THREE

What's at Stake?

European integration is unraveling the very policies and institutions that have made the Nordic area the focus of study for generations of comparative politics and international relations scholars. By internalizing EC norms and conforming to another level of governance, these states are abandoning the Nordic model of political and economic relations and the Nordic balance of security relations between East and West. As Nordic governments trade membership in EFTA for membership in the EC, they also diminish their unique role in international relations.[1] As Nordic societies embrace integration, they lose their identity as a group of nations that has defined itself as distinct, and better off than the rest of Europe.[2]

This chapter specifies the consequences of European integration for two Nordic models: the distinctive economic and security policies adopted during the cold war period. What is at stake as Nordic governments accept European integration is much more than merely a redirection of foreign policy. In the words of Lars Lundberg, "transforming a [Nordic] welfare state into a low-tax, low-cost society with higher income inequality and a much smaller public sector means transforming the fabric of society—not just the social policy sector."[3] In order to

[1] Sweden has been viewed as a model of organized capitalism. See, for example, Robert Isaak, *Managing World Economic Change: International Political Economy* (Englewood Cliffs, N.J.: Prentice Hall, 1995), p. 309; and Olof Petersson, *Swedish Government and Politics* (Stockholm: Fritzes, 1994), pp. 34–43.

[2] See Ole Wæver, "Nordic Nostalgia: Northern Europe after the Cold War," *International Affairs* 68 (January 1992), 77–102.

[3] Lars Lundberg, "Nordic Industry and the EEC Internal Market," in *The Nordic Coun-*

have access to the internal market program, Nordic governments accepted a normative change in national policies by trading social democratic policy regimes for EC policy regimes.[4] By signing the EEA agreement, Nordic governments agreed to "regulation without representation" and have accepted numerous rules and technical standards determined outside their national borders.[5] To have a voice in European institutions, Nordic governments have given up policies central to the egalitarian model of economic development and policies central to maintaining the greatest possible freedom from entangling alliances. In doing so, Nordic governments can play a new kind of politics, justifying reforms in domestic institutions and policies necessitated by cooperation with the EC.

Why do *all* Nordic states abandon economic interdependence for political integration, when the costs of European policy coordination are so high? The Nordic states have more to lose than any other group of states that have sought membership in the EC. European integration alters the social relations in these countries, has longlasting affects on the balance of state-society relations, and diminishes the capacity of the state to pursue independent policies.

The costs of accession are particularly high in northern Europe. In contrast to states such as Spain, Greece, and Portugal, which had more to gain from accession (such as economic development and the consolidation of democracy), the Nordic states have more to lose and the stakes are higher as they pursue a path of integration with their largest trading partner.[6] This has to do with the unique features of the middle way between capitalism and socialism and the peaceful model of regional security between East and West. Once the Nordic states accept that economic and security policy problems cannot be solved by national means alone, and once they agree to joint policymaking in European institutions, they also secure the end of exceptionalism. In my

---

tries and the Internal Market of the EC, ed. Lise Lyck (Copenhagen: School of Economics and Business Administration, 1990), p. 223.

[4] The internal market program, or the "four freedoms," refers to the liberalizations in capital, services, goods, and persons introduced by the EC in 1985.

[5] Speech by British foreign secretary Malcolm Rifkind to the European Policy Forum, London, Wednesday, May 1, 1996, p. 6.

[6] For a discussion of the southern European view of integration, see Michael Marks and Susannah Verney, "Influence and Institutions: EU Relations with Spain and Greece," paper presented at the annual meeting of the American Political Science Association, Chicago, 1995; and the chapter by Michael Marks in Peter J. Katzenstein, *Tamed Power* (Ithaca: Cornell University Press, 1997).

analysis, pursuit of political autonomy has been critical to retaining a Nordic model in political economy and security policymaking. European integration, however, consolidates a process of political change already under way in the Nordic states.

The Nordic countries were already undergoing profound changes when European integration deepened.[7] "The relative autonomy of these countries diminished already in the 1980s as a consequence of deregulation in the monetary markets (which were until recently highly regulated)."[8] Because of the extent of policy coordination at the European level, however, the capacity for states to retain independent policies diminishes even further. As Paul Pierson and Stephan Leibfried argue, European collaboration alters member-state power as more and more decisions are made by European-level organizations.[9] By participating in the European project, the Nordic states accept a menu of acceptable reforms and thereby lock in the direction and substance of changes in domestic institutions and policies.

The first section of this chapter outlines the shared features of the Nordic model. The second section discusses how the Nordic models of economic and security policy have experienced increasing pressures for change and how many of these changes have emanated from the EC. Core policies, central to retaining a Nordic model, have been adapted to changes in the EC. Nordic governments have found that it is no longer possible, as it was in previous periods of European integration, to sign a trade agreement with the EC and retain national policies. Instead, there have been profound consequences for domestic politics. European integration has diminished the power of some domestic interests while empowering others, thereby altering the balance of power among corporatist actors in national politics.

---

[7] See Christine Ingebritsen, "Pulling in Different Directions: The Europeanization of Scandinavian Political Economies," in Katzenstein, *Tamed Power*, and James Fulcher, "The Social Democratic Model in Sweden: Termination or Restoration?" *Political Quarterly* 65, no. 2 (1994), 203–213.

[8] Pekka Kosonen, "The Scandinavian Welfare Model in the New Europe," in *Scandinavia in a New Europe*, ed. Thomas Boje and Sven Olsson Hort (Oslo: Scandinavian University Press, 1993), p. 65.

[9] Paul Pierson and Stephan Leibfried see four characteristics of European integration as challenging the authority of member states: autonomous activity of regional institutions, policy legacies or past commitments, unintended consequences, and actors such as the European Court of Justice operating independently from states. See *European Social Policy* (Washington, D.C.: Brookings Institution, 1995), p. 10.

THE NORDIC MODEL

What is the Nordic model, and how has it changed? When scholars study northern Europe, they typically focus on its exceptional institutions and policies.[10] Even though Nordic scholars reject the notion of a Nordic model per se, there have been institutional, ideational, and policy characteristics of these five states that are distinct from other advanced industrial nations.[11] The Nordic, or Scandinavian model, has been used widely by comparativists and international relations scholars. The Nordic model may refer to as diverse an array of unique political and economic features as the system of universal social welfare; the distinctive position of women in politics; the cooperative, institutionalized relationship between employers and trade unions in the formation of industrial policy; the export-led economic development path; the regional cooperation agreements of Nordic governments; and the combination of deterrence and reassurance in national security policymaking. A brief discussion of each of these dimensions of Nordic uniqueness will be followed by a discussion of how the two models of economic and security policy that are the focus of my analysis have changed.

Northern Europe was the first and only group of states to award welfare benefits to members of its society on the basis of citizenship. Prior to the turn of the century, Denmark, Norway and Sweden adopted social welfare laws that established a norm of universalism.[12] From the early development of the welfare state, welfare benefits were extended to all members of society. In contrast to the German conception of social policies, which were directed at a particular class of workers (in-

---

[10] As Lars Mjøset argues, there is no one Nordic model. This chapter specifies the commonalities shared by all five states.

[11] See Marquis Childs, *Sweden: The Middle Way* (New Haven: Yale University Press, 1936); Eric Einhorn and John Logue, *Modern Welfare States: Politics and Policies in Social Democratic Scandinavia* (New York: Praeger, 1989); Walter Korpi, *The Working Class in Welfare Capitalism: Work, Unions and Politics in Sweden* (London: Routledge, 1978); Jonas Pontusson, *Swedish Social Democracy and British Labor: Essays on the Nature and Condition of Social Democratic Hegemony* (Ithaca: Cornell University Press, 1988); Olof Petersson, *The Government and Politics of the Nordic Countries* (Stockholm: Fritzes I, 1994); and John Stephens, *The Transition from Capitalism to Socialism* (London: Macmillan, 1979).

[12] See Hugh Heclo, *Modern Social Policies in Britain and Sweden* (New Haven: Yale University Press, 1974); Einhorn and Logue, *Modern Welfare States*; and Øyvind Bjørnson and Inger Elisabeth Haavet, *Langsomt ble landet et velfardssamfunn: Trygdens historie, 1894–1994* (Oslo, Norway: Ad Notam Gyldendal, 1994).

dustrial labor), the model encompassed both rural and urban workers.[13] "Cradle to grave" welfare policies were intended to eradicate inequalities and cushion the society from the unpredictability of market forces. Under the social democratic welfare regime, "the state is not a second or last resort, but the primary agency for enabling every citizen to enjoy the highest attainable degree of economic security and to benefit from a wide range of high class social services."[14]

As Norwegian political scientist Stein Kuhnle argues, the Nordic model of social welfare shares distinctive features.[15] These countries have a higher level of state involvement in the provision of welfare than do other countries, a larger share of employment in social and educational sectors, similar organizational systems, and a more legitimate role for the state. Class differences have been de-emphasized, and the provision of benefits has been comparatively more generous and comprehensive than in other states. The most important goals of northern European welfare systems are the elimination of poverty and the provision of jobs for everyone in the society. The governments are committed to full employment for all citizens.

The Nordic social democratic welfare state has been studied extensively to isolate the conditions for its success. Scholars have focused on trade union strength or cohesiveness, the weakness of the right, enduring compromises between labor and business, the political allegiance of the Social Democratic Party to working class interests, political coalitions between social democrats and agrarians, as well as the position of the state in the international economy, in order to account for the distinctiveness of the Nordic models of welfare capitalism.[16]

In *The Three Worlds of Welfare Capitalism*, Gøsta Esping-Andersen differentiates solidaristic, Nordic models of welfare capitalism from the more liberal UK/U.S. variant.[17] The continental, or German model, is less comprehensive than the Nordic policy regime and does not share

[13] Aksel Hatland, Stein Kuhnle, and Tor Inge Romøren, *Den norske velferdsstaten* (Oslo: Ad Notam Gyldendal, 1994), pp. 10–11.

[14] David Purdy and Pat Devine, "Social Policy," in *The Economics of the European Union: Policy and Analysis*, ed. M. J. Artis and N. Lee (Oxford: Oxford University Press, 1994), p. 277.

[15] See Petersson, *The Government and Politics of the Nordic Countries*, p. 32.

[16] For an overview of the historic development of research on the Social Democratic model, see Kees van Kersbergen, *Social Capitalism* (London: Routledge, 1995), pp. 12–23.

[17] Gøsta Esping-Andersen, *The Three Worlds of Welfare Capitalism* (Cambridge: Polity Press, 1990).

the commitment to full employment, to universal welfare rights tied to social citizenship, or to the degree of state intervention in the economy. The social democratic model represents a political and institutional commitment to full employment, and it depends for its success on a well-organized working class and political allies among the farmers or the new, white-collar middle class. The differences in unemployment levels, labor-market participation rates, levels of taxation, and public transfers are outlined in Table 3.1.

As also indicated in Table 3.1, the Nordic states have the highest level of female participation in the labor force. Many scholars have examined the power of women in politics and the ways in which the Nordic states encourage greater participation of women in the labor force.[18] Compared to women in the United States, women in northern Europe enjoy substantial benefits (state-sponsored day-care services, generous family-leave policies, legal guarantees protecting participation in the labor market and treatment on the job).[19] Thus, when examining the extent of female participation in the economy and in national politics, scholars view the Nordic countries as a model.[20] For political economists, the Nordic states are a model of cooperation in industrial relations. Two historic compromises forged in the 1930s institutionalized agreements that came to play a critical role in the postwar period. The cross-class alliances between employers and trade unions and a political coalition between the independent farmer's party and the Social Democrats led to the rise of a particular kind of politics.[21] As Jonas Pontusson argues, the reformist policies adopted by Swedish Social Democrats depended on a unified trade union movement and cooperation with the business sector.[22] The inclusion of unions in national politics led some scholars to view Sweden as a prom-

---

[18] See Petersson, *The Government and Politics of the Nordic Countries*, pp. 179–184.

[19] Lauri Karvonen and Per Selle, *Women in Nordic Politics* (Aldershot, England: Dartmouth, 1995).

[20] See "Gender Equality—the Nordic Model" (Copenhagen: Nordic Council of Ministers, 1995).

[21] The partnership between an independent farmer's party and the Social Democrats in Sweden ushered in the period of postwar Labor party hegemony. The other Nordic states had similar Social Democratic ascendancies, yet none as lengthy or as formative as in Sweden. See Gøsta Esping-Andersen, *Politics Against Markets* (Princeton: Princeton University Press, 1985); and Peter Swenson, "Bringing Capital Back In, or Social Democracy Reconsidered," *World Politics* 43 (July 1991), 513–544.

[22] Jonas Pontusson, *The Limits of Social Democracy* (Ithaca: Cornell University Press, 1993).

Table 3.1. Three models of welfare capitalism

	Sweden	Germany	United Kingdom
Unemployment (mean 1980–88)	2.6	6.6	10.7
Labor-market participation	81.3	65.5	75.5
Female labor-market rates	78.3	51.3	62.6
Taxes*	29.7	22.5	16.9
Public transfers*	28.2	17.2	16.5

*% of gross income, 1980
Sources: S. Ringen, *The Possibility of Politics* (Oxford: Clarendon, 1987), p. 260; G. Esping-Andersen, *The Three Worlds of Welfare Capitalism* (Cambridge: Polity Press, 1990), p. 85; and Thomas Boje and Sven Olsson Hort, eds., *Scandinavia in a New Europe* (Oslo: Scandinavia University Press, 1994), p. 97.

ising example of the possibility for achieving socialist aims through parliamentary reforms.[23] During the postwar period, reducing dependence on markets, known as *decommodification,* was a core strategy of Nordic social democracy.[24]

Other scholars view northern Europe as a model of economic development.[25] At the end of the nineteenth century, these states were among the poorest in Europe. The hardship of surviving on the farm led to a mass exodus, particularly from Norway and Sweden, to the United States during the latter half of the nineteenth century and early part of the twentieth century. Although the five Nordic states were late industrializers, they managed to avert economic backwardness by converting export earnings from raw materials to the production of semi-finished goods.[26] While they promoted free trade outside their territories, Nordic governments were extremely protectionist within their territories. Foreign direct investment was restricted by state authorities, and foreigners were not permitted to own property. The highest levels of taxation in the modern world, sustained periods of export-led economic growth, and governments committed to social democratic goals (universal social welfare, full employment, and equality) distinguished Nordic political economies from other societies.[27]

[23] See Esping-Andersen, *Politics Against Markets.*
[24] Ibid.
[25] See Johan Myhrman, *Hur Sverige blev rikt* (Stockholm: Nordstedts, 1994) for an excellent analysis of the importance of social, political, and economic institutions in Sweden's economic development.
[26] See Dieter Senghaas, *The European Experience* (Leamington Spa: Berg, 1985).
[27] See Lars Mjøset, "Nordic Economic Policies in the 1980s and 1990s," paper pre-

Northern Europe is also a model of peaceful regional security. Nordic cooperation agreements have been extensive, particularly in the area of social policy. While foreign and security cooperation was never formalized in Nordic arrangements, however, the extent of informal consultation and collaboration has been extremely high. The combination of geographic proximity to a nuclear threat, conflict avoidance, and the legacy of neutrality policy led many peace researchers to focus on northern Europe during the cold war period. Many analysts have praised the bridge-building effects of Nordic policies and diplomatic initiatives as responsible for dissipating conflict between East and West.[28]

My analysis examines recent reforms in economic and security policies emanating from closer cooperation with the European Community. Not all of the Nordic models are changing: the universal norms of welfare provision have thus far been retained, despite cutbacks and privatization measures in social welfare systems. Women retain a powerful position in national politics and a relatively high rate of participation in the labor market. Nordic levels of intergovernmental cooperation are high, and diplomatic efforts to negotiate the peaceful resolution of conflict continue—from Bosnia to the Middle East. What *has* changed is an ability to go it alone and pursue a policy agenda independent from the European Community in economic and security policymaking, two areas once considered to be the business of national governments.

CHANGES IN THE NORDIC MODEL

Since the 1930s, the Nordic governments have shared a commitment to the pursuit of full employment, a centralized system of wage bargaining, universal social policies, and the pursuit of equality. By the early 1990s, unemployment had soared to continental levels, wage bargaining had been decentralized, universal social policies were subjected to cutbacks, and the Nordic states, to a varying degree, were more willing

---

sented to the Tenth International Conference of Europeanists, Chicago, March 14–16, 1996.

[28] See Bruce Olav Solheim, *The Nordic Nexus: A Lesson in Peaceful Security* (Westport: Praeger, 1994); and Janie Leatherman, "Conflict Transformation in the CSCE: Learning and Institutionalization," *Cooperation and Conflict* 28 (December 1993), 403–431.

than in the past to embrace efficiency over equality in economic policymaking. The transformation did not occur overnight, nor was it inevitable. There was widespread recognition in northern Europe, however,
that the traditional means of intervening in the economy were no
longer working. The European option must be seen against these
changes.

Scholars disagree about the sources of change in the Nordic model
but agree that in the 1970s and the 1980s the capacity to retain social
democratic institutions and policies diminished. The international oil
crisis led to an expansionary fiscal policy and expansion of the public
sector, particularly in Sweden. Growing disillusionment with Keynesian
solutions and the desire to control inflation led Nordic governments to
pursue alternative economic policies. The economic pressures on these
states were far from uniform, however, because of important differences in export markets. For example, economic planners in Norway
were preoccupied with the consequences of changes in the international oil price, while across the border in Sweden, economic planners
were more concerned about the competitive position of multinational
firms. Nor were particular reforms implemented at lightning speed because of the institutional rigidities of the welfare state, the controversial
nature of social policy retrenchment, and institutional differences
among agencies within the state.[29]

The increasingly competitive international economy led to a realignment in domestic political coalitions and policy change.[30] Timothy
Tilton's analysis of Swedish politics emphasizes the ideological swing to
the right in Social Democratic strategy and the desire to open the
economy to global markets, which predated European integration.[31]
From the perspective of Eric Einhorn, "the main sources for changes in
Swedish social policy were internal, reflecting severe budgetary and in-
flationary pressures that have forced both social democratic and non-

---

[29] See Paul Pierson's discussion of the Swedish bourgeois coalition government's incli-
nation to proceed cautiously in restructuring the welfare state, although there were tremendous economic pressures in this direction, in "The New Politics of the Welfare
State," *World Politics* 48 (January 1996), 170–173; and institutional variations in Swedish
agencies responsible for implementing reforms in Bo Rothstein, *The Social Democratic
State: The Swedish Model and the Bureaucratic Problem of Social Reforms* (Pittsburgh: Pittsburgh
University Press, 1996).
[30] See Herman Schwartz, "Small States in Big Trouble," *World Politics* 46 (July 1994),
527–555.
[31] Discussions with Timothy Tilton, Bo Rothstein, and Jonas Pontusson.

socialist governments to reassess their policies."[32] Other scholars, such as Jonathon Moses and Ton Notermans, attribute changes in social democracy to internationalization and the inability to retain national controls over capital movement or to sustain the full employment model. These structural imperatives are contested by scholars, including Andrew Martin, who give more weight in their analyses to political choices, path dependence, and policy legacies. If macroeconomic conditions had been more favorable, the system of centralized wage bargaining might not have been terminated in Sweden in the 1980s.[33] The pressures of responding to the imperatives of the business sector (engineering had grown in importance to the Swedish economy, although these firms were less dependent on Swedish markets than on international markets) led to the decision to reform the institution of centralized wage bargaining—one of the unique characteristics of the Nordic systems of industrial relations.

These debates on the threshold of international political economy and comparative politics will not be resolved here. Instead, I take these considerations as a point of departure for discussing the relationship between the Nordic states and the European project.

The Nordic model, it is widely accepted, has been in crisis since the 1970s and has faced even greater external and internal challenges in the 1980s. From my perspective, the Nordic model was already in flux when these states experienced two profound changes that have led to a fundamental, lasting redirection in national policies.

For the international system and for the five Nordic states 1985 was a watershed year. Cooperation among EC member states moved well beyond previous periods of integration, and cooperation between the United States and the Soviet Union diminished the possibility of war in Europe. Beginning in 1985, these changes in the European environment put severe pressures on all Nordic states. They entered a new era of politics. In Chapter 4, we will look more closely at how these changes affected the Nordic states. For the moment, the analysis will focus on what actually changed in Nordic polities.

[32] Eric Einhorn, "A Farewell to Alms? From Scandinavian Welfare States to Euro-Welfare Sates," paper presented at the Seminar on Sweden and the New Europe, University of Washington, Seattle, November 1992, p. 11.

[33] Andrew Martin, "Macroeconomic Policy, Politics and the Demise of Central Wage Negotiations in Sweden," paper presented to the Peder Sather Symposium, University of California, Berkeley, March 21–22, 1996.

THE CONSEQUENCES OF INTEGRATION

What were the consequences of European integration for the Nordic states? When the European Community introduced its internal market program in 1985, all of the Nordic governments pursued deeper commitments with the EC. By adhering to the provisions outlined in the Single European Act, Nordic governments accepted new infringements on national policymaking that have altered state-society relations in each country. When security relations between East and West evolved from confrontation to collaboration, the Nordic strategy of balancing between the two blocs was rendered obsolete, raising new concerns about how to avoid marginalization and isolation from the rest of Europe. As NATO's role came into question and U.S. military power was withdrawn from the continent, the EC expanded its cooperation in foreign and security policy by forging ahead with the Maastricht Treaty. During the postwar period, social democracy and political integration with the EC were deemed incompatible. Nevertheless, the growing awareness that national policies were no longer tenable led governments to prefer regional collaboration. This shift in government strategies led to a transformation in the Nordic models and an important change in governance.

As the Nordic states pursued closer political integration with the EC, there have been three profound consequences for domestic politics. First, even the most minimal pact with Europe unravels national policies. All five states have signed the EEA agreement, an expanded trade agreement with the EC, and a regulatory policy regime. To conform to the EEA agreement, the Nordic states have liberalized capital markets and restrictions on foreign direct investment and opened up national labor markets. Second, even further reforms in economic policies are required by EC membership, as listed in Table 3.2. As a consequence of joining the EC, the Nordic states must reduce agricultural subsidies to be compatible with the Common Agricultural Policy (CAP), accept downward pressure on levels of indirect taxation, subsidize the EC's structural funds program, and agree to all the terms for the creation of political and economic union negotiated at Maastricht. These foreign-policy decisions do not leave the domestic political sphere unscathed. Instead, the internalization of European policies alters relationships between corporatist actors, runs counter to the ideology of social democ-

Table 3.2. Forms of European integration: Policy consequences

Issue Area	EFTA	EEA	EC
Goods			
Eliminate tariffs on industrial goods	X	X	X
Remove technical barriers to trade		X	X
Free trade in fish products		(X)	X
Common regulations, state subsidies		X	X
No rules of origin		(X)	X
Elimination of antidumping practices		X	X
Free trade in agriculture			(X)
Border controls		(X)	X
Capital			
Free movement of capital		X	X
Harmonization of indirect taxes			X
Peg currency to ECU/EMS			X
Nondiscriminatory rights of establishment		X	X
Services			
Transport (car, plane, ship, train)		X	X
Financial services		(X)	X
Wire services		X	X
Persons			
Common labor market		X	X
Mutual acceptance of degrees		X	X
Mutual recognition of social rights		X	X
Other			
Common rules of competition		X	X
Common rules for regional policies		(X)	X
Common trade policies			X
Common energy policy			(X)
Common agricultural policy			X
Common fisheries policy			X
Access to EC funds			X
Contribute to EC budget			X
Contribute to EFTA fund	X		

Note: X = required area of policy adaptation; (X) = some exceptions, safe-guards, limitations

Source: "Informasjon om EØS Avtalen" (Oslo: 1992), p. 30.

racy, promotes urban interests over rural interests, imposes macro-economic discipline from Brussels, and requires Nordic states to take a more active role in European policymaking than ever before. A third change in domestic politics is institutional: integration has contributed to an unraveling of the Nordic models of political economy and security policymaking by altering the power of some corporatist actors and diminishing the capacity of national authorities to maintain domestic policies unique to the Nordic model. Although the Nordic model was already in trouble when these governments opted for EC membership, political integration leads to further reform. From the perspective of Europe's northernmost states, the introduction of the Single European Act led to formative changes in national policies.

Consider now the scope of institutional and policy changes within the EC and the implications for the small, trade-dependent, social democratic states of northern Europe.

THE TRANSFORMATION OF EUROPEAN POLITICS

In a tour of European capitals in 1985, EC president Jacques Delors introduced the "Project 1992" reform program. The program was not new per se but revitalized the visions of the founders of the idea of European unity, such as French industrialist Jean Monnet. According to that argument, not only would further collaboration in economic affairs revive the health of Europe in relation to the United States and Japan, but Europe would increasingly take on the responsibilities formerly designated to nation-states. These include plans for political union (to include foreign and security policy coordination) and economic union (the creation of a common currency and a central European bank). In addition, plans were adopted to improve the decision-making capacity of the EC's core institutions (the Council of Ministers, the Commission, the Court of Justice, and the Parliament).

The Nordic states engage a more centralized European policy regime than in the past, in which more and more decisions are made at the supranational level. The EC's capacity to infringe on the sovereignty of member and nonmember states has expanded significantly since its founding. Although the EC was initially a loose federation of states, in today's Europe more and more sectors and policy areas are the business of EC-level representatives in Brussels, Strasbourg, or Luxembourg. Since the implementation of the Single European Act (1987), the decision-making capacity of European Community institutions has become more effective. Cooperation within the EC is the outcome of intergovernmental bargaining, yet the effect of those bargains has been to create federalist forms of cooperation within the EC.[34] The

[34] See Andrew Moravcsik, "Negotiating the Single European Act: National Interests and Conventional Statecraft in the European Community," *International Organization* 45, no. 1 (1991), 651–688; and Martin Sæter, "EC Developments Since 1972: The Changed Relationship between Supranationalism and Intergovernmentalism," *Internasjonal Politikk* 1–2 (1987), 37–52.

centralization of power in the EC has been particularly intrusive for northern European social democracies accustomed to determining economic and security policies independently from the more powerful European states. In European institutions, the position of small states is changing.

One of the most profound changes affecting the states with smaller populations in Europe is the revised voting system in the EC's executive body, the Council of Ministers. The system of qualified majority voting, adopted by the Council of Ministers in 1987, improves the efficiency of decision-making within the EC but diminishes the power of small states by removing the consensus requirement. Where once a single state could stall the process of integration, the system of qualified majority voting requires a bloc of resistant states.[35] Under the new system, small states are required to ally with other states to advance their interests. When votes in the Council of Ministers are allocated to the Nordic states according to population size, Sweden receives four votes, Norway and Finland three votes, and Iceland two votes.[36] Just how democratic is this European policy regime if the larger powers carry more weight in the core decision-making institutions? The centralization of authority in European-wide institutions diminishes the capacity of these governments to resist further integration. It is thus not surprising that many northern Europeans stress the democratic deficit in European institutions and are concerned about the elite nature of European policymaking.

As further evidence of the high stakes of European integration, consider how difficult it is for the Nordic states to retain national policies and implement domestic political goals once they pursue political integration. The Nordic states have not been passive bystanders as European policies and institutions have changed. With the extent of political and institutional reform within the EC, however, the capacity of the Nordic states to pursue independent policies has diminished.

[35] See Dermot McAleese and Alan Matthews, "The Single European Act and Ireland: Implications for a Small Member State," *Journal of Common Market Studies* 26, no. 1 (1987), 39–60.

[36] Madeleine O. Hosli, "Admission of European Free Trade Association States to the European Community: Effects on Voting Power in the European Community Council of Ministers," *International Organization* 47 (Autumn 1993), 638.

CHANGES IN NATIONAL POLICY

The sweeping changes in Nordic economic policies have included the liberalization of capital, opening private and public sectors to foreign investment, and expanding the boundaries of the Nordic labor market to include all of Europe. These reforms have been required for the five signatories of the EEA agreement.[37] Even more profound changes in domestic policies, such as liberalizing state protection of agriculture, reducing levels of indirect taxation, and creating new pressures to reform the national system of alcohol sales and distribution, are consequences of joining the EC. These are just some of the numerous changes underway that alter virtually every aspect of daily life in Nordic societies.

In this section, I will briefly survey key reforms implemented by the Nordic countries as governments traded economic interdependence for political integration. These include the liberalization of laws governing currency, banking, insurance, financial services, foreign investment, labor movement, taxation, alcohol regulation, and agriculture. In each policy area, EC-mandated reforms had profound effects on longstanding social and state-society relations.

The EC's liberalization of capital and services required member states and the Nordic signatories of the EEA agreement to reform national laws and regulations that restrict international participation in European currency markets, banking, insurance, and securities.[38] In the Nordic states, currency transactions have been conducted by national banking institutions. This has changed; the European Community requires this sector to adhere to principles of nondiscrimination, and new participants (foreign banks) are permitted to carry out currency transactions.

Nordic banking regulations have been protectionist and have deliberately restricted the participation of international banks.[39] Although

---

[37] The five signatories of the EEA agreement are Iceland, Norway, Finland, Sweden, and Austria. Swiss voters rejected the EEA agreement in a national referendum.

[38] Edward Gardener and Jonathan Teppet, *The Economic Impact of 1992 on the Norwegian Financial Services Sector* (Bangor, Wales: Institute of European Finance, University College of North Wales, 1990); and Sveriges Riksbank, *Finansiell Integration: Sverige och EG* (Stockholm: December 1989).

[39] See Søren Jensen and Christian Lotz, "The Prospects for the Scandinavian Banking Industry under Deregulation," in *The Nordic Countries and the Internal Market of the EEC.*

the Danish banks are the most internationally integrated of the Nordic banks, there are common characteristics of the banking sector across all Nordic states. A typical visitor to Oslo, Stockholm, Helsinki, Copenhagen, and Reykjavik would not find foreign banks open to the public—only Skandinaviska Enskilda Banken, Den Danske Banken, Kreditbanken, the postal banking service, and other Nordic institutions. International banks could only establish independent subsidiaries in the Nordic states, with limited drawing rights on their home institutions. International banks were unable to offer services to the public and were limited to providing commercial banking services.

Nordic laws also prevented the acquisition of national banks by foreigners. Liberalizations of the banking sector have contributed to severe losses for national banks resulting from a deregulation of lending practices and an inability of lenders to repay their loans. In 1991, the Norwegian government intervened to rescue its largest commercial banks (Den Norske Banken and Christiania Bank).[40] As Nordic banks confront more competitive market conditions, the sector will face even greater pressures to restructure and consolidate lending institutions. If the private banking sector suffers further shocks, Nordic governments will be required to intervene at tremendous cost to the taxpayers.

National regulations in each state have also restricted foreign participation in financial services and industry. For example, foreign ownership could not exceed 10 percent of a bank or 20 percent of an insurance company in Norway. Firms registered on the Oslo stock market limited foreign ownership to 10 percent.[41] Regulations also limited foreign ownership of industry. These regulations were particularly restrictive in Norway. The changes in Norwegian concession laws introduced in 1990 allow up to 33 percent foreign ownership of industry, instead of 25 percent. In Finland, we have witnessed a similar liberalization permitting foreigners to own a 40 percent share in joint stock companies instead of a 20 percent limit on ownership.[42] The Swedish Company Law Committee was created by the government in 1990 to adapt the Swedish Companies Act to EC regulations. The committee proposed that rules restricting foreign ownership of shares be repealed by

[40] Robert Peston, "Slippery Slopes," *Financial Times*, October 31, 1991.

[41] Jensen and Lotz, "The Prospects for the Scandinavian Banking Industry," p. 18.

[42] Riitta Hjerppe, "Finland's Foreign Trade and Trade Policy in the 20th Century," *Scandinavian Journal of History* 18, no. 1 (1993), 73.

January 1, 1993, consistent with the deadline adopted in Brussels.[43] Since the reform in rules governing foreign direct investment was implemented in 1993, it is no longer permitted to discriminate against foreign shareholders, nor are foreigners required to request permission from the government to operate businesses in Sweden.[44]

Under the EEA agreement, governments have been required to liberalize national restrictions on foreign investors. This change was designed to meet the requirements of the EC's nondiscriminatory right of establishment based on principles stated in the Treaty of Rome.[45] Thus, all Nordic governments have become more friendly to foreign direct investment since the implementation of the Single European Act.

In the public sector, northern Europe's growth industry since the 1970s, Nordic states have also been compelled to open up to European investors. According to the EC Commission's White Paper, "public procurement covers a sizeable part of GDP and is still marked by the tendency of the authorities concerned to keep their purchases and contracts within their own country. This continued partitioning of individual national markets is one of the most evident barriers to the achievement of a real internal market."[46] Nordic restrictions on bids for public sector projects have been subject to internationalization and liberalization as the European Community harmonized its public procurement policies.[47] Transport, energy, telecommunications, and the building and construction industries are just a few examples of state sectors that have had to become more open to bids by other European investors. In February 1991, the Swedish government announced its intent to privatize three state monopolies: Televerket (the telecommunications group), Vattenfall (the power generation authority), and Domanverket (state-owned forests), a move that conforms to the EC's requirements for public sector reform.

Nordic labor markets are an example of how individuals can move

[43] For details on the changes in Swedish Company Law affecting foreign ownership of firms, see Rolf Skog, "Foreign Acquisitions of Shares in Swedish Companies," *Current Sweden* (Stockholm: Swedish Institute, May 1992).
[44] Ministry of Industry and Commerce, *Economic Restructuring and Industrial Policy in Sweden* (Stockholm: Norstedts, 1996), p. 29.
[45] Article 67 of the Treaty of Rome requires EC member states to eliminate discriminatory practices that constitute obstacles to the free movement of capital.
[46] *Completing the Internal Market: White Paper from the Commission to the European Council* (Brussels: Commission of the European Communities, 1985), p. 23.
[47] Norwegian Foreign Ministry, *Offentilige Innkjøp og EFs Indre Marked* (Oslo: UD, 1990).

freely to work and study in neighboring states.[48] The EEA agreement required the Nordic states to extend the boundaries of this exchange to the continent. According to the free movement of persons, individuals have the right to seek and be granted employment in another state and are also entitled to the same social benefits that they receive at home. The free movement of persons also includes crossnational recognition of academic degrees.[49]

Northern European governments have tended to downplay the effects of labor mobility on the welfare state. According to interviews with representatives from the ministries in Sweden, Denmark, and Norway, more Nordic citizens are likely to work abroad, offsetting the number of foreigners coming to work in the Nordic states. Cultural, language, and climatic barriers may also discourage the relocation of southern Europeans to northern Europe.

Many of the trade unionists are skeptical about the consequences of joining a group of states that do not share Nordic priorities.[50] The unions express concern about two types of social dumping associated with the free movement of labor: the economic burden of providing benefits for an influx of new workers and the exit of capital from northern Europe to lower-wage areas.[51] In the EC's internal market program, there is one market for capital yet separate, national markets for labor and no commonly agreed-upon principles to restrict social dumping. As signatories of the EEA agreement and as EC member states, the Nordic states are obliged to open the regional labor market to other European workers. Yet at the same time, these states have experienced the highest levels of unemployment in the postwar period.

As EC member states, Nordic governments face new pressures to reduce levels of indirect taxation. Nordic levels of indirect taxation are, on average, higher than those of EC member states. The realization of a common market implies a harmonization of levels of value-added or

[48] Nordic cooperation includes the free movement of persons within the region. The passport union was approved in 1952, allowing Nordic citizens to move freely from one state to another without documentation.

[49] The obstacle here is to make sure that individuals receive comparable academic or vocational training. Until a system of mutual recognition of degrees or certificates is established, a worker is judged and tested by the employer.

[50] Author's interview with trade union representatives in Sweden, 1990.

[51] Interviews with representatives from LO in Denmark and Sweden, 1991. See also *Fackliga perspecktiv på den europeiska integrationen* (Stockholm: LO, 1989); and *The Internal Market and the Social Dimension: The Position, Objectives and Strategy of the Danish Trade Union Movement* (Copenhagen: LO, 1989).

indirect tax. As individuals move within the market to take advantage of lower levels of indirect taxation, there are pressures on the state to reduce the value-added tax (VAT). The harmonization of indirect taxes, however, constitutes a net loss of state revenue for Nordic governments and requires a revision of state revenue sources. Several proposals have been made to bring Nordic levels in line with EC levels of indirect taxation. According to a study by Norwegian economist Andreas Gaarder, "if Norway were to adapt the proposals of indirect taxes as specified by the Commission in August 1987, it would first of all lead to a significant change in prices."[52] This would be beneficial for consumers and constitute an increase in real income. Nevertheless, public revenue from indirect taxation would be significantly reduced. In Sweden, the challenge would be similar: indirect tax rates would have to be cut, reducing income to the state, which worries the Swedish minister of finance.[53] Among EC member states, Denmark has the highest ratio of indirect taxes to gross domestic product (GDP). According to one analyst, the Danes would incur a budgetary loss of approximately 6.8 percent of GDP if the original proposals introduced by the European Commission on tax harmonization were implemented.[54]

In addition to the loss of state revenue associated with EC membership, Nordic governments have had to defend the retention of an important policy tool: the excise tax. The excise tax has been used by these governments as a means to limit consumption of alcohol, tobacco products, energy resources, and imported foodstuffs. For example, in Sweden, the price of alcohol is two to three times the EC average, and prices are intended to deter consumption of strong drink.[55] It is precisely these areas where the largest reductions in price levels are likely to occur in EC proposals to harmonize indirect taxes.[56]

A traditional means of regulating the society has been contested as a consequence of pursuing closer cooperation with the EC. State control of the import and distribution of alcoholic beverages has been a mechanism of social policy designed to reduce consumption of alcohol. Al-

[52] Lyck, *The Nordic Countries and the Internal Market,* p. 119.

[53] Carl B. Hamilton and Carl-Einar Stålvant, *A Swedish View of 1992* (London: Royal Institute of International Affairs, 1989), p. 7.

[54] Jørn Henrik Petersen, "Harmonization of Social Security in the EC Revisited," *Journal of Common Market Studies* 29 (September 1991), pp. 515–517.

[55] Beverages with a higher alcohol content are three times the EC average price (hard liquor and spirits). Wine and beer are sold at twice the EC average price. See *Sverige, EG och alkoholpolitiken* (Stockholm: CAN, 1990), p. 10.

[56] See Lyck, *The Nordic Countries and the Internal Market,* pp. 119–120.

cohol abuse has a long, dark history in northern Europe, which some attribute to the cold climate or to deeply rooted social traditions.[57] Whatever the cause, governments have intervened to try to curb excessive consumption in order to protect public health. In Sweden, Finland, and Norway, national monopolies are responsible for the import and distribution of alcoholic beverages.[58] In Denmark, however, regulations governing the distribution of alcohol are more liberal, and price levels are markedly lower.

According to the Treaty of Rome, states are forbidden to operate monopolies. In a case before the European Court of Justice, an Italian tobacco monopoly was required to liberalize its control over the domestic market and permit other importers to compete. These liberalizations have also been requested in Sweden, Finland, and Norway but have already been adopted in Denmark. In Denmark and the other EC member states, it is the responsibility of the individual to regulate his or her consumption of alcohol, whereas in Sweden, Finland, and Norway it is the responsibility of the state.[59] According to representatives from the anti-EC movement in Norway, "a liberalization of alcohol policy will increase the use of alcohol, and adversely affect health, the state of mind, and the society at large."[60] In Sweden and Finland health policy officials also feared a substantial rise in alcohol-related deaths if excise taxes on alcohol were reduced by Systembolaget or Alko, the state alcohol monopolies.

Previously, the regulation of alcohol consumption was solely the concern of national governments. In this area of social policy, however, the retention of Nordic solutions has been contested by the EC.[61] During the accession debates, the Swedes were informed that glögg, a mulled wine spiced with cardamom and cinnamon, was too sweet and too strong to qualify as wine and would have to be diluted to meet EC standards. The EC Commission also questioned the widespread use of

[57] See Childs, *Sweden: The Middle Way*, pp. 112–114.

[58] For excellent discussions of state regulation of alcohol, see Svante Nycander, *Svenskarna och spriten* (Oskarshamn: Tryckeri AB Primo, 1967); and Bo Rothstein, *Den korporativa staten: Intresse-organisationer och statsforvaltning i svensk politik* (Stockholm: Nordstedts, 1992), pp. 136–158.

[59] See James Shiffer, "Sweden and Denmark: Contrasting Alcohol Policies," *Scandinavian Review* 79 (Winter 1991), 29–35.

[60] Translated from *EØS-avtalen: Virkninger for Norge* (Oslo: Nei til EF, 1991), p. 39.

[61] See Svante Nycander, "Tid för en folkkampanj mot EG's alkoholpolitik," *Dagens Nyheter*, March 25, 1990; "Stå upp for alkoholmonopolet!" *Dagens Nyheter*, July 27, 1993; "Att undervisa EG om alkohol," *Dagens Nyheter*, May 9, 1993.

snuff, a moist tobacco product consumed by 20 percent of the adult male population in Sweden.[62] The media reported widely on the efforts to defend national products from criteria adopted in Brussels. National monopolies and products have been contested by EC officials and have thus far been defended by Nordic governments. In Sweden's accession agreement, the National Monopoly for the Retail Sale of Alcoholic Beverages (Systembolaget) was retained; but the import, export, wholesale, and production monopolies were phased out.[63] Norwegians appealed to the European Court of Justice to retain the existing system. Thus, in new policy areas, where national and regional norms of governance interact, solutions must be negotiated between Nordic and EC officials.

European Community membership also requires Nordic governments to liberalize agricultural policies. Complying with the EC's Common Agricultural Policy (CAP) is a major adjustment for northern European states that have long traditions of providing support to the agricultural sector.[64] The legacy of a strong farmer's movement in the north led to the adoption of agricultural policies designed to promote self-sufficiency in agricultural production, to retain a dispersed settlement pattern by providing jobs in peripheral areas, and to promote income equality between rural and urban workers.[65] For the Nordic states with the highest levels of agricultural protection (Norway and Finland), liberalization of state subsidies to farmers has been particularly problematic. Norwegian farmers were among the strongest opponents of entry into the EC and helped block the government's efforts to join. In a stunning effort to align domestic policies to the EC norm, the Swedish government liberalized its agricultural sector directly prior to accession. In the other Nordic states, liberalizations have occurred more gradually, yet these serve to undermine the support for the

[62] Jan Berg, "Swedish Public Opinion and the European Community" (Stockholm: Ministry of Foreign Affairs, 1992), p. 2.

[63] Swedish Ministry of Foreign Affairs, "Sweden's Negotiations on Membership of the EU," April 7, 1994, p. 4.

[64] In comparison to EC member states, Nordic agriculture receives higher levels of support. According to 1993 figures, Norway spent 3.7 percent of GDP on agriculture, Finland 4.1 percent, while Sweden liberalized its agricultural support to 1.3 percent of GDP, closer to the EC average of 2.0 percent of GDP. See *Agricultural Policies, Markets and Trade, Monitoring and Outlook* (Paris: OECD, 1993).

[65] See Michele Micheletti, *The Swedish Farmers' Movement and Government Agricultural Policy* (New York: Praeger, 1990); Finnish Ministry of Foreign Affairs, *Finnish Position on Agriculture* (Helsinki: September 1993); Lauri Kettunen and Jyrki Niemi, *The EU Settlement of Finnish Agriculture and National Support* (Helsinki: Agricultural Economics Research Institute, July 1994); and Zenon Tederko, *Agricultural Policy and Trends in Norwegian Agriculture* (Oslo: Norwegian Agricultural Economics Research Institute, 1992).

farmer central to the historic development of these social democratic states.[66]

In another policy area, support for regions, pressure on the Nordic states to accept European-wide solutions has intensified. In 1991, the Danes abolished the Regional Development Act and the Regional Development Fund in order to correspond to EC requests.[67] The change represents a regime shift, transferring authority for administering regional aid to the EC level in cooperation with state and local authorities. A normative change is also visible in national planning policy. In contrast to the traditional social democratic model endorsing parallel development of all regions (and promoting the periphery), the new orientation is toward the center, supporting regional development in the Copenhagen area.

These are just a few examples of the sweeping changes in these countries as the Nordic states become entangled in the web of European policy networks. European integration has not only led to changes in Nordic policies, but it also infringes on state capacity in new and intrusive ways.

CHANGES IN STATE CAPACITY

Legal, fiscal, and monetary cooperation among EC member states alters the capacity of Nordic governments to pursue independent policies. For example, the legal system in northern Europe is dualist: the decisions of international authorities are subject to national approval. The EC relies on a monist legal system, where international law is binding on the state. Under the European Community's legal system, national courts are bound by decisions made by the European Court of Justice.[68]

Not only has the reform imposed by European institutions affected social democratic policies and state-society relations, it has undermined the options available to Nordic governments. I will look at the dimin-

[66] See, for example, Esping-Andersen's *Politics Against Markets* for a discussion of the political role of the peasantry in Scandinavian politics and Micheletti's *The Swedish Farmers' Movement* for an analysis of the historic power of farmers in Swedish society and politics.

[67] Ib Jørgensen and Jens Tonboe, "Space and Welfare: The EC and the Eclipse of the Scandinavian Model," in *Scandinavia in a New Europe*, p. 365.

[68] See "The New Constitutional Politics of Europe," special issue of *Comparative Political Studies* 26 (January 1994).

ishing capacity of the Nordic governments to act independently in two critical areas, currency policy and full employment policy.

By accepting the provisions of the Maastricht Treaty, Nordic governments, in effect, subordinate fiscal and macroeconomic policy decisions to European institutions. The five Nordic states have, to a varying degree, relied on currency devaluation as a means of controlling inflation. Their ability to act unilaterally is severely curtailed in this regard. By joining the EC, Nordic governments coordinate monetary policy decisions with representatives from other EC governments. When the EC develops an independent central bank and common currency, Nordic banks will become even more dependent on European financial institutions—particularly the Bundesbank. Danish banks have followed the lead of the Bundesbank in determining rates of interest, and the other Nordic banks are increasingly pursuing a European monetary policy.

Between 1990 and 1991, the Swedish, Finnish, and Norwegian governments pegged the value of their currencies to the ECU in order to demonstrate political commitment to the European project and to receive the long-term economic benefits associated with monetary cooperation.[69] The destabilizing effects of linking to the ECU were visible in the fall 1992 currency crisis. When the Bundesbank introduced a tight monetary policy to combat inflation, the Nordic economies also experienced a sharp increase in interest rates under the fixed exchange rate regime. The Swedish government attempted to keep the value of the currency on par with those of other European states. Domestic bank interest rates soared from 75 percent to 500 percent in less than a week. Despite the destabilizing effects on the Swedish economy, the government initially refused to devalue the krona. The Swedish Riksbank was finally forced to abandon its peg of the krona to the ECU on November 19, following a week when approximately Skr 158 billion in reserves ($29 billion) had been depleted.[70] Nordic governments allowed the value of their currencies to float in the aftermath of the crisis. Yet European Community membership compels Nordic govern-

---

[69] Norway pegged its currency to the ECU on October 19, 1990, followed by Sweden in May 1991 and Finland in June 1991. Jonathon Moses speculates that this process reflects a deliberate strategy on behalf of Nordic elites to bring these countries into the EC. See Jonathon Moses, "Fixing the Agenda: ECU-Linkage and the EU Ambitions of Nordic Elites," paper prepared for APSA, New York City, September 1–4, 1994.

[70] David Cameron, "British Exit, German Voice, French Loyalty," p. 34. Unpublished manuscript, 1993.

ments to abandon unilateral devaluations of their currency and accept the roller-coaster economic effects of linking national currencies more closely with those of other European states.

In a second core policy area, the pursuit of full employment, the Nordic states have had more difficulty meeting national policy goals. While northern Europe traditionally maintained some of the lowest levels of unemployment (2 to 3 percent) in the industrialized world, integration with the EC has corresponded to higher levels of jobless-ness. In the 1980s, the priorities of Nordic governments shifted from the goal of full employment to combating inflation. During the 1990s, Nordic societies experienced the highest levels of unemployment in the postwar period.[71] An open labor market required by the EEA agree-ment made it even more difficult for these states to pursue the tradi-tional social democratic goal of full employment. Nordic governments have become increasingly concerned with implementing anti-inflation-ary measures as they integrate with Europe, which is more consistent with German macroeconomic policymaking than with the full employ-ment goal of Nordic social democracy.[72]

A final yet profound effect of European integration on the domestic politics of these small social democratic welfare states has been a change in the balance of state-society relations. The relations between the institutions of democratic corporatism (government, business, and trade unions) have been altered by the forces unleashed by the liberal-izations of capital, goods, services, and persons initiated in Brussels.

TRANSNATIONAL CAPITAL AND CORPORATIST BARGAINING

By encouraging the movement of industry across state boundaries, European policy coordination has weakened the bargaining power of labor in domestic politics. In response to the internal market program, Nordic industries launched what some business analysts referred to as "the second Viking invasion." The psychological effects of "fortress Eu-rope" led to an exodus of capital investment. Nordic industry moved south to EC member states in order to position themselves within their largest market. Nevertheless, the cost to labor in jobs and bargaining

---

[71] Unemployment in Finland soared to 19 percent of the work force in 1994; Sweden recorded a record high level of unemployment at 13 percent, above the Danish average of 10 percent, and the Norwegian unemployment level of 5 percent.

[72] See Ingebritsen, "Pulling in Different Directions."

power within the Nordic states was severe. The strategy of some Nordic trade unions changed from resisting capitalist Europe to promoting accession in order to attract foreign direct investment to the north.[73] According to representatives from the trade union movement in Sweden, the loss of jobs associated with capital flight required a new, European-wide strategy.

The relationship among labor, capital, and government (referred to by Peter Katzenstein as "democratic corporatism") experienced two consequences of capital flight. The preferences of blue-collar trade unionists in Sweden changed from resistance to support for collaboration with Europe in order to secure employment. In doing so, these trade unions effectively aligned with Nordic export-oriented industry and completely reversed their historic position of retaining the greatest possible distance from the market-oriented, less solidaristic member states of the EC. Yet the public sector unions, which have grown in importance throughout northern Europe since the 1970s, remained more resistant to European integration. Public sector unions anticipated a rationalization of jobs associated with accession. Thus, in Sweden, the debate over joining the EC drove a wedge between those workers employed by the state and those employed in other sectors. As Jonas Pontusson argues in *The Limits of Social Democracy*, divisions within the trade union movement have contributed to undermining the strength of the left. European integration moves northern Europe farther down this path to dismantling the pacts associated with the golden years of social democracy (1935–73).

Gone are the days when Nordic societies were sheltered from international capital markets by national regulations, when national authorities had the capacity to pursue independent policies, when governments could establish acceptable levels of taxation to sustain solidaristic social policies, and when restrictions on the participation of foreign workers and investors were considered an acceptable means of sustaining a nationally directed economy. These were elements that were critical to the survival of a distinctive Nordic economic model. Politics in the Nordic states is losing its exceptional status in contrast to the pre-1985 period. Yet despite the consequences for state-society relations, Nordic governments increasingly consider their future to be in the European Community, where decisions depend on multilateral co-

---

[73] Interviews with Nordic trade union representatives, 1989–94.

operation and pooled sovereignty. The remarkable nature of this transition, however, can only be understood by looking back on an earlier period of foreign policymaking, when distinct political choices were made.

Chapter 4 contrasts the pursuit of political integration (1985–95) with the pursuit of political autonomy (1945–85) to demonstrate just how radical the transformation has been in the history of northern European politics. To establish what is at stake is to recall the golden age of the Nordic models, a historic moment when these states successfully combined domestic compensation with economic growth and Nordic security policies were tailored to a bipolar distribution of military power.

CHAPTER FOUR

From Economic Interdependence
to Political Integration

While the period beginning in 1985 demanded changes in the Nordic countries' social charter and in the capacity of the state to act domestically, in contrast to two earlier periods of European integration, the range of choices available to the Nordic states narrowed considerably. In two earlier periods of alliance building (the 1940s) and economic policy coordination (the 1970s), northern European governments preferred political autonomy to integration and sought compatible yet independent solutions to international change.

Whenever possible, Nordic states resisted joining intrusive forms of multilateral cooperation or signing defense agreements that compromised political autonomy. For example, Norway and Denmark reluctantly agreed to participate in NATO only after regional cooperation efforts broke down and the appropriate restrictions on alliance activities were agreed upon.[1] Finland combined economic and security partnerships with the East and the West in order to enhance its political autonomy. Iceland initially denounced the U.S. proposal to maintain a base on its territory after the Second World War and has been referred to as the "reluctant ally." Yet the Icelanders, along with the other Nordic states, have preferred less binding forms of economic cooperation, such as bilateral free trade agreements, to membership in the EC. When the Danish people voted in the fall of 1972, 64 percent of the

[1] Three restrictions were agreed upon: limitations on NATO exercises in northern Norway and east of the island of Bornholm in the Baltic Sea, no stationing of foreign troops on Norwegian and Danish territory during peacetime, and no nuclear weapons permitted aboard ships or on territories of these states.

participants endorsed membership in the EC. Yet domestic opposition to the "supranational, capitalist" EC has remained so strong that the Danish people voted against the Maastricht Treaty on June 2, 1992.

Thus, in response to previous periods of European economic and security integration, the Nordic states adopted five distinct combinations of economic and security policies. In the current phase of European integration, the Nordic states have fewer roads to choose from. In fact, all roads lead to Europe. The deepening and widening of European integration required northern Europe to relinquish autonomous policies or risk marginalization. The end of the cold war pulled Sweden and Finland into the European Community once neutrality was no longer an obstacle.

Nordic political choices have narrowed with the deepening of European integration and the breakup of the cold war defense system. From choosing between two blocs and a policy of Europe at arms' length to determining the pace of European integration, Nordic foreign policy options have qualitatively changed. Consider now the range of Nordic solutions to international change prior to 1985.

COLD WAR SECURITY CHOICES

As Karl Deutsch has argued, the Nordic countries form a "security community" where the prospect of war as a means of solving conflict has become unthinkable.[2] While the five northern European states no longer fear the prospect of war among themselves, the German occupation of Norway and Denmark during the Second World War (1940–45), the occupation of Iceland by Allied forces (1940–44), and Finland's Winter War (1939–40) and War of Continuation (1941–44) with the Soviet Union are reminders of how small neutral states can be strategically important in the military plans of larger powers.[3]

[2] Northern Europe has not always been at peace. In the last five hundred years, there have been at least 50 wars within or among the Nordic states.

[3] For a historical analysis of postwar discussion of northern European security issues, problems, and how U.S. policies affected Nordic security during the cold war see Rolf Tamnes, *The United States and the Cold War in the High North* (Aldershot, England: Dartmouth, 1991). For an analysis of the German invasion and occupation of Denmark and Norway during World War II, see Richard Petrow, *The Bitter Years* (New York: Morrow Quill, 1974); and for an explanation for the failure of the allied campaign to defend Norway, see Jack Adams, *The Doomed Expedition* (London: Mandarin, 1989). For analyses of the Soviet invasions of Finland during World War II, see Tomas Ries, *Cold Will* (Lon-

Prior to World War II, the Nordic states preferred to maintain policies of neutrality. Alliances with other states could unwillingly draw them into the military affairs of larger powers. Following the war, the Norwegian, Danish, and Swedish governments attempted to form a regional pact, the Nordic Defense Union. The negotiations broke down over differences between Norwegians and Swedes over the appropriate relationship to external powers. The Swedish government envisioned a partnership of neutral states, whereas the Norwegian government insisted that a defense pact must include a security guarantee from the West.[4] Norway negotiated a restricted agreement with the Atlantic Alliance, and in 1949 Denmark followed Norway into NATO.

Finland allied with Germany during the war and was required to pay heavy war reparations (approximately 300 million U.S. dollars) to the Soviet Union.[5] In February 1947, Finland signed the Paris Peace Treaty, which specified restrictions on the size of the Finnish armed forces.[6] At the initiative of the Soviets, Finland concluded a Treaty of Friendship Cooperation and Mutual Assistance (TFCMA) in the spring of 1948. The treaty provided reassurance that Finland would repel any attack on Soviet territory. Despite these infringements on Finland's political autonomy, the state managed to remain outside the Warsaw Pact and to develop its own independent military force. Iceland, on the other hand, pursued an entirely different security guarantee.

An editorial in the Icelandic daily *Morgunbladid* on April 10, 1940, warned that the invasion and occupation of Denmark and Norway by Hitler's armies demonstrated how great powers ignore declarations of neutrality.[7] When British forces preemptively occupied Icelandic territory on May 10, 1940, and violated Icelandic neutrality, many Ice-

don: Brassey's, 1988); Jukka Tarkka, *Neither Stalin nor Hitler* (Helsinki: Otava, 1991); and Tuomo Polvinen, *Between East and West* (Minneapolis: University of Minnesota Press, 1986).

[4] For an analysis of the negotiations to create a Nordic Defense Union, see Bernt Schiller, "At Gun Point: A Critical Perspective on the Attempts of Nordic Governments to Achieve Unity after the Second World War," *Scandinavian Journal of History* 9 (1984), 228–229; Magne Skodvin, *Norden eller NATO* (Oslo: Universitetsforlaget, 1971); Tamnes, *The United States and the Cold War in the High North*, pp. 42–44; and Sverker Åström, "Swedish Neutrality," in *The Committed Neutral*, ed. Bengt Sundelius (Boulder: Westview Press, 1989), p. 23.

[5] See T. K. Derry, *A History of Scandinavia* (Minneapolis: University of Minnesota Press, 1979), pp. 354–355.

[6] See Pekka Visuri, *Evolution of the Finnish Military Doctrine, 1945–1985* (Helsinki: War College, 1990), pp. 21–23.

[7] Donald Neuchterlein, *Iceland: Reluctant Ally* (Ithaca: Cornell University Press, 1961), p. 23.

79

landers were caught by surprise. The withdrawal of British forces needed for the North African campaign led President Roosevelt to commit U.S. troops to defend Icelandic territory in an agreement signed on July 1, 1941. Icelanders anticipated the full withdrawal of U.S. forces at the end of the war and sought to reestablish a policy of neutrality. The U.S. request for a base on Icelandic territory was met with heavy resistance during the 1946–49 period. After a lengthy domestic debate and aggressive Soviet actions in Czechoslovakia and Berlin, however, Iceland agreed to join NATO and to allow the alliance to maintain a base at Keflavik. Iceland is the only Nordic state without an independent military force.

After World War II, all five Nordic states responded to the emerging bipolar security system by combining the strategies of deterrence and reassurance. Iceland joined NATO and permitted a base on its territory only as a last resort to deter Soviet military action. To reassure the Soviet Union and to reduce tensions in northern Europe, Denmark and Norway restricted NATO's military activities in the proximity of Soviet territory and the surrounding seas. Sweden and Finland sought to dissipate conflict between East and West by creating new institutions such as the Conference on Security Cooperation in Europe (CSCE) and by refusing to participate in Western military or economic alliances.

The Nordic states, while pursuing separate alliance relationships with the two great powers, learned to live under conditions of vulnerability. In the cold war period, the principal military threat to northern Europe was the prospect of a limited attack: the Danes envisioned a sudden Soviet move to seize the island of Bornholm; Norwegians and Icelanders feared Soviet control of territory or airspace along the coast or on the island of Spitzbergen, adjacent to the Atlantic access point for U.S. and Soviet submarines; and the Swedes and Finns were concerned about the prospect of Soviet control of the Baltic.

In the early 1980s, the Soviet naval buildup on the Kola Peninsula, submarine maneuvers in the Greenland-Iceland-U.K. gap, repeated submarine incursions into Swedish and Norwegian inland waterways, and the U.S. forward naval strategy heightened an old concern: the fear that deterioration in relations between the great powers could result in a war in or around Scandinavia. After 1985, the rapprochement between the Soviet Union and the United States brought with it an entirely new security situation, and a reassessment of foreign policy strategies.

I have discussed the Nordic preference for neutrality and the desire to keep from becoming entangled in the military affairs of larger powers. To do this, these states opted for separate types of security arrangements (Swedish armed neutrality, Iceland's base agreement with NATO, Danish and Norwegian membership in the alliance with restrictions, and Finnish semineutrality). The following discussion focuses on similar efforts designed to maintain independence from larger powers visible in the cold war economic policies of the Nordic states.

COLD WAR ECONOMIC CHOICES

All Nordic states have shared reservations about subordinating economic policies to supranational authorities. Yet the cold war system imposed more constraints on neutral Nordic states than on NATO member states. For Sweden and Finland, political integration with the European Community (whose membership predominantly included NATO member states) would have undermined the credibility of each state's policy of neutrality. For Iceland, Denmark, and Norway, membership in NATO was a choice of last resort. It did not compel these states to comply with the intrusive forms of policy coordination embodied in the EC's Treaty of Rome. As in security relations, the Nordic states sought the greatest possible degree of autonomy from intrusive international institutions during the cold war period.

When Britain proposed to create EFTA, a free trade agreement designed to be an alternative to the ambitious plans for union sought by the EC, most of the Nordic states preferred this option. In 1959, just two years after the signing of the Rome Treaty, Denmark, Sweden, Norway, Britain, Switzerland, Austria, and Portugal signed an agreement to create a free trade area (EFTA) with the EC. Iceland and Finland, however, were latecomers to the EFTA agreement. Iceland joined EFTA in 1970. Finland negotiated a separate agreement (FIN-EFTA) in 1961 and also maintained an agreement with Comecon. Finland did not become a full member of EFTA until 1986 because of its special relationship to the Soviet Union. EFTA was established because its members preferred solutions other than those that were adopted by the European Community.

EFTA's institutions were deliberately weak because these states objected to the supranational character of the EC. No provisions were established by the EFTA states in important sectors such as agriculture. The members did not adopt a common tariff because of Britain's status as a commonwealth. The only imposition on state autonomy was the requirement that members eliminate tariffs on industrial goods. The EFTA agreement provided an ideal solution for the Nordic participants by securing access to the EC market (France, West Germany, Italy, Belgium, the Netherlands, and Luxembourg) without sacrificing autonomy over economic policy. The organization was an economic arrangement, not a political body. A small secretariat was established in Geneva to provide administrative support for the organization, yet it did not have the capacity to act independently. EFTA's form and objective have been defined by the EC, just as the periphery is subject to the core.[8] EFTA also resulted in the reduction of trade barriers among Nordic member states—something that had proved impossible in the failed effort to create a Nordic customs union, Nordek.[9]

Although British leadership was crucial to the formation of EFTA, power disparities among EFTA member states have been inconsequential. Leadership is shared on a rotating basis, and no single state acts as a hegemon within the organization. The structure of EFTA is nonhierarchical, the capacity of the institution to infringe on the political autonomy of its members or on other states is weak, and power is shared equally among its members. For states desiring autonomy from supranationalism and greater access to European markets, EFTA was the ideal solution.

When Britain announced its intent to join the EC in the 1960s, a debate ensued in Denmark, Norway, and Sweden over how to resolve economic dependence on the British market with the desire to remain outside the EC. As indicated in Table 4.1, Britain was one of the most important markets for Nordic exports. De Gaulle's rejection of Britain's application put the EC debate on ice. When Britain reapplied to join the EC, however, the domestic debate in three of the Nordic states revealed essential differences in each state's relationship to Europe.[10] According to the Swedish government, the policy of neutrality pre-

[8] Per Magnus Wijkman, "Policy Options Facing EFTA," *EFTA Occasional Paper* 22 (January 1988), 2.
[9] See Clive Archer, "Britain and Scandinavia: Their Relations within EFTA, 1960–68," *Cooperation and Conflict* 1 (1976), 1–23; and Bo Strath, *Nordic Industry and Nordic Economic Cooperation* (Stockholm: Almqvist and Wiksell, 1978).
[10] For a discussion of the importance of the British decision in Norway, see Martin

Table 4.1. Value of Nordic exports to the
three largest recipients, 1970 (millions of
U.S. $)

Destination of Danish Exports	
United Kingdom	626
Sweden	556
Germany	424
Destination of Norwegian Exports	
United Kingdom	440
Germany	439
Sweden	398
Destination of Swedish Exports	
United Kingdom	847
Germany	796
Denmark	665
Destination of Icelandic Exports	
United States	44
United Kingdom	19
Germany	16
Destination of Finnish Exports	
United Kingdom	402
Sweden	349
Germany	243

Source: Direction of Trade Annual, 1969–75
(Washington, D.C.: International Monetary
Fund, 1976).

vented the state from participating in the Common Market. Swedish
Social Democrats viewed the proposals for monetary and political
union embodied in the Dauvignon and Werner Plans as incompatible
with nationally determined economic and security policies. For the
Nordic members of NATO, on the other hand, security policy concerns
were not an obstacle to membership in the EC. A majority of Norwegians rejected EC membership (53.5 percent), however, while a majority of Danes (64 percent) agreed to join the EC in the fall of 1972.
In the 1970s, Sweden, Finland, Norway, and Iceland agreed to form a
closer partnership with the European Community through EFTA in
order to secure access to markets without sacrificing political autonomy
over national economic or security policies.

Sæter, "Norway and European Integration: External Challenges and Domestic Constraints," paper presented to the Conference on EFTA Countries' Integration Strategies,
Helsinki, September 1988.

The End of Political Autonomy

During the cold war period, the Nordic states adopted separate combinations of security and economic policies in order to minimize subordination to larger powers, to maintain access to vital markets, to dissipate East-West conflict, and to minimize the risk of a superpower war in Europe. When the EC created new forms of economic and security policy coordination and the polarized relations between East and West broke down, the Nordic preference for political autonomy from international institutions fundamentally changed. Nordic political leaders expressed concern about the prospects of economic exclusion or marginalization and an increased vulnerability to new security risks. Thus, policy coordination with the European Community became the priority of Nordic political leaders. In some Nordic states, however, resistance to regional governance was far more extensive than in other Nordic states. These domestic political differences will be discussed at length in Chapter 6.

What was critical in the transformation of international relations after 1985 for the small northern European states has been the loss of options associated with political change. These states have been pulled into greater cooperation with the European Community: the only questions are what form integration will take, how long until the state can join, and what deal can be struck with Brussels in the accession process.

The following section outlines how the Nordic states evolved from an EFTA solution to an EC solution in the decade of the Europeanization of Nordic security and economic policymaking (1985–95).

The Pursuit of Political Integration

After 1985, Nordic states became much more willing to exchange political autonomy for integration and cooperate with the European Community. The old solutions became inappropriate, as one Nordic leader argues: "As an institution, EFTA has served its purpose well. But in the opinion of our EFTA partners it is no longer adequate. Ensuring permanent success requires more extensive multilateral commitments and closer cooperation among the states of Europe."[11] Yet as in the 1970s, the first preference of Nordic states was for a more limited part-

[11] Icelandic foreign minister's address to the Althing (Icelandic parliament), October 27, 1994, p. 8.

nership with the EC, the EEA agreement. In the process of negotiating the EEA agreement, important differences emerged in the European strategies of the EFTA states.

In the Luxembourg Declaration (1984) the Alpine and Nordic member states of EFTA (Switzerland, Austria, Iceland, Finland, Sweden, and Norway) initiated negotiations to create a new form of partnership with the EC, a European Economic Space (EES), or EEA.[12] The precise nature of this partnership was not specified. The EC's publication of the White Paper and its revival of plans to create a single European market convinced the six EFTA governments that the Luxembourg Declaration required more specificity. It became clear that the 1973 bilateral agreements could no longer guarantee access to an internal market for capital, goods, services, and persons.

In June 1988, the EFTA ministers met in Tampere, Finland, to specify alternative forms of cooperation with the EC. In response to a series of EFTA proposals, EC President Jacques Delors outlined two alternatives: expanded bilateral agreements between the EC and EFTA or a new and more structured form of partnership with common decision-making and administrative institutions. At the March 1989 EFTA meeting in Oslo, the six states agreed to pursue a new form of partnership and negotiate with the EC to create an expanded free trade area. In December 1989, the EFTA members made a critical decision: they agreed to liberalize economic policies to the EC's "four freedoms." At the request of EFTA representatives, the environment, safety, health, research, education, and social security ("the flanking issues") were added to the agenda for negotiation. Finally, EFTA states were assured that they would be able to have a formal voice in EC decisions.[13]

While the EFTA states negotiated a draft EEA treaty, the international situation changed dramatically. The collapse of communism encouraged the newly independent states of Czechoslovakia, Poland, and Hungary to look to the European Community for political and eco-

[12] See Helen Wallace and Wolfgang Wessels, "Towards a New Partnership: The EC and EFTA in the Wider Western Europe" (Geneva: EFTA Working Paper, March 1989); and the special issue of the *Journal of Common Market Studies* 28 (June 1990), on EC-EFTA relations.

[13] Four institutional questions were also included on the EC-EFTA agenda. With respect to political decision-making, EC directives issued by the Council of Ministers would apply directly only to member states. EFTA members should adopt corresponding arrangements. A common court should be established to resolve disputes and ensure that legislation is applied uniformly. A common framework of supervision should be established to uphold compliance with Community rules.

nomic support. For the Nordic states, this move created a dilemma. Would central and northern Europe share the same relationship with the EC in a Europe of concentric circles? These changes also created an opportunity for the four neutral states in EFTA (Finland, Sweden, Switzerland, and Austria) to reassess their policies, which were intended to address the particularities of the cold war period. German unification diverted diplomatic attention away from the creation of the EEA and led the Danish foreign minister to encourage the Nordic states to join the EC. A Nordic bloc in the Community, it was argued, would have more voting power in the Council of Ministers than a united Germany would.[14]

In June 1990, two signals came from the European Community. In a speech at Harvard University, Helmut Kohl indicated that the European Community would welcome new members from EFTA. And in a speech made at an EFTA meeting in Gothenburg, Sweden, Jacques Delors indicated that EFTA's inclusion in EC political decision-making would only be possible if they agreed to join the Community. EFTA states could not merely "take the raisins from the cake" and expect to free ride on the EC's internal market. The membership option was not the original goal of the six EFTA states, nor did EFTA anticipate exclusion from EC decision-making institutions based on the initial phase of negotiations.

Three conceptions of the EEA emerged among the six EFTA states following these changes in the international context of negotiations. One group (Sweden and Austria) perceived the EEA as a stepping-stone to full membership in the EC. The policy changes required by the EEA would also be required if these states were full members of the EC. A second group (Finland and Switzerland) viewed the EEA as an anteroom. It would not be appropriate to apply for full membership yet, but the EEA enabled these governments to keep that option open. A third group (Norway and Iceland) viewed the EEA as an alternative to EC membership. The EEA extends the 1973 trade agreement to the four freedoms, provides the possibility of institutional mechanisms to safeguard national interests, and preserves greater political autonomy than EC membership implies.[15] But the options for EFTA states had narrowed: all governments sought closer ties to the EC. The two alter-

---

[14] This argument was made by the Danish foreign minister, Uffe Ullemann-Jensen.
[15] See Finn Laursen, ed., *EFTA and the EC: Implications of 1992* (The Netherlands: European Institute of Public Administration, 1990).

natives were starkly presented by Norwegian prime minister Gro Harlem Brundtland in a debate held in the Parliament on December 13, 1990: "Since 1985, the EC countries have systematically reduced internal trade barriers. The inner market will have common regulations by 1992. It is this development that we must meet, and we have two choices: by forming an agreement between EFTA and the EC; or by joining the European Community."[16] As Nordic governments collectively pursued political integration (a move from the free movement of industrial goods to acceptance of the acquis communitaire negotiated in the EEA agreement), political differences among the EFTA governments emerged.

During the summer of 1991, the EEA negotiations suffered a severe setback. Clearly, intra-EFTA relations had reached a new low. Switzerland and Austria were dissatisfied with EC demands for truck transport through the Alpine area. Iceland and Norway contested the Spanish and Portuguese request for access to domestic fishing resources. The Swedish government requested to bypass the EEA negotiations and deal directly with the EC on its membership application. Representatives from the EC indicated that compromise solutions should be worked out by issue area and that the Swedish government would have to work within the EEA framework. By October 1991, the negotiations were back on track, and a draft treaty was sent to the European Court of Justice for approval. The EEA treaty also required approval by the national assemblies of each EFTA member state and ratification by the European Parliament.

The final version of the EEA agreement committed the EFTA states to contribute $2 billion to the EC's structural funds; established an EFTA court; created an EFTA equivalent of the Council of Ministers; and required the EFTA states to adopt economic policies consistent with the free movement of capital, services, goods, and persons (see Appendix, Agreement on the EEA). The treaty also committed the EFTA states to liberalize their agricultural policies so as not to impose excessive import duties, particularly on goods originating from less developed regions within the EC. Of particular importance to the Nordic states was the inclusion of safeguard clauses in the agreement.[17] These clauses can be activated whenever policy adaptation incurs "serious

[16] UD-Informasjon, "EØS-debatt i Stortinget," December 12, 1990, p. 44.
[17] Discussion with Ulf Dinkelspiel, chief negotiator for Sweden in the EEA negotiations, 1990–91.

economic, societal, and/or environmental difficulties of a sectoral or regional nature."[18]

The EEA agreement requires adherence to EC legislation without offering EFTA states the possibility to influence the decision-making process. The EEA agreement specifies which of the EC's existing body of legal regulations, or acquis communitaire, apply to EFTA states. According to representatives from the Norwegian foreign ministry, in the negotiations between EFTA delegations and the EC, 1,400 decisions were discussed in detail and became the basis for the final agreement.[19] EFTA countries retained formal decision-making autonomy yet abdicated control over the direction and substance of policy changes implemented in the EC. For many Nordic political leaders, pooling sovereignty at the EC level was preferable to the automatic reflexive adjustments required by the EEA. In sum, as the EC consolidated its internal market program, it made retaining autonomous economic policies more difficult for EFTA members.

While EFTA states no longer had the options associated with the period of economic interdependence prior to 1985, the EC also increasingly infringed on the independence of its members in two important policy areas in the implementation of the Maastricht Treaty. Only for Denmark was an exception made. For a majority of Danes, economic union (the creation of a central European bank, common currency, and coordinated macroeconomic policies) and political union (common foreign and security policies) were considered unacceptable forms of supranational cooperation. The Danish people rejected the Maastricht Treaty on the grounds that these types of policies should be decided in Copenhagen, not in Brussels. The treaty was implemented, however, once the Danes approved the limitations on EC cooperation specified in the Edinburgh protocol.

The new entrants to the European Community in 1995 (Austria, Finland, and Sweden) were required to abide by the conditions negotiated at Maastricht. A Danish solution was not possible for the EFTA states seeking to join the EC yet desiring to retain national economic and security policies. Thus, in contrast to the past, when northern European states had greater independence from supranational institutions, the Nordic states have become more embedded in the European

[18] EFTA-EC document in *EFTA Bulletin* (1991), 9.
[19] Norwegian Foreign Ministry, "Status i EØS-forhandlingene," Ambassador Berg, January 1, 1990, p. 1.

trading regime (EC) and the European security system (WEU) than ever before.

At stake as the Nordic states trade political autonomy for European integration is more than merely a redirection of foreign policy. Instead, the very structure of state-society relations, the policy legacies of years of social democratic leadership, and the capacity of the state to act are in jeopardy. In contrast to the bilateral agreements eliminating tariffs on industrial goods, European integration requires liberalizations in national controls on the movement of capital, goods, services, and persons. The middle way between capitalism and socialism depended on national intervention and tight controls over the domestic economy. To liberalize these policies is to accept greater dependence on foreign capital movements, more diversity in the labor market, less solidaristic social policies, and diminished national control over the determination of macroeconomic policy. European cooperation also requires giving up political autonomy in the formation of foreign and security policies.

When we consider the high stakes of European collaboration for this particular group of states and the traditional desire for distinctive economic and security policies, it is even more remarkable that Nordic governments willingly trade national solutions for multilateral collaboration. Chapter 5 explains why all Nordic states chose to collaborate more fully with the EC after 1985, before turning to an analysis of why some are more resistant to European unity than others are.

PART III

The Argument

CHAPTER FIVE

International Security: Nordic Preferences Change

The dramatic changes in European security after 1985 required all Nordic governments to reevaluate their foreign policy strategies. From a tense period of balancing between East and West during the cold war to the changes unleashed by perestroika, the withdrawal of scores of U.S. troops and weapons from Europe, the relocation of Russian military forces from central Europe to the flanks, the unification of Germany, and the creation of new, post–cold war security structures (CSCE, WEU, NACC), the Nordic states faced a new yet in many ways less stable situation. As the threat of a major war in Europe receded and the ideological and political divisions between the superpowers diminished, the major European powers sought new forms of political and military cooperation. The effect of these systemic changes on Nordic preferences was profound. In response to the emerging multipolar system, all of the Nordic states reevaluated their national security policies in relation to the European Community.

In this chapter, I outline how the transformation of international security played out in northern Europe. No Nordic defense ministry proclaimed that peace was breaking out. The security concerns of military planners throughout northern Europe were remarkably similar: all shared a fear of isolation and were wary of the cold war military forces that remained in the proximity of Nordic territory.[1] The dismantling of the Warsaw Pact and the withdrawal of military forces from the Baltic states altered the composition of forces in the north. Despite a funda-

[1] See, for example, Pertti Joenniemi, "Europe Changes, the Nordic System Remains," *Bulletin of Peace Proposals* 21 (June 1990), 205–217.

93

mental change in intentions, Russian capabilities improved in northern Europe.[2] With the presence of troops and equipment and the absence of political stability, the situation to the east required new thinking in the north. In addition to the relative improvement in military capabilities in the region, previously unimaginable security risks confronted Nordic political leaders and defense planners. These included images of Russians crossing the Finnish border by the thousands, environmental risks associated with dismantling cold war weapons systems, the continued existence of a vast nuclear arsenal in the former Soviet Union, and remnants of animosities predating the First World War resurgent throughout Europe. At the same time, the United States appeared both less capable and less willing to accept responsibility for European security problems. America's passive reaction to the war in Yugoslavia was a sign that European defense matters were a European problem more than an American one.

This chapter returns to the first question posed in the book: why do *all* Nordic states give up political autonomy after 1985? Changes in the military/security environment surrounding the Nordic states led to a major redirection in foreign policies. With the resolution of the East-West conflict, the EC became the new regional core, requiring the Nordic states to position themselves in relation to European economic and security structures. The changes were, in many ways, greater than the Nordics could have hoped for. "The change in Europe had gone far beyond detente to define a major transformation in which the traditional conflict pattern was broken up."[3]

Without the opening provided by the breakup of the cold war security system, it would have been impossible to conceive of Nordic accession to the European Community. In short, the major economic policy changes came about only because of a transformation in international security. Economic policy changes can be understood only in the context of the transition from a bipolar, East-West division to the process of institution-building in the European Community. Previously, Finland and Sweden were prevented from joining the EC because of their policies of neutrality. As the domestic political debates on accession in the other Nordic states reveal, security concerns were an important motiva-

[2] The transfer of forces from the continent to the flanks was referred to as the *pøl-seeffekt*, or sausage effect. Russian tanks in the Leningrad military district were upgraded to the newest version, as were aircraft and helicopters.

[3] Ole Wæver, "Nordic Nostalgia: Northern Europe after the Cold War," *International Affairs* 68 (January 1992), 70.

tion for cooperating with the EC. Political elites presented Europe as a solution to managing the post–cold war security risks faced by the Nordic states. One of the primary fears for Nordic elites was the possibility of isolation, or to "be left out in the cold," as the rest of Europe created a Deutschian security community.

The first section of this chapter focuses on the effect of changes in European security on the two neutral states in northern Europe. Finnish and Swedish policies of neutrality prevented these states from joining an economic partnership with other European states during the cold war period. As the rigid postwar division of Europe into two ideological blocs broke down, so did the constraints on Finnish and Swedish foreign policy. Even Russia has expressed interest in forming some kind of partnership with the European Community—a radical reversal from the pre-1985 period. Thus, as a consequence of the profound changes in international security, the neutral Nordic states had political choices comparable to those of their NATO neighbors.

The second section outlines how the preferences of Nordic governments changed once the system was transformed from a bipolar distribution of capabilities to a multipolar one. Nordic political leaders increasingly viewed European security cooperation as a possible long-term guarantee and a necessary supplement to the security umbrella provided by the United States. Even states firmly committed to the NATO alliance (Norway) sought cooperation with the European Community's defense pillar, the Western European Union (WEU). Thus there was a visible change in the domestic debates throughout northern Europe over what the EC could offer the Nordic states. This shift should be interpreted on two levels: an effort to redefine national interests and an effort to build new political coalitions. Societal interests were less concerned with the new security threat, however, and more preoccupied with the economic and social consequences of integration.

The third section draws some important conclusions about the implications of these changes in international security on Nordic politics. In contrast to previous periods of integration, it was the neutral states that were the first to apply to join the EC. The political process was relatively closed, however, and seemed more similar to a security policy crisis than did other types of foreign policymaking. Meetings were held in secret, the process was elite-centered, and the public was informed of a redirection in national policy after the fact. A second important change illustrates the effect of the inversion of high politics and low politics on domestic institutions. The relative importance of defense and security departments has diminished as more EC responsibilities are handled by the representatives from the Foreign Ministry and officials trained in economics and trade.

Despite the fact that the changes in European politics created a level playing field among the Nordic states (all feared isolation and sought new forms of security cooperation), security changes were a necessary but not a sufficient explanation for Nordic responses to international change.

SYSTEMIC CHANGE: EFFECT ON THE NORDIC NEUTRALS, SWEDEN AND FINLAND

The opening provided by the end of the cold war permitted the unthinkable: Finland was released from an intrusive defense pact with the Soviet Union and free to join any military alliance or economic trading regime, and Sweden was no longer preoccupied with Moscow's interpretation of its trade and political relations with the West. Instead, these states assumed a new role as active participants in European institution-building.

During the summer of 1990, Swedish political elites actively debated the meaning of a neutrality policy in the absence of the cold war military threat. In the political forum provided by *Dagens Nyheter*, Social Democratic prime minister Ingvar Carlsson initially resisted European Community membership since it would threaten the credibility of the policy of neutrality.[4] The prime minister maintained that Sweden should draw the line at defense and security policy collaboration with the EC. Carlsson was criticized for hiding behind neutrality and for failing to adjust to important changes in the security situation. The EC debate intensified as members of Carlsson's party and the Conservative opposition leader Carl Bildt strongly disagreed with the Social Democratic leader.

Former Social Democratic cabinet secretary and security policy expert Sverker Åström took issue with Carlsson's position as an unnecessary restriction of Sweden's negotiating ability. Åström maintained that, precisely because of the profound changes in European politics (the

---

[4] See Ingvar Carlsson, *Dagens Nyheter*, Debatt, May 27, 1990.

erosion of military blocs and a diminished threat of war), neutral states such as Sweden have an important role to play in the transition process. Neutrality should not rule out Swedish participation in broad changes occurring in European politics. "It is possible that Sweden, together with the other Nordic countries, may further its own interests through the EC and give meaning to the new security structure in Europe (which is the big project of the 1990s) rather than by remaining outside the EC's institutional framework."[5]

In an effort to sway support for EC membership, Conservative Party leader Carl Bildt used security policy arguments in the summer 1990 debate on Sweden's role in the new Europe. Bildt contributed a column to *Dagens Nyheter*, entitled "Political Union Is Advantageous for Sweden!" He maintained that the EC's proposals to cooperate in the formation of common foreign and security policies made Swedish membership in the EC *more* attractive. Just as we cast aside our reservations with the United Nations in 1947, so must we adapt in the aftermath of the 1989 European revolution, argued Bildt. Otherwise, Sweden risks "sterile isolation" while Europe continues building a common security policy framework.[6]

During the fall of 1990, Carlsson reversed his position on the EC, and in so doing he initiated a fundamental shift in the direction of Swedish foreign policy. In a statement to the Swedish Parliament on October 2, 1990, the Social Democratic leader presented a rather different view of the international security situation. Carlsson's statement left open the possibility of Swedish EC membership. In a Europe without blocs, where cooperation has replaced the threat of war, neutrality policy no longer hinders participation in the EC.[7] The government announced its intent to join the EC on October 26 as part of an economic crisis package.

In July 1991, just prior to the national elections, Ingvar Carlsson's government submitted Sweden's application to join the EC. The Social Democrats sought to recapture the EC issue from the right in a campaign that featured positive images of Sweden in the EC. Television advertisements portrayed Swedes as European citizens, relaxing in Pari-

---

[5] Translated from Sverker Åström, "En onödig inskränkning," *Dagens Nyheter*, June 1, 1990, p. A4.

[6] Translated from "Politisk union gynnar Sverige!" Carl Bildt, *Dagens Nyheter*, June 3, 1990, p. A4.

[7] See Lauri Karvonen and Bengt Sundelius, "The Nordic Neutrals Facing the European Union," unpublished paper (mimeo), 1994, p. 3.

sian cafés and enjoying the amenities of the internal market. At bus stops and public places, numerous posters featured a red rose placed over the EC flag, with the motto "a Social Democratic Europe." Despite efforts by Ingvar Carlsson to capitalize on widespread public support for entry into the EC, the 1991 elections ushered in a new government led by Carl Bildt. The details of the Swedish accession treaty were finalized under Bildt's leadership. To negotiate the deal, Bildt relied heavily on the expertise of one of the most optimistic Europeanists in the north, chief negotiator Ulf Dinkelspiel in the Ministry of Foreign Affairs.

On September 16, 1993, in a speech made in Brussels on Sweden's EC policy, Prime Minister Carl Bildt presented the government's interpretation of systemic changes: "We are now watching the emergence in Europe of a more complex pattern of security policy. It is becoming more important to establish, by a process of continuous consultation, common solutions to common problems. And in this process, no institution will be as important as the European Union [EC]." With respect to Sweden's role in this new European architecture, he went on to say, "Sweden will be an active and committed participant in the evolution of the common foreign and security policy. Foreign observers who think otherwise have not really understood the Swedish mentality. When we join international cooperation, we intend to have an influence, and we want to make a difference. We look upon the European Union, of which we hope shortly to be a member, as the hub of the new European security order."[8] Under Bildt's leadership, Sweden positioned itself to be a player in the European Community. "The Union will have the central role in promoting peace and stability throughout Europe. We have stated on a number of occasions that we intend to be an active and full participant in the Union's common foreign and security policy."[9] The rapid reversal in Sweden's foreign policy had an important demonstration effect on Finland's security policy and its relationship to the EC.

The transition from bipolarity to multipolarity and the breakup of the Soviet empire also had profound effects on Finnish foreign policy. The Finnish defense minister Elizabeth Rehn interpreted the end of the cold war as a "seismic wave that has shaken the political and mili-

[8] Address by Prime Minister Carl Bildt to La Fondation Paul-Henri Spaak, Palais des Académies, Brussels, September 16, 1993, p. 15.
[9] Ibid.

tary structures of the Old Continent. Finland, following the pragmatic tradition characteristic of its foreign policy, has reshaped its foreign and security policies to reflect its new geopolitical position."[10]

Within a relatively short period of time, three important changes occurred in Finnish foreign policy that could not have occurred in the absence of international events: the end of the Finnish-Soviet cold war defense agreement; an application to participate in the North Atlantic Cooperation Council (NACC); and, most important, an application to join the EC.

On January 20, 1992, the Russian and Finnish governments agreed to declare null and void the Treaty of Friendship, Cooperation, and Mutual Assistance (TFCMA) of 1948. The treaty committed Finland to resist an attack by Germany or any of its allies and required consultation between Finland and the Soviet Union in case of such an attack. Finland was also prohibited from joining any alliance directed against the Soviet Union and pledged to respect the sovereignty and integrity of its neighbor.[11] The era some disparagingly referred to as "Finlandization" was over.[12] For the first time since the end of the Second World War, Finland had the chance to ally with the West. Some Finnish elites entertained the option of joining NATO, although the government never fully endorsed this idea.[13] Instead, Finland was granted observer status in NATO's political council, NACC. According to Finnish political leaders, the ambitions of the CSCE, which were to foster greater cooperation between East and West, were also served by participating in NACC.

Once the Swedes indicated that they were pursuing the fast track to Europe, the Finns were not far behind. In March 1992, the Finnish government applied to join the EC and willingly accepted the conditions negotiated by the EC member states at Maastricht. Recognizing the end of the era of bipolarity, the Finns also reformulated their security policy in a manner parallel to the Swedish realignment and thereby accepted a much more activist role in relation to Europe. "In a divided

---

[10] Elisabeth Rehn, "Finland in the New Europe," speech given at the Center for Strategic and International Studies, Washington, D.C., October 16, 1992, p. 1.

[11] See William Taylor and Paul Cole, *Nordic Defense: Comparative Decision Making* (Lexington, Mass.: D. C. Heath, 1985), p. 38.

[12] See, for example, James Clarity, "Shadow of the Russian Bear over Finland Is Lifted," *New York Times*, Tuesday, January 21, 1992.

[13] Discussions with Finnish defense policy expert Pauli Järvenpää during his visit to the University of Washington, Seattle, 1993.

Europe, the Finnish policy of neutrality was a means of staying outside conflicts between the great powers. . . . The end of the division of Europe and confrontation between the superpowers means that there is no longer ground for a broadly applied policy of neutrality."[14]

An important concern for the Finnish government was the possibility of abandonment by the West. In the words of Nordic security analyst Arne Olav Brundtland, "Finland applied for EC membership in the wake of the Swedish application in fear of otherwise being isolated as a grey area between the EC and Russia."[15] Since Finland shares a lengthy border with the former Soviet Union, the political and economic stability of its neighbor continues to be of primary concern to national security. The cold war trading regime that led Finland to be referred to as "the Japan of the North" collapsed with the end of the Soviet empire.[16] Finnish leaders have viewed involvement in the European Community as a means to prevent right-wing, antimarket forces from becoming too powerful in Russia. From the perspective of Prime Minister Esko Aho, the situation in Russia (often referred to as the "Zhironovsky factor") contributed to a more positive attitude toward European integration in Finland.[17] The Russian politician's infamous article in *Pravda* expressing his desire to reinstate the empire (including Finland and the Baltic states) may have encouraged support for closer ties to the EC to stabilize Finland's security. Yet efforts to use the Russian threat as a means of garnering public support for EC membership were criticized by the anti-integrationists, who viewed this strategy as vulgar.[18]

As in Sweden, the government advocated EC membership as a means of shoring up Finnish national security. "For a country in the position of Finland, Union membership offers—also without military alliance—significant added security which we must actively exploit."[19] Finland has no intention of being a free rider and is open to coopera-

---

[14] "Finnish Foreign Policy and EC Membership," *Finnish Features* (Helsinki: Ministry for Foreign Affairs, October 1992), p. 2.

[15] Arne Olav Brundtland, "Nordic Security at the End of the Cold War," paper presented at the Baltic and Nordic Security Conference, Oslo, September 21–23, 1993, p. 34.

[16] Finland maintained a barter relationship with the Soviet Union, trading domestically manufactured goods for petroleum products. The crisis of the Finnish economy can, in part, be explained by the end of the Soviet trading regime.

[17] Bjarne Nitovuori, "Ryska osäkerheten förklarar EG-opinioner," *Huvudstadsbladet*, October 26, 1993.

[18] Karvonen and Sundelius, "The Nordic Neutrals Facing Europe," p. 13.

[19] Speech by Undersecretary of State Jaako Blomberg in Kuopio, Finland, September 28, 1994, p. 6.

tion in the provision of defense forces within European security structures. According to the revised conception of national policy, full participation in the West European Union conforms with Finnish national
security interests.[20]

In an address to the European Parliament in November 1993 Finnish president Koivisto stated: "In the European Union, we are fully prepared to take an active part in the common foreign and security policy
and in its further development as foreseen in the Treaty. We do not
exclude any options."[21] According to a representative from the Ministry
of Foreign Affairs:

> Finland's relations with the Western European Union (WEU), which is to be
> used as an instrument of the European Union in preparing and implement-
> ing decisions with defence implications, will be determined in the light of the
> development of European security structures. As a member, Finland would
> commit itself, in a spirit of solidarity and without reservation, to join the
> other EC Member States in promoting the objectives of the Union.[22]

Following Finnish entry into the European Community in January
1995, the government became an observer in the WEU, the EC's organization for regional military cooperation.

For the two neutral states in the north, Sweden and Finland, the
conditions for EC membership required a major redirection in security
policy. This change could not have occurred independently of international politics. The collapse of the Soviet empire and the breakup of
the Warsaw Pact entirely changed the interests of the neutral states.
The European Community structured the playing field by restricting
entry to those states committed to the entire European project. Denmark's Edinburgh exemptions could not be extended to the other Nordic states.[23] The EC maintained that all new entrants must comply with

[20] Ibid., p. 9.
[21] "Finland and the Evolution of Europe," address by Dr. Mauno Koivisto, president of
the Republic of Finland, at the Plenary Session of the European Parliament, Strasbourg,
November 16, 1993, p. 4.
[22] "Finnish Foreign Policy and EU Membership," *Finnish Features* (Helsinki: Finnish Foreign Ministry, November 1993), p. 2.
[23] The Edinburgh Protocol defined the limits of Danish integration. After the public
vetoed the Maastricht Treaty, the EC and representatives from the Danish government
negotiated a compromise settlement that enables Denmark to opt out of the economic
union (creation of a common monetary system) and the political union (formation of
common foreign, security, and defense policies). Denmark also objected to the EC's
notion of common citizenship and criticized the democratic deficit in EC institutions.

the political union dimension of integration and could not accept integration à la carte.[24] Nor was security the only interest involved: Finland and Sweden, to a greater extent than Norway, Iceland, and Denmark, had more at stake in the integration of European markets, as I discuss in Chapter 6.

As the international security situation fundamentally changed, so did the discussion of national interests in the Nordic states. Neutrality policy came under scrutiny with the fear of isolation from the rest of Europe. An integrated neutral, with greater access to the European market and new security structures (following the Irish and Austrian examples), became much more attractive to Swedish and Finnish political leaders. In the domestic debates over accession, leading Social Democrats and Conservatives advocated EC membership as a security guarantee and viewed participation in the EC's security structure (the Western European Union) as a means of enhancing state influence.

The foreign policies of the Nordic neutrals changed much more rapidly than those of their NATO neighbors in the aftermath of the cold war. Other Nordic elites, however, also sought to ally with the European Community to meet national security policy needs. The security argument became prominent after 1993, representing a fundamental change in national preferences and a means to deflect attention away from the controversial bread-and-butter issues of integration. The public and Euro-skeptics were less enthusiastic than political leaders in the government yet were forced to respond to the appeal of European Community membership as "the best way to achieve a European security order."[25]

NATIONAL SECURITY AND EUROPEAN INTEGRATION

As each of the Nordic states contemplated its relationship to the European Community, a new, pro-EC argument based on national security considerations was voiced by Nordic political leaders. Changes in the security environment, it was argued, called for a multilateral solution. Promoting European Community membership as a vital security interest reflected a change in the ways in which the Nordic states con-

[24] See, for example, "Beredskap utvecklar försvarsdimensionen," *Hufvudstadsbladet*, November 5, 1992, p. 5.
[25] See Mikael Holmström, "Inga alternativ vid nej till EU," *Svenska Dagbladet*, January 8, 1994, p. 8.

ceived of Europe—as not only an important trading partner but a political entity. It also represented, I believe, a significant attempt to garner support for the European project at home by attempting, at best, to build new coalitions and, at the very least, to deflect consideration from the more controversial aspects of European Community membership for the state, society, and the economy. The warnings were made by members of Nordic cabinets, who stressed the risk of isolation and marginalization associated with standing outside the efforts of the EC to create common security and foreign policies.

In Norway, the call for active participation in common European initiatives was led by the foreign and defense ministers and endorsed by the prime minister. In an article entitled "Fearing Isolation," which appeared in *Aftenposten* in February 1992, Norwegian foreign minister Thorvald Stoltenberg emphasized the stark choices facing the country: "Either we will be a part of a multilateral project (EC), or we will stand alone with one or two other European countries outside this cooperative project."[26] For Stoltenberg, the EC's role has fundamentally changed. The EC has become "the most attractive international organization in Europe." According to Stoltenberg, Norway confronted three foreign policy alternatives: (1) Norway returns to bilateral relations with Russia and other countries, which it had before the First World War; (2) Norway (like Iceland) establishes a bilateral security policy agreement with the United States; or (3) Norway becomes a member of the European Community and its security policy entity, the Western European Union. After the Maastricht Agreement, the EC established itself as the unrivaled guarantor of welfare and stability for all of Europe. Norway, he implied, should be a player—not an observer—of that process.[27] Stoltenberg's call for Norwegian membership in the EC on the basis of "our security policy interests" was also a theme taken up by his successor, Johan Jørgen Holst.

Johan Jørgen Holst, who served under Social Democratic prime minister Gro Harlem Brundtland as defense minister and later became Norway's foreign minister, repeatedly argued in the Norwegian media for an activist role in the new Europe. In one of many articles in *Aftenposten*, he said, "Today the entire European architecture is taking shape. It is becoming a new Europe. The contours are unclear. There

---

[26] Translated from Per Nordrum, "Frykter Isolation," in *Aftenposten*, February 4, 1992, p. 9.
[27] Ibid.

is no clear picture, but it is under way. Some structures are clear. The EU will become the central pillar of the new political order."[28]

Norway's proximity to the former Soviet Union was an additional motivation for securing a new partnership with Europe.[29] As Holst stated, "The last large empire in Europe is breaking up, with all the unpredictabilities that go with that. . . . Norway shares a border with nuclear-armed Russia. The EC can also offer support to Russia, and enhance political stability."[30] The Norwegian minister's view struck the same themes and relied on the same images as the words of the Finnish foreign minister. Holst repeated in October 1993: "For the first time we can see in reality the dream of an all-European security community based on economic and political integration—in contrast to the old divisions between the blocs. One of the opposition's main arguments against the EC in 1972 was that expansion of the EC would aggravate those divisions. Now the argument is reversed: an expanded EC offers the prospect of diminishing conflict between east and west."[31]

State secretary in the Norwegian prime minister's office Eldrid Nordbø also stressed the foreign and security policy motivations for Norwegian membership in the EC: "Norway shares fundamental interests with its NATO allies inside the Community. Throughout the 1980s we have witnessed an increasing degree of foreign policy cooperation between the EC member states. . . . Viewed in isolation, it would have been in Norway's interest to join the foreign policy cooperation of the European Community."[32]

Norwegian officials emphasized the distinct security problems on the northern flank. The director of strategic studies at the Norwegian Defense Research Institute, a lieutenant general in the armed services and editor of the Norwegian military journal, warned that the strategic situation in the north should be decoupled from changes on the continent. The former Norwegian defense minister, Per Ditlev-Simonsen, observed that "despite reduced tension, Norway remains in the shadow of the USSR's largest concentration of military forces."[33] According to the former chief of defense, General H. F. Zeiner-Gundersen, a paradoxi-

---

[28] Johan Jørgen Holst, "Vår vei til Europa," Aftenposten (Spring 1990).
[29] Interview conducted with Holst at the Norwegian Institute of International Affairs in Oslo, 1991.
[30] Ibid.
[31] Translated from Per Vassbotn, "Veiviseren Holst," Dagbladet, October 26, 1993, p. 2.
[32] "Europe and the Nordic Countries," European Affairs 4 (1989), 106.
[33] Interview with Per Ditlev-Simonsen in Jane's Defence Weekly, April 21, 1990, p. 764.

cal situation threatens Norway: as a consequence of glasnost and perestroika, there has been more uncertainty within the former Soviet
Union. It is less predictable what will evolve, and the substantial military capacity to the east has not weakened.[34]

In Norway, Denmark, and Iceland, affiliation with the WEU was controversial and pursued cautiously. No European government, it was argued, could provide an equivalent to the security guarantee provided
by the United States. The chairman of the Norwegian Parliamentary
Defense Committee, Hans Jacob Rosjørde, stated, "I have a great deal
of respect for history. . . . NATO is the only security guarantee and we
know it functions well."[35] Johan Jørgen Holst advocated "keeping the
options open," pursuing cooperation with European defense initiatives,
and maintaining allegiance to NATO.[36] Holst emphasized the special
relationship between Norway and the United States, which retains the
capability and the will to defend Norway. According to Holst, "if the
Alliance were to falter, we [the Norwegians] would be among the last
ones to leave the sinking ship."[37]

Helge Hernes, state secretary in the Norwegian Foreign Ministry in
1991, confirmed the importance of NATO to a post–cold war system of
European security. In the new European security architecture, NATO is
of fundamental importance to Norway because of its proximity to Europe's most powerful group of states, Russia and its near neighbors.
The new security dilemma for Norway, she warned, is the emergence of
a stronger and more defined EC in which the WEU becomes the European defense pillar. "We are not looking forward to the scenario of the
U.S. and EC members arriving at NATO meetings with pre-prepared
positions while flanking countries, Norway and Turkey, barely have an
opportunity to express their interests." Nor would Norway like to think
that the only way to find out about European security policymaking
would be to travel to neighboring Stockholm, since Sweden is much
more likely to be in the EC before Norway.[38] For defense planners in
Norway, it became more difficult to articulate security concerns than

[34] H. I. Zeiner-Gundersen, "Forsvar mot usikkerhet," *Aftenposten*, February 14, 1992, p.
2.
[35] Interview with Hans Rosjørde, "NATO på tegnebrettet," *Aftenposten*, November 11,
1991.
[36] Interview with Johan Jørgen Holst at the Norwegian Institute of International Affairs,
Oslo, 1991.
[37] Interview with Johan Jørgen Holst, *International Defense Review* 9 (1989), 116.
[38] "Store forandringer i NATO," *Aftenposten*, November 22, 1991.

before the end of the cold war. "There is an inner circle and an outer circle—EC countries are in the inner circle."[39]

In a statement made during the domestic debate over EC membership during the spring of 1994, Norwegian defense chief Admiral Torolf Rein endorsed EC membership as a means of promoting vital security interests. According to Rein, EC membership will enhance Norwegian security through participation in the European security organization, the WEU. Full voting rights in the WEU will be granted to Norway only when it becomes a member of the EC. The EC "will increasingly take over NATO's role in Europe."[40] For Norway, a loyal NATO ally, this position was novel.

Danish government officials also sought to cooperate with the strengthening of a European security entity yet were wary of creating a new "West European superpower."[41] The Danes, like the Norwegians, view the WEU as compatible with NATO membership but not a realistic alternative. According to Michael Clemmesen, the director of strategic studies at the Royal Danish Defense College, an adviser in the preparation of the National Defense Report, and lieutenant colonel in the army: "NATO's original mission still holds true today: keep the Americans in, the Germans down, and the Russians out—except today, this refers to Russian civilians."[42] From the Danish perspective, changes in the East make it even more important to rely on the alliance. "NATO is still necessary to provide the balance and to function as a crisis control instrument in relation to the destabilizing developments in the [former] Soviet Union."[43] Even though the Danish Parliament approved the Maastricht Treaty by a clear majority of 130 members in favor and 25 against, the Danish people were more skeptical. The voters rejected the treaty by a narrow margin of 48,000 (50.7 percent to 49.3 percent).[44] Denmark was the only European state to reject the provisions for European unity and the plans for deepening security policy cooperation outlined in Maastricht.[45]

[39] Interview with Johan Jørgen Holst, "Trang Norsk EF-debatt," by Svein Thompson, *Dagens Næringsliv*, December 11, 1991, p. 4.
[40] "The Case for Defence," in *Norway Now* (August 1994), 2.
[41] See "NATO ændrer struktur," *Berlingske Tidende*, May 30, 1991, p. 8; and "Europeisk sikkerhed," *Berlingske Tidende*, April 10, 1991, p. 11.
[42] Interview with Michael Clemmesen, Royal Danish Defense College, Copenhagen, 1991.
[43] Danish Commission on Security and Disarmament, 1991 report, p. 41.
[44] Gunnar Selgård, "Uventet nei til EF-unionen," *Aftenposten*, June 3, 1992, p. 4.
[45] In response to the Danish people's no to Maastricht, the government drafted a mem-

The security interests of Norway became a prominent theme in the EC debate on the eve of the national referendum.[46] For Prime Minister Brundtland, Norway's most ardent supporter of EC membership, security policy considerations were not only important to national interests but also a crucial part of the political process of convincing Norwegians to support European Union membership. On a tour of western Norway (the heartland of Euro-skepticism amid fisheries and rural communities) in August 1994, she stressed the importance of Norwegian security policy concerns. "Norway should not become a second-rate power in Europe. There are important foreign and security policy reasons for becoming full members of the European Union."[47] The Norwegian public, however, was less convinced by the security imperative in the EC debate.[48]

Following the EC's meeting in Maastricht, Norway was invited to participate in the European security pillar (WEU) as an associate member. Full membership is only granted to EC member states. Associate member status, according to representatives in the Foreign Ministry, will enable Norway to engage in "important consultations that affect our security" and is not incompatible with participation in NATO.[49]

Even in Iceland, where the resistance to European integration remains the strongest, representatives from the government sought to redefine national interests. Jón Baldvin Hannibalsson, minister for foreign affairs and external trade, described Iceland's situation: "Now we are in the middle of a storm and we do not know what awaits us when it abates: The role of NATO has changed with the withering away of its former enemy in the east and the strategic importance of Iceland has diminished. The Western European Union is increasingly becoming the core of security and defence policy identity for the European

orandum outlining the post-referendum position of Denmark. The Danish memorandum was accepted by other EC member states in the December 1992 meeting in Edinburgh. The Edinburgh Amendments to Maastricht outline Denmark's aspirations for European unity and the exemptions from economic and political union.

[46] See, for example, speech by Gro Harlem Brundtland, "Norway and Europe," at the European Institute, Washington, D.C., 1994, reprinted in *News of Norway* (July/August 1994), 8–11.

[47] "Gro på EU-tokt i nei-land," *Nytt fra Norge*, August 23, 1994, p. 11.

[48] Henry Valen, "The EU Situation in Norwegian Politics," lecture at the University of Bergen, April 26, 1995.

[49] Helge Hernes, "Norge i Vestunionen?" *Aftenposten*, December 18, 1991, p. 2.

Union."[50] For Iceland, "a common foreign and security policy only adds to the EU's attractions."[51]

Although it was once considered high treason to mention EC membership in national politics, Hannibalsson left open the possibility of Icelandic accession. "It is a tried and true fact that one can never hope to win if one does not participate in the game. If the Union becomes a real pan-European organisation of democratic European States, it becomes increasingly difficult for a democratic, European country with a developed market economy such as Iceland to justify a decision to abstain from membership."[52] The foreign minister stressed the long-standing historical and cultural ties to the continent to justify an internationalist orientation. The Icelanders, however, like the Danes, have a much greater skepticism toward European integration than do their respective governments. And the real obstacles to cooperation with the European project lie not in relatively abstract notions of achieving peace through allying with continental powers in the WEU but in the real and perceived costs to societal interests of integrating with the European Community. These domestic political obstacles will be discussed in Chapter 6.

STRUCTURAL CHANGE AND THE EFFECTS ON NORDIC POLITICS

As a consequence of systemic changes, Nordic domestic politics has changed in three fundamental ways. First, the decision-making process has become more secretive, suggesting that more is perceived to be at stake than in previous periods of integration. Second, national security concerns have been broadened to include environmental risks, refugees from the East, and transnational criminal organizations. Finally, the relative importance of actors has changed. Within bureaucracies, power has shifted away from experts in military and defense affairs to those who work in offices for commercial, economic, or trade relations.

More and more decisions have been made behind the scenes by Nordic elites who are well informed and frequently travel to Brussels.

[50] Speech by Jón Baldvin Hannibalsson, "Iceland and the Enlargement of the European Union," presented at the Conference of the French-Icelandic Chamber of Commerce, Paris, October 21, 1994, p. 3.

[51] Jón Baldvin Hannibalsson, "European Integration: A View From High Latitudes," speech to the Office of the European Union, Bonn, July 14, 1994, p. 7.

[52] Ibid., p. 9.

When a Swedish advisory council on European questions was created by Ingvar Carlsson, the public was not informed, nor is it possible to obtain a text of the issues raised in those discussions.[53] Because of the depth of changes in national policies required by integration, the decision-making process took on the character of a security policy crisis.

The security threats to Nordic territories require new solutions, according to political leaders and defense planners in northern Europe. From a Finnish perspective, "the collapse of the totalitarian regimes in Europe has brought along both hope and agony. We will be faced with a complex security situation for years to come. Ideological confrontation has been replace by ethnic strife, border disputes, and ecological concerns. Now we need a dynamic concept for security."[54]

The definition of a security risk to northern Europe has been expanded to include problems of border controls associated with the influx of non-Nordics from the East, the smuggling of nuclear or conventional weapons through Nordic territories, and the crime networks operating in Moscow that infiltrate the Nordic states. For countries whose airport security could be described as porous, these new security risks require alternative types of security forces and equipment. Collaboration with other European states also appears more attractive to Nordic governments. These new security risks by their very nature require multilateral solutions.

We have also witnessed an inversion of high and low politics. The prominence of security policy making, or so-called "high politics," has lost its status, while economic and trade policy making, or "low politics," has become much more important. This inversion has affected who is involved in foreign policy making. In the words of Finnish scholar Raimo Väyrynen, "the transition from the predominance of security policy during the Cold War to the primacy of functional integration has had repercussions throughout the society."[55]

The negotiations to create the EEA involved, to a much greater extent than previous foreign policy making, economic officers from the foreign ministry. The defense and military planners have lost the mystique they held during the cold war. They are no longer exclusively

[53] See "Hemligt råd styr Sverige mot EG," *Svenska Dagbladet,* June 30, 1991, p. 6.
[54] Speech by Martti Ahtisaari, president of Finland, "Finland in the New Europe," Paris, February 21, 1995, p. 1.
[55] See Raimo Väyrynen, "Security of Small States in Europe: Finland," paper prepared for the Conference on Small State Security in Post–Cold War Europe, University of British Columbia, Vancouver, March 24–25, 1994, p. 14.

responsible for information important to the formation of foreign policy in the Nordic states.

As Europe changes, so have the foreign policy strategies of the Nordic states. For the Nordic neutrals, systemic changes created opportunities unthinkable during the cold war. In Sweden and Finland, political leaders viewed the concept of neutrality and the political strategy of the bipolar period as irrelevant. "Neutral from whom?" became the most frequently raised question in the domestic political debate. Those most strongly advocating membership in the EC maintained that the continued use of the concept would unnecessarily constrain negotiations over membership. The EC had set the development of a common foreign and security policy as one of its central goals, and the Nordic neutrals considered this goal to be in their interest as well.[56]

In the domestic debates over European unity, the security interests of the Nordic states increasingly became a motivation to participate. Even though those structures were not fully created, it would be better to be at the table to have a say in Europe's evolution, according to Nordic political leaders. For all of northern Europe, the end of the cold war brought new uncertainties. Pollution, poverty, risk of a sudden outbreak of civil unrest in the former Soviet Union and eastern Europe, crime syndicates, and nuclear proliferation required a multilateral response, and Nordic governments sought closer cooperation with European institutions (the WEU and the EC). As Finnish scholar Kari Möttölä aptly put it, "EC membership has also a strong security policy content. . . . the EC is a key actor in promoting a new security order for Europe as a whole that will not create new divisions, isolate Russia or leave the Baltic states out in the cold."[57] All the Nordic states charted a European course, and security policy motivations can account for this common pattern. If international politics had not been transformed, Finland and Sweden would still be constrained by the East-West division and unable to conceive of multilateral solutions.

As a consequence of changes in international security, the five Nordic governments all sought cooperation with the European Community. Yet changes in international security cannot effectively answer my

[56] Ibid., p. 16.
[57] Kari Möttölä, "The New Security Environment of the Baltic Area," presented to the Seminar on the International Relations of the Baltic Region, London School of Economics and Political Science, February 16, 1994, p. 10.

second question: why do some Nordic states adopt a German model of European unity and embed their political economies and security policies in European institutions while others follow a British model of European unity and resist cooperation? To explain these diverging responses, we must turn to each state's leading sector. It is the political influence of leading sectors that accounts for the fact that some Nordic governments face far greater societal resistance to European accession than others do.

By far the most pressing new security risk to the Nordic states was the possibility of exclusion from their largest export market, the EC. Some sectors had more at stake than others did, and the capacity of economic interest groups to influence the state varied within the Nordic region—from petroleum-dependent Norway to manufacturing-dependent Sweden.

CHAPTER SIX

The Political Influence of Leading Sectors

The Norwegian and Swedish paths to Europe are two models of how the Nordic states have pursued integration with the European Community. The Norwegian government has been compelled to defend important domestic economic interests in its EC relations, while the Swedish government deliberately joined the European confederation of states with fewer exemptions and a desire to influence the system from within.[1] These alternative routes in European politics are visible in the statements of key representatives from each government during the accession period. For Norwegian foreign minister Thorvald Stoltenberg, Norwegian entry means that "we will also bring with us national interests, which will have to be respected, in for example agriculture, fisheries, and energy."[2] Swedish bank director Nils Lundgren summarized the effects of European integration on national policy: "For many years all preparations for new legislation in Sweden have been made subject to the constraint that the proposals which emanate must be compatible with the existing and expected regulatory system in the EC."[3] These divergent approaches to European integration are not merely window dressing. They represent two distinct ways of responding to the political and economic changes on the European continent. This chapter reveals the structural explanation underpinning these choices. For in the absence of petroleum, Norwegian political choices

[1] These strategies are reminiscent of G. John Ikenberry's offensive and defensive typologies of state adaptation to international change in *Reasons of State* (Ithaca: Cornell University Press, 1988), pp. 14–18.
[2] Speech by Norwegian foreign minister, 1990.
[3] Speech by Nils Lundgren, Nordbanken, Sweden.

would be far more limited. If Swedish capital had remained in Sweden and the pressures for accession on the Social Democratic government were not as great, we might have witnessed a situation rather different from the rapid reversal in foreign policy that occurred between May and October of 1990. The choices were not inevitable but were shaped by powerful economic groups that mobilized for or against European integration within each state.

In this chapter, we return to the second puzzle raised in this book. Why do some Nordic states readily accept greater cooperation in supranational institutions (the EC), while others are more resistant? To explain why Nordic responses to European integration vary from the desire to protect particular economic interests (Norway) to the intent to embed the political economy fully in European institutions (Sweden), we turn to a comparison of the political influence of leading sectors. The other Nordic states have, to a varying degree, been resistant (Denmark, Iceland) or acquiescent (Finland) as European integration deepened.

European integration created different imperatives for the five northern European political economies. The source of those disparities and the reasons why some of the Nordic states have embraced European integration and others have resisted are inextricably tied to the very nature of economic production and the political influence of leading sectors. Social coalitions formed around the idea of European unity within each state, from fishermen in Iceland, and petroleum exporters in Norway to industrialists in Sweden, and forestry workers in Finland. Interest groups representing leading sectors had distinct preferences and vital interests at stake in the accession process.

In the first section of the chapter, I present a comparative analysis of how economic dependence varies within the Nordic area. The Nordic political economies depend on different international markets and vary in the mix of mobile or immobile factors of production. As European integration has deepened, these differences have had profound political consequences for each government.

In the second section, I specify how and why sectors influence each government's integration strategy. In small, export-dependent economies, the preferences of leading sectors are critical to foreign economic policymaking. How do sectors act to influence governments? The relationship between sectors and political institutions varies from party representation, to direct consultation as a peak association, to involvement in social movements.

In the final section I compare and contrast how domestic political coalitions acted to promote or resist European integration and what effect this had on state capacity in each of the Nordic countries.

WHEN SECTORS HAVE POLITICAL INFLUENCE

In response to European integration, Sweden's manufacturing-dependent economy experienced the most dramatic effects. As Swedish firms invested heavily in order to be positioned inside the European market, the Social Democratic prime minister was under tremendous pressure to follow the lead of prominent export firms and join the European Community. No similar exodus of capital occurred in Norway despite the threat made by industrialists to relocate their production and investment to the continent. With the exception of the international shipping sector, which did not view accession as necessary or appropriate, Norwegian industries do not have the international orientation or the domestic political clout of Volvo, Electrolux, or other Swedish conglomerates. In Iceland, where the economy has been the least diversified and the opposition to the EC has been the strongest, the Common Fisheries Policy was the most important obstacle to European integration. Sharing Iceland's most precious commodity was highly undesirable, even for those who did not engage in fishing. In Finland the forestry and manufacturing sectors endorsed membership in the European Community. As in Norway, the resistance to integration was strongest in the agricultural sector. Farmers protested the consequences of adjusting national policies to the EC's more liberal regime, the Common Agricultural Policy.

Collectively, the preferences of economic sectors became politically important to Nordic governments in the accession process. The institutional requirement for approval of the decision by the public and by the parliaments gave social coalitions several opportunities to influence the decision to join the EC.

In the national referenda held in Finland, Sweden, and Norway, during the fall of 1994, patterns of voting reflected the sectoral composition of the electorate. The urban-industrial centers voted in favor of EC membership, while the rural/agricultural areas were the strongest opponents of EC membership. (See Maps 7.1 and 7.2 on pages

173 and 174.) The leading sectors, however, had profound effects on state strategies well before the referenda were scheduled.

As my analysis reveals, the economic effects of closer policy coordination with the EC was divisive within and across Nordic societies. Not only were the most important leading sectors affected, but so were sectors that are marginal to the economy yet symbolically important to the society. In Norwegian politics, the close affiliation between traditional sectors (agriculture and fishing) and the party system was a political obstacle to government accession plans. Norway's Center Party is the only truly agrarian party in northern Europe, and the party stubbornly resisted efforts by the Conservatives and Social Democrats to join the EC. The Center Parties in Sweden and Finland endorsed EC membership and no longer represented strictly rural communties. The only other state in northern Europe with a major political party blocking entry into the EC was Iceland, where the Independence Party led by David Oddson endorsed the EEA agreement but opposed accession.

By disaggregating Nordic dependence on international markets and focusing on the domestic political influence of sectors, it is possible to trace the distinct challenges (or opportunities) of European integration for each government. The diverging paths to Europe conformed to the specificities of sectoral politics, not to the structure of the state, to membership in international institutions, or to class divisions within the society.

INDUSTRIAL STRUCTURES AND EC POLICY COORDINATION

As Norwegian political economist Lars Mjøset argues, there are important differences in the industrial structures of the five Nordic states.[4] Each Nordic government had to respond to a different set of interest groups—some that anticipated positive benefits of European integration and others that anticipated undesirable costs. Despite the inclusiveness and openness typically associated with northern European political systems, some groups had a much more influential role than others did in the accession process. Collectively, leading sectors represented by economic interest groups mobilized to exert pressure on

[4] See Lars Mjøset, ed., *Norden Dagen Derpå* (Oslo: Norwegian University Press, 1986); and Lars Mjøset, "Nordic Economic Policies in the 1970s and the 1980s," *International Organization* 41, 3 (Summer 1987).

governments in order to receive safeguards, exemptions, and special conditions in the respective treaties on EC membership; to block membership; or, alternatively, to facilitate a relatively smooth and unhindered entry into the European political and economic union. While we tend to think of northern Europe as a group of similar nations, the European integration process offers insight into just how diverse these countries really are.

A critical difference between the Nordic political economies in the integration process is the degree of dependence on manufacturing and raw materials production. On one extreme, the export structure of Iceland is virtually entirely dependent on fishing. Very few manufacturing firms exist, and of these many are linked to the fishing industry. Norway, on the other hand, has a capital-intensive petroleum sector that dominates the national production structure. Denmark, when it entered the EC, depended primarily on the export of agricultural products. A raw material–based economy that has undergone a boom into niche markets with small electronics firms, chemicals, and pharmaceuticals, Denmark has depended for its wealth during the twentieth century on diversification of the agricultural sector.[5] In Sweden, on the other hand, raw materials dependence is limited to the forestry sector. Sweden's leading sector is manufacturing, where a small group of influential firms dominates the domestic market. Finland has a mix of internationally oriented manufacturing and engineering firms yet continues to be dependent on the export of forestry products. As indicated in Table 6.1, the Swedish and Danish economies have been more dependent on the export of manufactured goods to the EC than the Norwegian economy has. When European integration deepened, these central differences became politicized.

Henry Milner points to the importance of sectoral differences in his analysis of the future prospects for Nordic social democracy in an integrated Europe: "The question of adjusting to the new international (and especially Europe) environment poses itself differently. . . . Natural resource–based industries such as Finland's pulp and paper and, especially Norway's oil and gas, are constrained primarily by world prices. It is in Norway where, as we shall see, the very assumptions of the pro-European orientation are contested, especially by farmers, fishermen,

[5] See, for example, Dieter Senghaas, *The European Experience* (Leamington Spa, England: Berg, 1985).

Table 6.1. Principal exports

	$ Million	% Total
Sweden		
Machinery (including electric)	16,424	29
Wood products, pulp, and paper	10,226	18
Transport equipment	8,460	15
Chemicals	4,083	7
Iron and steel	3,419	6
Food, beverages, and tobacco	1,118	2
Total, including others	57,504	
Denmark		
Machinery (including electric)	8,396	24
Food	6,826	20
Chemicals	3,277	9
Furniture	1,383	4
Fuels and energy	1,253	4
Transport equipment	957	3
Total, including others	34,967	
Norway		
Oil, gas, and petroleum products	14,143	42
Nonferrous metals	2,947	9
Machinery (including electric)	2,374	7
Fish and fish products	2,012	6
Ship and oil platforms	1,675	5
Iron and steel	984	3
Total, including others	33,799	
Finland		
Metals and engineering	7,978	33
Paper industry products	7,274	30
Chemicals	2,717	11
Wood industry products	1,762	7
Total, including others	23,989	
Iceland		
Fish and fish products	1,239	83
Aluminum and alloys	155	10
Diatomite and ferrosilicon	46	3
Agricultural products	30	2
Woolen products, skins, and hides	18	1

Source: Country Surveys, Norway, Sweden, Denmark, Finland, Iceland, *Economist Intelligence Unit* (1991–1996).

and workers in hinterland communities whose industries are based on cheap energy and other state subsidies tied to these resources."[6]

Sectoral cooperation varies extensively at the EC level with important consequences for the divergent interest groups affected by integration

[6] Henry Milner, *Social Democracy and Rational Choice: The Scandinavian Experience and Beyond* (London: Routledge, 1994), pp. 155–156.

within Nordic political economies. The perceived costs and benefits of accession are also contingent on the depth of European policy coordination. Some regimes, such as agriculture, offer social compensation to those who join. The Common Fisheries Policy, on the other hand, exposes domestic fisheries to greater competition. The elaborate system of price supports and subsidies for farmers (the Common Agricultural Program, or CAP) reduces uncertainty for EC agricultural producers and discriminates against nonparticipants. The Common Agricultural Policy is one area where European government collaboration has been particularly high. The CAP, however, is somewhat atypical if we look at other sectors. Despite the intent of the Commission, policy coordination in other sectors, such as energy, has not been as extensive and thus does not threaten to impose comparable opportunity costs on energy-producing states (such as Norway) outside the EC. Thus, the pull of European cooperation in farming was attractive to the Danes, whose agricultural sector became eligible to receive subsidies above those the national government could provide. Icelandic and Norwegian fisheries organizations, however, have viewed the EC's Common Fisheries Policy with skepticism: both groups have effective national resource management regimes and support from their respective governments and do not relish the idea of tougher competition from Portuguese and Spanish trawlers. When Spanish foreign minister Javier Solana lamented to members of Parliament that the Norwegian no to European Community membership on November 28, 1994, would mean the loss of seven thousand tons of cod for Spanish fishermen, the fishermen in Norway were even more convinced that membership was the wrong option. In another area, energy, Norwegians have long-term interests at stake. The European Energy Policy, however, was not an incentive to join the EC. When Norway contemplated EC membership in the early 1990s, there was no significant benefit to energy exporters other than the prospect of being included in European-level discussions of future cooperation in energy.

The characteristics of particular sectors have political consequences. For example, the integration of European markets pulled manufacturers into the EC, yet raw materials exporters did not have the capacity to exit. In response to the European Community's internal market program, Swedish companies relocated production on a massive scale to EC member states between 1985 and 1990. In that time, Sweden doubled its foreign direct investment in the EC every year until the decision was announced to join the European Community.[7] Engineering firms accounted for one-half of total outward investment; followed by finance, insurance, real estate, and transport at 15 percent; and wholesale/retail trade for 6 percent.[8] When firms decided to move within the European market, they thereby narrowed the choices available to the state. The government and trade unions confronted two macroeconomic consequences of capital flight: the loss of jobs at home and the difficulty of attracting foreign capital to Sweden if the country remained outside the EC. "If corporate Sweden moves its production to the EC," Swedish government representatives noted, "it is only logical that the government should also fully participate in the European Community."[9] To prevent further capital flight, Carlsson's government was compelled to join the EC.

Norway's economic dependence on the petroleum sector had entirely different political consequences. Energy products could be sold to the EC without price discrimination, so there was no comparable push to enter the EC. Instead, the Norwegian government faced the strongest resistance to integration from relatively small yet politically influential sectoral interests. Groups representing sectors of the economy sheltered by state subsidies (agriculture, coastal fisheries, and small manufacturers) mobilized against governmental cooperation with the EC; energy interests requested special exemptions from EEA liberalization requirements; and export-oriented sectors (metals, fish farming, and chemicals) promoted cooperation with the European Community. As a petroleum exporter free riding on an open European energy market, Norway found its subsidized traditional sectors a major obstacle to accession.

In sum, the preferences of economic interest organizations provide an indication of what was at stake as each government set sail for Brussels. These preferences should be understood as relational: the interaction of industrial structures and the degree of EC policy coordination by sector.

The following section analyzes how sectoral interests mattered in the political process of integrating with Europe—from Danish entry in the early 1970s, when the Norwegians first vetoed Europe; to Swedish and

[7] Jukka Leskelä and Seija Parviainen, "EFTA Countries' Foreign Direct Investments," Occasional Paper No. 34 (Geneva: EFTA, September 1990), p. 11.
[8] Ibid., p. 16.
[9] Interview at the Swedish Foreign Ministry, 1991.

Finnish entry in 1995. The discussion focuses on the political consequences of sectoral dependence and specifies how European integration affected domestic coalitions within each state by documenting when, why, and how sectors had influence.

My analysis begins with a discussion of Denmark, an ambivalent European. Denmark was the first of the Nordic states to join the EC, with social coalitions supporting membership in 1972 precisely because of the anticipated economic benefits to Denmark's leading sector, agriculture. In the 1980s, domestic coalitions supported the Single European Act to improve Danish economic competitiveness. Yet anti-EC sentiment remains high even after more than twenty years of membership. I then turn to a paired comparison of the two Nordic states where societal interests have been the most resistant to European integration, Iceland and Norway, and the two most cooperative members of the EC's 1995 entering class, Sweden and Finland.

DANISH FARMERS AND EXPORT INDUSTRY: THE PULL OF EC POLICY REGIMES

Denmark's economic development depended on the relative abundance of fertile land for farming and the export of agricultural products to the European market. Agriculture has been the engine behind Danish prosperity. Denmark's economic dependence on Britain and access to stabilization measures provided by the EC's Common Agricultural Policy influenced the government's decision to join the EC in 1972. Agricultural products were Denmark's dominant export in the 1960s, and the political leadership shared concerns with the agro-industry: how to maintain market access and promote agricultural trade. Britain was the recipient of half of Denmark's agricultural exports, and two EC member states, Italy and Germany, accounted for an additional quarter of agricultural exports.[10] Agricultural organizations consistently endorsed a foreign economic policy that secured profitability to Danish exports.[11] When Denmark's most important customer ap-

[10] Anders Ølgaard, *The Danish Economy* (Brussels: Commission of the European Communities, 1979), p. 181.

[11] Danish agricultural organizations advocated maintaining close parity between the Danish krone and the British pound because of the importance of the British market to the export economy. See Hans Chr. Johansen, "The Danish Economy at the Crossroads between Scandinavia and Europe," *Scandinavian Journal of History* 18, no. 1 (1993), 40–41.

plied to join the EC, the CAP guaranteed protection and subsidies to the agricultural sector that could not be provided at home, and Danish agriculture viewed its prospects as better in the EC than outside it.

In contrast to other agricultural sectors in northern Europe, farmers in Denmark have been much more in favor of free trade than of protectionism. The government endorsed economic liberalism in its trade relations throughout the twentieth century. Free trade in agricultural products has been more popular in Denmark than elsewhere in Europe. For example, the Danish delegation ran into conflict with the British and the French when it proposed free trade in agriculture in the EC-EFTA negotiations held in the 1950s.[12]

Danish farmers were well represented in the national parliament when Denmark negotiated its application with the EC. As evidence of concern for the farmer in national economic policymaking, the Danes stepped in to assist agriculture during the 1960s, when Britain was denied entry into the EC. The government enacted a national system of subsidies to support agriculture until the sector could fully participate in the Common Agricultural Policy. The Danes implemented subsidies only as an emergency measure and did so to promote the export economy.

In the domestic debate over accession in Denmark, the pro-EC forces emphasized the economic advantages of membership and downplayed the political dimension. As Danish political scientist Hans Branner acknowledges, "by pointing out the concrete economic advantages that Denmark and each citizen would achieve through membership, supporters succeeded in bringing home a comfortable majority for Danish consent to the EC."[13] Following Britain, the Danish government joined the EC on January 1, 1973.

Thus, the dependence of Danish farming on the British market and the prospect of support for export-oriented agriculture from the CAP were critical to Denmark's decision to join the European Community. Since Danish entry in 1973, Danish farmers have received price supports and subsidies from participation in the CAP. EC subsidies to agriculture exceed $27 billion and account for 55 percent of the annual European Community budget.[14]

---

[12] Johansen, "The Danish Economy at the Crossroads," pp. 49–52.

[13] Morten Kelstrup, ed., *European Integration and Denmark's Participation* (Copenhagen: Political Studies Press, 1992), p. 316.

[14] Timothy Devinney, "A Bigger Europe Is Bad News for Free Trade," *Wall Street Journal*, November 5, 1991.

The Danish economy has diversified since it entered the EC in 1973, and in recent years manufactured goods have surpassed agriculture as the largest contributor to national income. The manufacturing sector, however, is dominated by a large number of small, specialized firms that produce for niche markets. Denmark's post-Fordist economy is in sharp contrast to the large multinational firms more typical of Sweden or the small to medium-sized firms found in Norway. Economists praise the internationally oriented microfirms that have become dominant in very specialized markets: "The president of the Confederation of Danish Industries, Svend Nielsen, leads the world in making fittings used in draught beer pumps. Novo Nordisk is the world's number two producer of insulin and has 90% of the market in fountain pen–size capsule injectors. It claims 55% of the industrial enzyme market. FLS, Denmark's largest conglomerate, is a niche-hunter ranging from airliner maintenance to cement-producing equipment."[15]

The capacity for Danish firms to influence the government's EC policy has changed since it joined the EC, as more and more producers entered manufacturing and service-oriented industries. Yet in contrast to Norway, firms have not been heavily subsidized by the state and thus have not requested protection from internationalization. Nor do Danish manufacturers exert influence in the political economy equivalent to the power of business in Sweden. There is no Danish rival to Swedish Volvo, Saab-Scandia, or Ericsson.

As in the 1970s, economic motivations encouraged cooperation with the EC when the Danes debated whether to approve the Single European Act. The anticipated economic benefits from participation in the internal market program for EC member states were a motivation for participation in the EC's internal market project according to representatives of the Danish government, business leaders, and the trade union confederation, LO. The Danes referred to the findings of the Cecchini Report that outlined the microeconomic and macroeconomic improvements associated with completing the internal market program.[16]

A coalition of organizations representing Denmark's leading sectors and the largest trade union confederations supported the Single European Act. In response to the EC's internal market program, the inter-

---

[15] "Denmark: How It Works," *Economist*, October 31–November 6, 1992, p. 51.
[16] Discussions with Mary Dau, Ole Wæver, Ralf Pittelkow, and Ole Karup Pedersen in Copenhagen, 1991.

est organizations representing Denmark's leading export sectors (machinery, agricultural products, and chemicals)—the Danish Federation of Industries and the Danish Federation of Crafts and Smaller Industries—endorsed the government's adaptation of economic policies. Since 1987, Danish small and medium-sized businesses have expressed concern about their competitive position vis-à-vis other European firms and cooperate with other European companies in the EC's association of small businesses (SBA). The Danish Employers' Federation praised the implementation of competition regulations for European business activities at the EC level. Danish trade unions also supported the Single European Act. "The trade union movement supports the completion of the internal market," an LO brochure states, "including the removal of the technical and physical barriers to trade, and the liberalization of competition within the EC."[17]

Denmark's political parties are predominantly pro-European.[18] The degree of European collaboration, however, has increasingly been contested. From the EC campaign in 1972 until 1986, consensual agreements were negotiated among the major parties on Community policy questions. On January 14, 1986, however, Danish Social Democratic Party leader Anker Jørgensen announced that the party intended to veto the Single European Act in the Folketing (Danish Parliament), ushering in a new era of more divisive EC politics. Prime Minister Schlüter called a referendum on the question, and the Single European Act was approved decisively by the public and then by the Danish Parliament.[19]

The Danish government and the representatives of leading sectors are committed Europeanists. The challenge for the government, however, has been to convince skeptics within Danish society to allow supranational authorities more authority over economic and foreign policies. Prominent representatives of Denmark's Social Democratic and Radical Parties have also objected to specific forms of European collaboration in recent years.

[17] *The Internal Market and the Social Dimension* (Copenhagen: Danish Federation of Trade Unions, 1989), p. 12.

[18] The Conservatives, Liberals, Center Democrats, and the Christian People's Party are the most pro-European; Social Democrats and Radicals are divided over EC policy yet support Denmark's participation in the EC. The Socialist People's party, the Left Socialists, Justice, and the Communists actively oppose Denmark's membership in the EC.

[19] For an excellent analysis of Danish approval of the Single European Act, see Torben Worre, "Denmark at the Crossroads: The Danish Referendum of 28 February 1986 on the EC Reform Package," *Journal of Common Market Studies* 26 (June 1988), 361–388.

THE ARGUMENT

Despite Denmark's reputation as a reluctant European, the Danes have a stellar record when it comes to implementing EC directives.[20] Following the approval of the Single European Act, the government substantially reformed its economic policies, as indicated in Table 6.2. In some areas, such as alcohol policy and rules governing public procurement, Danish regulations have more in common with other EC member states than with Nordic traditions.[21] Yet many Danes share concerns visible in the Norwegian political debates over European unity. When it comes to union, the Danish government is compelled to abide by the public's reticence to transfer sovereignty to supranational institutions.

On June 2, 1992, the Danish people voted no to the Maastricht Treaty on political and economic union by a narrow margin—50.7 percent against, 49.3 percent in favor. This vote was not a rejection of Danish participation in the European Community, nor did it affect the government's willingness to adjust its economic policies to the EC's internal market program. A June 1992 Gallup poll confirmed Danish support for EC membership: 67 percent of Danes were in favor of EC membership. The Maastricht veto expressed Danish concerns about the loss of sovereignty associated with economic and political union. According to discussions with Danish foreign policy analysts, the coordination of economic policies is fundamentally different from the creation of a common currency, common foreign policies, or common defense policies. Danes are wary of the creation of a European superpower where decisions are made by unelected Eurocrats in Brussels.

Here the Danish role in European politics differs from that of Sweden and Finland, who joined the EC in 1995. Danes have had the longest tenure in the EC, yet the anti-EC forces remain an influential political coalition to be reckoned with, both in national politics and at the EC level. In the early 1990s, four representatives of the Danish anti-EC people's movement, *Nej til EF*, were part of the Danish delegation in the European Parliament. As a consequence of reservations over the European conception of centralized federalism, Danes prefer to influence the development of Europe within EC institutions, and

[20] See Christine Barbour, "Domestic Politics and Policy Compliance within the European Community," paper presented to the annual meeting for the Midwest Political Science Association, Chicago, April 1992.

[21] In 1990, the government opened up public projects to competitive bids. Alcoholic beverages are sold in grocery stores, not in state-run monopolies, as in Sweden and Norway.

Table 6.2. Implementation of single market directives, EC member states, 1992

Member State	% of 170 Directives Implemented
Denmark	89.8
France	83.4
Germany	78.6
Portugal	78.4
Greece	75.3
Netherlands	75.0
Britain	73.1
Ireland	72.5
Italy	70.6
Luxembourg	69.9
Spain	67.3
Belgium	64.3

Source: Richard W. Stevenson, "Europe Copes with Details of Unity," *New York Times,* November 16, 1992, p. D1. Copyright © 1992 by the New York Times Company. Reprinted by permission.

they promote a British vision of unity. The Danes, like the British, believe the locus of power in EC policymaking should reside at the national level. In Sweden, the pull of European integration evoked an entirely separate response, and powerful economic interests promoted a pro-integrationist strategy at the EC level above and beyond the Danish commitment to the European project.

Sectoral differences between the Nordic applicants to the EC in the 1970s (Norway and Denmark) can account for the reason why the Danes decided to enter the EC and the Norwegian government failed to achieve a majority in favor of joining the EC. Those same groups prevented the Norwegian government from fully participating in European Community integration in the 1990s. Ironically, the oil economy has frozen the pattern of opposition to the EC by permitting the state to sustain lavish subsidies to the periphery (farmers, fishermen, and small industry). As in other forms of welfare provision, the social and political costs of liberalizing support to the Norwegian periphery were unacceptably high. The Norwegian Social Democrats were in many ways victims of their own success: they have successfully achieved their goal of eliminating income inequalities between agricultural and industrial workers, yet the legacy of that policy has been to create a political constituency dependent on the maintenance of support from the center and inherently against the reduction of state subsidies and protection associated with European integration. Without oil, the periphery would be forced to accept the forces of internationalization and integrate more rapidly into the European market. If, however, the economy depends on the natural resources of the sea, there are other interests at stake. This is the situation in Iceland, the northern European state that has been the most skeptical to European integration.

ICELAND: WHEN FISH *ARE* THE NATIONAL INTEREST

Iceland is an island economy with one of the highest GDPs per capita in the advanced industrial world, and many outsiders wonder how the people have managed so well with so little.[22] Fishing has been the backbone of Iceland's economy, employing up to 12 percent of the work force, and providing the primary source of export revenue.[23] "Iceland's role," economist Birgir Bjorn Sigurjónsson states, "is to supply raw fish for processing and marketing to the main centers of the capitalist world."[24]

Icelanders have an international reputation as skilled fishermen. According to an economist with the Overseas Development Council, Icelanders "catch as much fish as the French with one-tenth of the manpower."[25] National policies are geared to protect Iceland's most vital resource. The Icelandic government maintains a strict national fisheries regime, which preserves particular species and seeks to avoid the depletion of the resources of the sea through reliance on a quota system.

The Icelanders are wary of depending too heavily on the fishing industry. They have sought to diversify the economy into manufacturing. Like the Danes, manufacturers have been in search of niche markets in the world economy. So far, they have had some success with this strategy by producing electronic gadgets for the fishing sector. Yet the biggest change in Iceland's economy was a joint venture initiated by the government in the 1980s. To balance the dependence on fisheries, the government has also sought to diversify production and encouraged

[22] See, for example, Peter Passell, "A Little Economy That Can," *New York Times*, June 26, 1994.

[23] Central Bank of Iceland, *The Economy of Iceland* (Reykjavik, 1994), p. 14.

[24] Birgir Bjorn Sigurjónsson, "National Sovereignty and Economic Policy: The Case of Iceland," *Scandinavian Economic History Review* 1 (1985), 60.

[25] Passell, "A Little Economy That Can."

investment in energy-intensive industries, Iceland's comparative advantage. In a joint venture between the Japanese Sumitomo Corporation, Elkem A/S of Norway, and the Icelandic government, a manufacturing facility was established to produce the industrial compound ferrosilicon. Swiss Alusuisse is the owner of a large aluminum smelter operated by the Icelandic Aluminum Company, and in 1991 aluminum accounted for approximately 9 percent of total exports.[26]

As is typical of the Nordic states, the EC is Iceland's most important trading partner. More than 60 percent of Icelandic exports goes to the European Community, of which approximately 25 percent goes to the United Kingdom and 12 percent to Germany, according to 1992 figures.[27] The changes initiated by the EC, combined with the bandwagoning effect of more and more members of EFTA applying to join the Community, should have given Icelanders more than enough reasons to consider submitting an application to Brussels. How have Iceland's leading sectors—fishing, aluminum products, and manufactured goods—influenced the integration process? The importance of fisheries and the anticipated negative consequences for that industry have dominated any discussion of the EC in national politics.

In Iceland, European unity has been viewed with extreme skepticism. Nowhere are the interests of one particular sector so important to the state as in Iceland. The economy continues to depend heavily on the resources from the sea, and the government has defended its territorial waters from foreign fishermen on numerous occasions.[28]

The prospect of integrating with Europe is a trade-off that the Icelanders have thus far been unwilling to make. Unless special terms were negotiated by government authorities, the conditions for Icelandic entry could require the state to participate in the Common Fisheries Policy and share vital national resources with other European states. The Icelandic fishing industry fears the consequences of joining the EC and thereby opening up the prospect of Spanish and Portuguese boats fishing in Icelandic waters and surrounding seas.

In Iceland, fishing is a strategic sector: the interests of fishermen are synonymous with government policy goals. Icelanders are uncompromising when it comes to fish. "The common consensus is that Ice-

---

[26] Central Bank of Iceland, *The Economy of Iceland*, p. 15.

[27] Ibid., p. 26.

[28] In the cod wars between Britain and Iceland and the dispute between Denmark and Iceland over fishing rights adjacent to Greenland in 1996, Iceland demonstrated its intent to use force to restrict access to national fishing zones.

land will never enter any international treaty which does not guarantee it sovereignty over its seafood resources, which account for over half of all gross domestic product and represent the basis for the future habitability of the country."[29] Although Iceland has no independent military force and relies on a defense commitment to NATO, the state has been willing to wage war with the British on three separate occasions to preserve its territorial fishing zone out to two hundred miles.

Icelanders prefer to trade with the EC and get the best possible deal for their exports. Icelandic foreign minister Jón Baldvin Hannibalsson explained to a group of French and Icelandic businessmen in 1994 the government's preference for signing the EEA agreement, which does not compel Iceland to take on the fisheries policy or the common agricultural regime of the EC: "The main obstacle to membership . . . has been the common fisheries policy. To try to put things in perspective let me make a comparison. The French have a tradition of making noble wine of incomparable quality. We would never dream of trying to teach the French how to make wine! I think the French would also hesitate before teaching us how to fish."[30] Although Hannibalsson has his own particular views of European politics, the expression of serious reservations about the consequences of deepening integration for the nation's most vital economic sector is common among Icelandic political leaders.

The Icelandic government has, however, managed to secure a good deal for the state's fishery interests with the EC. Fish and fish products enter the EC market without incurring duties under the EEA agreement.[31] Prime Minister David Oddsson of the Independence Party in the summer of 1994 could say, "The EEA agreement is satisfactory for us, and will remain so, even if the other (Nordic) states join the EU (EC)."[32] The most vital export industries in Iceland can have all the Europe they need by bilateral agreement. Is there pressure on the gov-

[29] Æsgir Fridgeirsson, "Will Iceland Apply for EC Membership? The Heat Is On," *News from Iceland* (August 1994), 5.

[30] "Iceland and the Enlargement of the European Union," speech by Jón Baldvin Hannibalsson to the Conference of the French-Icelandic Chamber of Commerce, October 21, 1994, Paris, p. 4.

[31] Iceland negotiated a special fisheries rights accord with the EC. Under the terms of the agreement set in place by Icelandic fisheries minister Thorsteinn Pálsson, EC trawlers are authorized to catch three thousand tons of ocean perch in Iceland's jurisdiction in exchange for a 30,000-ton quota for capelin in EC waters (*News from Iceland*, February 1993, p. 4).

[32] Marianne Nordstrøm, "Avslappet utenfor EU," *Aftenposten*, June 8, 1994, p. 13.

ernment to join the EC? From which interests within the society would it come? Instead, societal interests have prevented the state from following the lead of other Nordic governments and applying to join the EC. Fish are at the heart of Iceland's EC opposition.

Since the national interest in Iceland is the protection of the domestic fishing industry, EC membership has been politically undesirable. In 1993, none of the major political parties included EC membership on its platform. With the other Nordic states signing up to join, however, there was some, albeit limited, debate over whether to apply to the EC to see what kind of deal Iceland could get with respect to the fishery sector. The first party to suggest the possibility of membership in the EC, the Social Democrats, adopted a position similar to other parties in northern Europe in promoting the deep historic and cultural ties that Iceland has with the European continent. Nevertheless, the response from Icelandic voters was unfavorable. In the 1994 election, the Social Democrats (the only political party endorsing EC membership) did not fare as well as the opposition.[33] When Norway voted no to Europe in the fall of 1994, the Icelanders seemed to breathe a sigh of relief, knowing that they had a Nordic partner outside the Community.

Thus, in the Icelandic view, a cautious, incremental approach to integration where national policies can be retained has been preferable to joining a partnership of European powers. If and when Iceland eventually joins the EC, the exemptions requested for fisheries and the small agricultural sector are likely to be extensive. Iceland is following a Norwegian road to Europe yet with even stronger economic interests preventing the government from pursuing a closer partnership.

NORWAY: THE INFLUENCE OF OIL, AGRICULTURE, AND FISH

In Norway, the economy has been less dependent on an internationally oriented manufacturing sector and more reliant on a single industry for its export revenue: the petroleum sector.[34] Norway's principal export commodity, responsible for more than one-third of export revenue and the largest contributor to GDP, is oil and gas from the North Sea. The Norwegian economy has grown accustomed to income

---

[33] "Pro-EU Party Suffers in Iceland," *International Herald Tribune*, April 10, 1995, p. 5.

[34] Norway's export sectors (in order of importance to the economy) are oil, gas and petroleum products, nonferrous metals, machinery, fish and fish products, and ship and oil platforms.

from the sector, and the government has adopted policy options, such as a national petroleum fund, that are inconceivable elsewhere in northern Europe.[35] Petroleum companies, both Norwegian and multi-nationals operating on the continental shelf, are strategically important to the Norwegian state; yet these producers are not as committed to European policy coordination as the manufacturing sector is in Sweden.

With abundant hydroelectric power from the nation's waterfalls, Norway could easily convert into export earnings the oil and gas discovered off its continental shelf in the 1960s. In contrast to other petroleum-exporting countries, Norway established a national concession system, similar to the regime adopted to retain Norwegian control over hydro-electric power.[36] In the early 1990s, Norway produced more than ten times the country's own consumption of oil and one-sixth of western Europe's oil consumption.[37] Since the conclusion of the Troll gas contract, Norway has become the largest supplier of natural gas to the EC.[38] As the European energy market converts to natural gas, the Norwegian economy also stands to gain from this development.[39]

In contrast to the Danes, who anticipated economic advantages to farmers by joining the CAP, or to the Icelanders, who have opposed EC policy regimes that threaten to infringe on national fishing zones, the Norwegians have ready access to the most important market for petroleum. European importers of petroleum rely heavily on exports from the continental shelf. Norwegian petroleum companies reap the same economic benefits, regardless of whether the state is in EFTA, the EEA, or the EC. The European energy policy regime is relatively unde-

[35] See Torstein Moland, "The Norwegian Economy's Oil Dependence," *Economic Bulletin* 66 (June 1995), 195–206.

[36] The Norwegian government established a national concession system restricting foreign ownership of hydroelectric energy after a lengthy debate in the national Parliament held in 1909. See Knut Mykland, ed., *Norges Historie* (Oslo: Cappelens Forlag, 1978), p. 438.

[37] "Position Paper of Norway on the EC Directives Concerning Oil Stocks and Crisis Management," Norwegian Foreign Ministry, July 6, 1993.

[38] The Troll gas field contracts were signed in 1986, ten years before production. Deliveries to the continent (Germany, France, Belgium, Spain, the Netherlands, and Austria) are contracted through 2022. See "Norway's Shift to Natural Gas Picks Up As Ten Tugs Deliver a Huge Concrete Centerpiece," *International Herald Tribune*, May 12, 1995, p. 18.

[39] For a discussion of Norway's energy export position in relation to other states, see Janne Haaland Matlary, "Norway, the EC and Energy Policy," *Internasjonal Politikk* 1–2 (1987), 141–158; "Oljedirektivet et ideologisk problem," *Stavanger Aftenblad*, August 25, 1992, p. 48; and "Økt interesse for norsk gas i EF," *Profil* [newsletter of Norsk Hydro] (May 1989), 2.

veloped compared to regimes in agriculture or fisheries. Energy contracts are negotiated bilaterally between the Norwegian authorities and individual EC member states, and Norway is the principal European supplier of petroleum to the continent. Norwegian energy policy expert Janne Haaland Matlary believes that "for the next 20–40 years there will be a sufficient influx of oil revenue in order for exposure to the competition in the European marketplace to be deferred."[40]

At home, Norwegian oil revenue has become a way to support traditional sectors of the economy and enable a substantial proportion of the population to remain in peripheral areas.[41] Since 1975, when Norwegian oil first entered the international market, the state has come to rely on revenue from the continental shelf. Norwegian dependence on oil revenue has enabled the state to sustain policies abandoned by other Scandinavian governments, particularly in Sweden. As Stockholm sought to recover from the worst economic crisis since the Great Depression while at the same time entering the European Community, many Swedes may have regretted the peaceful dissolution of the Swedish-Norwegian union in 1905. The Norwegian oil economy subsidizes social democratic policies untenable elsewhere in the north.

A striking example of the egalitarian uses of oil income are found in the support of "district Norway." The Norwegian government retains an ideological commitment to sustaining employment in peripheral regions.[42] It has maintained generous regional support policies—in contrast to the Swedish government, which has reformed its regional and agricultural policies.[43] In the mid-1970s, the Norwegian government adopted policies intended to eliminate wage differentials between

[40] Janne Haaland Matlary, "And Never the Twain Shall Meet: Reflections on Norway, Europe, and Integration," in *The Nordic Countries and the EC*, ed. Teija Tiilikainen and Ib Damgaard Petersen (Copenhagen: Copenhagen Political Studies, 1993), p. 57.

[41] For an analysis of the effect of oil revenue on Norwegian domestic policy, see Øystein Noreng, "Petroleum Revenues and Industrial Income," in *Oil or Industry?* ed. Terry Barker and Vladimir Brailovsky (London: Academic Press, 1981), pp. 31–35.

[42] Norwegians are committed to preventing the depopulation of local areas. "By og land, hand i hand" (city and country, hand in hand) is the Social Democratic Party's slogan for the policy to transfer resources to localities. For a discussion of Norwegian ecopolitics, see Roland Bjørsne, *Populism och Ekopolitik: Framväxten av en ekopolitisk ideologi i Norge och dess relationer till et mångtydigt populismbegrepp*, Ph.D. diss., University of Stockholm, 1979; on regional assistance policies, see *Trade Policy Review: Norway* (Geneva: GATT, December 1991), p. 137.

[43] The Swedish government liberalized its regional subsidies in 1990 to "adapt better to the EC's norm" (SIND om regionalpolitiska propositionen, "Beklagligt att lokaliseringplänen forsvinner," no. 1, 1990, p. 4).

farmers and industrial workers and to expand economic opportunities in the periphery. The government supports small-scale coastal fishing industries and subsidizes single industries and agriculture, particularly in the less developed regions of northern Norway. Within these sheltered sectors of the economy the strongest opponents to EC integration can be found.

Agriculture is the largest recipient of government support, accounting for approximately 60 percent of total transfers each year.[44] The lavish subsidies to agriculture, small industries, and fisheries support a life-style that would otherwise be difficult, if not impossible, to maintain. In the pursuit of solidarity between rural and urban workers, oil monies have been used to enrich peripheral Norway. When the Social Democrats seek to join Europe, what do these same interests say? They reject the government's proposal on the grounds that they may not be able to maintain a livelihood in remote areas of the countryside as a consequence of accession.

Yet subsidies are not restricted to traditional sectors such as agriculture and fishing. Small industries far from urban centers are also recipients of state support. The logic is this: avoid depopulating rural areas and confront the problems associated with urbanization by providing jobs in the country. As a consequence of this policy, Norwegian firms tend to be more dependent on the state and less international in their orientation than are other Nordic firms. For example, direct subsidies to the business sector increased by 7 percent from 1989 to 1990. Subsidies to mining and manufacturing increased by 26 percent in 1990.[45] Of the six small European states that once comprised EFTA (Sweden, Switzerland, Finland, Norway, Iceland, and Austria), Norway recorded the highest level of support to industry, as indicated in Table 6.3. While other EFTA governments have substantially reduced state subsidies to industry since 1985, Norway was the only member of EFTA to increase support to industry. Between 1975 and 1990, the Norwegian manufacturing sector became more sheltered and less export oriented.[46] The international firm typical of Sweden's political economy or the niche market strategy of Danish business are not found in Norway. Norwegian companies have, on average, continued to rely more heavily on support

[44] *Trade Policy Review: Norway,* p. 134.
[45] OECD Economic Surveys, *Norway* (Paris: OECD, 1991), p. 21.
[46] *Trade Policy Review: Norway,* p. 184.

Table 6.3. EFTA members: State support to
industry (% of GDP)

State	1985	1988
Norway	.6	.65
Sweden	.9	.35
Austria	.75	.4
Finland	.35	.25
Iceland	.1	.05
Switzerland	.05	.01

Source: "Norge gir mest i industristøtte,"
Dagens Næringsliv, August 17, 1990, p. 13.

from the government and seem to be more immune to the so-called internationalization process than are firms elsewhere in northern Europe.[47]

In light of Norway's petroleum-subsidized political economy, how did European integration affect the state and society? The immobility of factors of production created an entirely different political and economic situation in Norway. A small entrepreneurial class of export-oriented managers and industrial Norway endorsed European integration.

Nevertheless, the pro-EC coalition in Norway was not as powerful as organized agriculture in Denmark or business in Sweden. Whereas in Sweden business exerted its influence by relocating to the continent, the effect was much less dramatic in Norway. Some companies purchased subsidiaries in the EC, and others threatened to leave. However, the ten largest Norwegian companies invested more in Norway than they did in European Community member states in 1991. Norsk Hydro (petroleum, aluminum, fertilizers) and Statoil (the national petroleum company) accounted for more than 50 percent of total direct investment, as indicated in Table 6.4.

After fifteen years of silence, Norwegian political leaders returned to the question of whether to join the EC in 1987. The prospect of membership, however, once again divided the political establishment and the society. While negotiating the EEA agreement, the Conservative-led coalition government was forced to resign when the anti-EC Center Party withdrew its support over what it deemed "the selling of Norway." When Gro Harlem Brundtland created a new government, her party

[47] The Norwegian company Norsk Hydro is an exception, with global corporate operations and an international reputation in the sale of fertilizer and petroleum products.

Table 6.4. Norwegian industry: investment, 1991 (*millions of kroner*)

Company	European Community	Norway
Statoil	1,200 (15%)	6,000 (75%)
Norsk Hydro	1,600 (21%)	5,400 (71%)
Kværner	290 (13%)	1,660 (74%)
Orkla	116 (9%)	1,190 (88%)
Aker	100 (6%)	1,400 (78%)
Norske Skog	230 (16%)	1,200 (84%)
Elkem	0 (0%)	335 (67%)
Dyno	246 (35%)	134 (19%)
Hafslund Nycomed	850 (39%)	1000 (45%)
Freia Marabou	70 (15%)	120 (25%)

Source: Adapted from a table that appeared in *Aftenposten,* June 16, 1992.

was internally divided over EC membership. As a committed internationalist, however, she was not going to take no for an answer. When she announced in November 1992 that the Social Democratic–led government would seek membership in the EC, prominent members of her own party voiced their disapproval. A strong anti-EC coalition emerged, led by the Center Party and supported by the Socialist Left Party and the Christian People's Party.

In the debate preceding the 1994 referendum, Norwegian society was as deeply divided over the EC question as in the 1970s. Two separate coalitions emerged, with economic interest groups lining up on each side to promote their view of European integration. The strongest protests came from rural Norway, where farmers and fishermen actively resisted the Social Democratic government's efforts to convince the public of the advantages of EC membership. The stakes for specific economic interests were just as high as in the 1972 referendum.[48]

The farmers had the most to lose and were united against European integration. Norway maintains the highest level of agricultural subsidies among the northern European states. The average farmer in Norway

[48] Discussions with Henry Valen, Stein Kuhnle, and Lars Svåsand at the Institute of Comparative Politics, University of Bergen, spring 1995. For analyses of the 1972 EC referendum in Norway, see Hilary Allen, *Norway and Europe in the 1970s* (Oslo: Universitetsforlaget, 1979); Truls Frogner, *En lang marsj mot Europa? Politiske perspektiver på Norge og EF* (Oslo: Gyldendal Norsk Forlag, 1988); Ottar Hellevik, "The Common Market Decision in Norway: A Clash between Direct and Indirect Democracy," *Scandinavian Political Studies* 9 (1974), 227–234; and Henry Valen, "Norway: 'No' to EEC," *Scandinavian Political Studies* 8 (1973), 214–225.

receives in subsidies much more than is granted to the typical EC farmer.[49] A trip to the western and northern regions of rural Norway illustrates the extraordinary conditions facing the Norwegian farmer. Rocky soil; difficult terrain; small valleys separated by fjords, rivers, and streams; and an extremely short growing season make it hard to imagine that anyone could survive producing agricultural products. Here the state has stepped in to enable traditional sectors to prosper. The farther away from the center and more remote the farm, the higher the state subsidy. At great costs to the consumer, the Norwegian government has an elaborate scheme of incentives that rewards domestic producers. "Norwegian agriculture receives extensive subsidies and is protected from foreign competition through restrictions on imports, although production costs for many of the industry's products are well above market prices. For instance, Norwegian consumers are constrained to buy costly Norwegian apples so long as they are available, and comparable restrictions on imported tomatoes and cucumbers have generated an unusual inverse relationship between their price and the height above the horizon of the midday sun," as one economist puts it.[50] As indicated in Table 6.5, subsidies to the agricultural sector accounted for 4.1 percent of Norwegian government expenditure in 1989, as compared to 0.5 percent of Swedish government expenditure.

Agriculture, coastal fisheries, and small manufacturers opposed closer ties to the EC through the political party system and as participants in the anti-EC social movement, *Nei til EF*. In contrast to the other Nordic countries debating EC membership in the 1990s, the Norwegian anti-EC forces had a prominent representative in the political party system. Anne Enger Lahnstein, chairperson of the anti-EC Center Party, became the champion of Norwegian opposition to European integration. The Center Party viewed the EC as a threat to traditional society. Her support in the 1994 anti-EC campaign was strongest in those areas outside of Oslo, among the same groups (farmers and fishermen) that led Norwegians to reject EC membership in the 1970s.

The Norwegian Farmer's Organization also protested the government's pro-EC stance and objected to both the EEA agreement and EC

---

[49] Norwegian Agricultural Economics Research Institute, 1994.

[50] Rognvaldur Hannesson, "Rent Seeking," working paper, Bergen, Norwegian School of Economics and Business Administration, 1986, cited in Thrainn Eggertsson, *Economic Behavior and Institutions* (Cambridge: Cambridge University Press, 1990), p. 273.

Table 6.5. Subsidies to agriculture: Sweden and Norway, 1989

	Producer Subsidy Equivalents (all products, % of production value)	Agriculture Spending (% of general government current expenditure)
Sweden	47	.5
Norway	74	4.1

Source: OECD Economic Surveys, Sweden (Paris: OECD, 1991), p. 92.

membership. According to the organization, the liberalization of state subsidies threatens the livelihood of Norwegian farmers and endangers the Norwegian way of life. During the EC debate in the early 1990s, the general secretary of the farmer's organization, Amund Venger, promised, "The farmers will use all means possible in the fight against EC membership. . . . we can expect a similar situation to the debate of 1972."[51] This proved to be the case as farmers painted barns and planted crops that read "no to the EC" in order to mobilize support against accession. Yet their strongest ally was in the Center Party, which has remained loyal to agricultural interests (in contrast to the Center Party in Sweden and Finland). When the 1993 national elections split the Parliament into two factions—EC and anti-EC—and the Center Party led the no bloc as Norway's second largest party, farmers had a voice in the accession process that defied their importance to the economy. In Sweden and Finland, on the other hand, the farmers' organizations supported closer ties to the EC and anticipated that agriculture would benefit from price supports provided by the special deal negotiated with the EC for Arctic agriculture.

The farmers had another ally in the anti-EC coalition, the fisheries sector. While only 2.2 percent of Norway's population works in the fishing industry, up to 7 percent of the total population is employed indirectly in the fisheries sector. In the northern and western areas of the country, fishing is the most important economic activity. For example, in Finnmark the municipality is 60 percent dependent on fisheries, and the western counties of Norway (Møre og Romsdal) are about 40 percent dependent on the fishing industry.[52] Fishing is a vital source of employment along the Norwegian coastline, and in recent years there

[51] Aslak Bonde, "Kompromissløse bønder mot EF," Aftenposten, June 19, 1992.
[52] "Norwegian Position Paper on Fisheries," Norwegian Foreign Ministry, July 6, 1993, p. 7.

has been an increase in exports from the fish farming industry.[53] Norwegians export 90 percent of their fish and fish products, and the EC is the largest customer, receiving 65 percent of exports from the sector. To the Norwegian economy, fishing accounts for a relatively minor proportion of annual export revenue (10 to 11 percent), but to Norwegian society the threat of greater competition associated with EC membership became another reason not to join.

Norwegian fisheries feared two possible consequences of EC membership. The boats used by coastal fishermen are typically smaller than EC boats, limiting the Norwegian catch. In addition, the Norwegian fisheries policy is designed to prevent overfishing. As in Iceland, the national regime is viewed much more favorably than is the EC's fisheries policy, which may lead to a more rapid depletion of fish stocks. These same concerns were voiced in the 1970s when Norway also submitted an application for EC membership.[54]

The fisheries organizations were active in the anti-EC social movement, contesting the government's accession strategy. In 1990, the Norwegian Fishermen's Organization blockaded the coastline to protest the government's proposal to open up Norwegian resources to Spanish and Portuguese trawlers in the EEA negotiations. In 1992, prior to the debate in the Parliament over the EEA treaty, a convoy of fishing boats traveled down the coast from Kirkenes to the Oslo fjord to demonstrate opposition to the EEA agreement. Representatives from the anti-EC organization, Nei til EF, and another group called Coast Action against the EEA also participated in the public demonstration.[55] According to leader Mariette Korsrud, "The EEA agreement is a catastrophe for coastal Norway. We will fight to maintain a viable coastal society, and therefore we must stop the EEA agreement."[56] These demonstrations against the government's decision to adapt policies to the EC's internal market program were unique to the Norwegian EC debate.

In the EC negotiations, the government endorsed many of the concerns raised by interest groups representing the fisheries sector, which receives more state support than do fisheries in Denmark, Sweden, or

---

[53] Fish farming employs approximately 14,000 workers, and 845 plants are located along the western and northern coast.

[54] See Arild Underdal, "Diverging Roads to Europe," *Cooperation and Conflict* 10 (1975), 70.

[55] See Erik Veigård, "Båtkonvoi mot EØS," *Aftenposten*, July 11, 1992.

[56] Eirik Ramberg, "Kyst-Norge til kamp mot EØS," *Aftenposten*, July 9, 1992.

the EC.[57] Under the terms of the EEA agreement, liberalization includes "the abolition of import duties on fish and fish products, direct landings of fish, right of establishment, price differentiation and state aids."[58] In response to demands from the fisheries' organizations, the governments of Iceland and Norway requested safeguard clauses to ensure national control over economic resources in the EFTA-EC trade negotiations. A compromise was reached between the Norwegian government and the EC that reduced tolls on fish exports in exchange for expanded fishing rights to EC trawlers.

The anti-EC social movement presented European integration as a fundamental threat to agricultural production and fisheries. According to the opposition, "In the EC negotiation process, Norway was granted the right to maintain national support to agriculture, but only for a five-year period. Then subsidies can only be given to a few areas. Very few Norwegian farms will be able to compete with industrialized agriculture in the EC after the transition period. Membership in the EC will require a major decrease in farming in Norway. At the same time we will have less control over food production."[59] As a consequence of joining the EC, Norway will also be required to give up sovereignty over the resources of the sea. "It is the EC that determines the total quota that can be taken in the Norwegian Sea, and how that quota is to be divided among the different countries. The EC also will take over the negotiations concerning quota sharing with third countries. The EC—and not Norway—will negotiate such vital issues as how to divide the Arctic cod catch with Russia."[60] In contrast to Norway's stringent fishing regime, the EC fisheries policy is less restrictive and thereby encourages overfishing. North Sea resources will be depleted, and it will be more difficult to make a living in the fisheries industry. The market-oriented EC policies will prevent Norway from retaining the viability of small farming communities and coastal fishing industries, according to the EC skeptics.

Norwegian entrepreneurs and exporters of nonpetroleum products who depend heavily on trade with the continent were the strongest proponents of EC membership. These included firms in paper and forest products, metal and aluminum, and fish farming. For example,

---

[57] See Odd Inge Skjævesland, "Fiskerifradrag truet av EØS," *Aftenposten*, August 8, 1992.
[58] *Trade Policy Review: Norway*, p. 177.
[59] Nei til EU, "Folkestyre Eller Union" (Oslo: Duplotrykk) 25.
[60] Ibid., p. 26.

the Prosess og foredlings-industriens landsforening (PIL) an association representing more than four hundred member companies throughout Norway in the metal, chemicals, and petrochemical industries, supported closer ties to the EC in the form of an expanded free trade area
(the EEA) and eventual EC membership. These industries are not
heavily subsidized by the state, nor do they produce exclusively for the
domestic market. Sixty percent of total Norwegian raw materials exports (excluding oil and gas) come from industries that are members
of PIL, and approximately 50,000 Norwegians are employed in this
sector. According to the director of the organization, Arve Thorvik,
"the EEA agreement opens doors to Europe and eliminates technical
barriers to trade. Transport costs will be reduced, and there will be
fewer obstacles to the the free movement of goods, capital, and workers."[61] To Norwegian businesses, the EEA is not a waiting station on the
way to Europe but is much more significant. "EC membership should
be the next step in the integration process. Those that say that we
should be satisfied with the EEA agreement have too short a time horizon for the development of Norwegian industry."[62]

The most important organization representing Norwegian industry
also promoted integration. The Norwegian Association of Industry
(NHO) endorsed European integration in the EC campaign. When
Terje Osmundsen served as director of NHO, he advocated membership to improve Norway's competitive position. According to Osmundsen, the Norwegian economy cannot survive solely on oil. Adaptation to
the EC's internal market program will prepare the economy to compete well into the next century. If Norway joins the EC, government
officials can participate directly in the development of a common European energy policy. As Osmundsen advocated accession, more finds
were made in the North Sea; and the necessity of making hard decisions in the present in order to reap future benefits was lost on many
groups within the society.

Norway's leading sector, petroleum, was influential in structuring the
choices available to the government. An abundance of oil gave Norway
options that were not available elsewhere in northern Europe: the economic capacity for the society to wait. "Because oil is a global commodity transcending membership in international regimes," Ulf Lindström

[61] Interview with Arve Thorvik, translated from Norsk Hydro's newsletter *Profil,* September 4, 1992, pp. 8–9.
[62] Ibid.

argues, "Norway's affluence was not immediately at stake as the country considered its relationship to Europe."[63] The favorable price of oil and the continued supply made it less imperative for Norway to rush into the European Community.

When the Norwegian national petroleum regime ran into conflict with the requirements of Europeanization, the state came to the defense of the industry in the negotiations. The petroleum sector, similar to hydroelectric power, has been heavily regulated by the Norwegian state.[64] Statoil, the Norwegian national petroleum company, is responsible for the sale of oil and natural gas to the continent. Licenses to participate in oil exploration, development, production, and sales are awarded by political authorities. A controversy developed about how to satisfy EC deregulation imperatives for the energy sector yet retain Statoil as a "privileged partner."[65] Adapting to the European Community's internal market requires deregulating national control of the energy sector and opening the sector to more competitive market conditions. This prospect was met with resistance by representatives from the petroleum industry and was brought to the negotiating table.

In 1992, the interest organization representing the major oil companies operating on the Norwegian continental shelf appealed to the government on this question. The petroleum industry requested that Norwegian authorities negotiate an exemption from EC directives that harmonize public procurement. Norwegian companies receive preferential treatment, and that may be subject to change.[66] The Norwegian government followed the lead of other North Sea petroleum producers. The governments of Denmark, Great Britain, and the Netherlands appealed to the EC to follow an alternative procedure that would allow the state to maintain restrictions on the development of the energy sector.[67] During 1990, Norwegian EC negotiator Kaci Kullman Five of the Conservative Party maintained that Norway would adhere to the EC's guidelines as soon as Britain decided to do so. According to the

[63] Ulf Lindström, "Scandinavia and the European Union: The Referenda in Denmark, Finland, Norway and Sweden 1992–1994" (University of Bergen, 1995), p. 14.
[64] See Merrie Klapp, *The Sovereign Entrepreneur* (Ithaca: Cornell University Press, 1987), pp. 76–90.
[65] Lars Mjøset, Adne Cappelen, Jan Fagerberg, and Bent Sofus Tranøy, *Norway: Changing the Model* (Oslo: Advanced Research on the Europeanization of the Nation-State, 1995), p. 73.
[66] See *Trade Policy Review: Norway*, pp. 115–116.
[67] Finn Kristensen, Norwegian oil and energy minister, "EØS-avtale og offentlige innkjøp," *Aftenposten*, August 11, 1992.

government, the Norwegian continental shelf has fewer obstacles to foreign participation than does the British continental shelf.[68] Thus, government officials accommodated the demands of the petroleum sector in their negotiations with the EC. The strategic interests of the Norwegian state and the specific interests of the petroleum sector were inseparable.

The political consequences of entry into the European Community also affected sectors that have a symbolic meaning to the society. For example, the Norwegian practice of whaling, which has been a traditional activity for hundreds of years, brought heavy criticism from EC officials. According to the EC commissioner of fisheries, all EC member states are required to abide by the decisions of the International Whaling Commission (IWC).[69] Norwegian membership in the EC and the practice of whaling are incompatible, according to EC officials. Sweden and Finland were unaffected by these problems in their accession negotiations. Iceland also avoided this controversy since the government announced its decision to abandon whaling in 1985.

Sectoral differences were also visible in the preferences of Nordic trade unions. Norway's largest blue collar trade union, LO, initially opposed EC integration. During 1991, the organization became more open to the prospect of closer ties to the European Community (the EEA agreement). After a lengthy debate within the organization over whether to support the EEA agreement, 80 percent of the members approved the EEA treaty in June 1992. LO approval was conditional: the leadership requested that the government and the Parliament implement Norwegian laws and regulations governing conditions for foreign workers seeking employment in Norway.[70] The trade union movement has never officially advocated EC membership, in contrast to the Swedish, Finnish, and Danish trade union movements.

As Norway negotiated its treaty with the EC, the state came to the defense of its leading sector, petroleum, and two influential, protected sectors of the economy dependent on support from the state, fisheries and agriculture. On regional policy, the Norwegian position is as follows:

---

[68] Ibid.
[69] "Hvalfangst eller EF," interview with EC commissioner of fisheries, Manuel Marin, in *Aftenposten*, July 16, 1992; and "Hvalfangst-forvirring i EF," *Aftenposten*, July 4, 1992.
[70] See "LO sa et endeligt ja til EØS," *Aftenposten*, June 23, 1992.

It is of great importance to Norway to have the necessary flexibility to be able to pursue, within the framework of EC legislation, active and ambitious regional policies. This implies that the special conditions of Norway must be taken into account with respect to regions eligible for support from the Structural Funds. We would also like to underscore the important role of agriculture and fisheries in promoting regional development in Norway. A viable agricultural and fisheries sector must be maintained in order to sustain the main features of existing settlement patterns.[71]

In Norway, state-supported industry and raw material producers, threatened by the prospect of liberalizations of Norwegian economic policies and more competition from abroad, resisted government efforts to forge closer ties to the EC. Coastal fishermen, farmers, and representatives from sheltered industries have been active in the anti-EC social movement, *Nei til EF*. For the anti-EC organization, any form of cooperation with the EC beyond the bilateral agreement signed in 1973 is unacceptable. Kristen Nygaard, the leader of *Nei til EF*, insists, "The European Community is a threat to the Scandinavian model. . . . The Rome Treaty is market-oriented, business interests are given priority over environmental concerns, and Norway will not be able to retain its national policies."[72] It was this view that carried the day when Norwegians, for the second time in twenty-two years, voted no to European integration.

The most important sector in Norway's economy is petroleum. Yet Norway's national resource is subject to market forces outside Europe. The determination of the oil price is international, subject to fluctuation in prices as a consequence of oil strikes as far away as Nigeria, disruptions in Middle East oil supplies, or upswings in the American market. The European Community is a market that Norwegian oil producers already have access to without further integration. Access to the European energy market has been guaranteed by bilateral deals negotiated between the Norwegian state and a group of EC members. The best argument that the pro-EC forces could make—that Norway should be at the table to influence the development of European politics—failed to sway economic interest groups who were threatened by the prospect of exchanging national policies for more market-oriented EC policies.

[71] Norwegian Foreign Ministry, "Position Paper of Norway on Regional Policy," 1993, p. 1.
[72] Interview with Kristen Nygaard, leader, Nei til EF, Oslo, September 1990.

The Norwegian state never experienced the economic consequences of capital flight that occurred in Sweden. More jobs stayed in Norway, and the government had the capacity to retain traditional social democratic policies intended to keep the population economically active in peripheral Norway. All in all, life looked pretty good outside the EC when Norwegian voters went to the polls in November 1994. As a consequence of societal resistance, the state was unable to join the EC in 1995, as the government had hoped. Nowhere else in northern Europe has a government been twice humiliated in its efforts to convince a majority of the population to join the EC. Nor was Norway's EC treaty a sign that the state would be a cooperative European. The treaty itself contained many requests for safeguard clauses and special conditions that were not to be found in the Swedish application.[73] The political and economic consequences of European integration for the manufacturing sector propelled Sweden toward the European core, while Norway, extracting its revenue from the North Sea, remained on the periphery of European politics.

SWEDEN: THE POLITICAL INFLUENCE OF BUSINESS

Sweden's industrial structure is dominated by a small number of relatively large manufacturing firms that are well integrated in international markets.[74] Sweden has paid for its imports with revenues from the manufacturing sector. Finance and industry have a close institutional relationship, and the economy depends primarily on the export of manufactured goods.[75]

Business has always been international in Sweden, yet only recently have national champion companies collectively moved their operations to European markets and, by doing so, convinced the government to follow their lead. The rapid, pro-EC response of economic interest organizations, political parties, trade unions, and the government to a

[73] In November 1992, Social Democratic party leader Gro Harlem Brundtland announced her party's intent to join the EC. But internal opposition within the party remains strong, public opinion is divided, and economic interest organizations (fishing, farmers) remain actively opposed. The anti-EC forces have a membership ten times the size of the pro-European movement.

[74] Sweden has 643 foreign-owned enterprises, followed by Denmark with 269, according to the Nordic Statistical Yearbook, 1992.

[75] See Jonas Pontusson, "Conditions of Labor-Party Dominance: Britain and Sweden Compared," in *Uncommon Democracies*, ed. T. J. Pempel (Ithaca: Cornell University Press, 1990), pp. 71–72.

more integrated Europe was in marked contrast to the situation in neighboring Norway. Only in Finland did we see such a well-coordinated pro-EC coalition and a broad endorsement of European integration throughout the society.

Sweden's primary export sectors are more capital-intensive than is characteristic of other Nordic states. In order of importance, these sectors are machinery, wood products (including pulp and paper), transport equipment, chemicals, iron and steel, food, beverages, and tobacco. In comparison to Norway, Sweden's production profile is more diversified and less sheltered. Capital is concentrated in the hands of a few important groups in the society, and there has been far less reliance on state subsidies to industry.

Swedish national champion companies (Ericsson, Pharmacia, Electrolux, Volvo, Saab-Scania, Alfa-Laval, SKF, ASEA, Sandvik) are internationally competitive and export oriented. As the European Community consolidated its internal market program, Swedish industry responded by relocating production facilities to EC member states. From 1989 to 1991, Swedish companies acquired eighty-two European companies, totaling $1.3 billion.[76] By 1988, the foreign concentration of industrial production was much higher in Sweden than in Norway, as indicated in Table 6.6. EFTA reported that "of the EFTA member-states, Sweden and Switzerland are the two most EC-oriented in their direct investment activity."[77]

The leaders of Sweden's holding companies (Axel Johnson, Wallenberg, Lundberg) and other representatives from Swedish industry actively encouraged the government to pursue deeper cooperation with the European Community.[78] Swedish business led the way into the European market, and the government was convinced to follow their lead. The argument was persuasive. In contrast to the EEA, membership guarantees equal access and fair competition for the business sector:

> This is necessary to assure investors that plants located in Sweden will have as secure market access to EU countries in the future as their competitors there and that identical terms of competition will continue to prevail in all countries. Membership thus provides a significant boost to investment in

[76] "Sweden Grasps EC Nettle," *European*, weekend edition, June 28–30, 1992, p. 25.

[77] Jukka Leskelä and Seija Parviainen, "EFTA Countries' Foreign Direct Investments," occasional paper no. 34 (Geneva: EFTA, September 1990), p. 11.

[78] For an in-depth discussion of Swedish industrialists' attitudes toward European integration, see Svenska Metallindustriarbetareförbundets, "Sverige, EG och Storföretagen," Stockholm, Sweden, 1990.

Table 6.6. Swedish and Norwegian employment in foreign subsidiaries, 1987–88 (% of total employment of the thirty largest manufacturing firms)

Sweden	52
Norway	24

Source: Growth and Integration in a Nordic Perspective (Stockholm: IUI, 1990); Lars Lundberg, "European Integration and Nordic Countries' Trade," *Journal of Common Market Studies* 30, no. 2 (June 1992), 160.

Sweden—an important consideration for a troubled economy on the periphery of Europe.[79]

A visitor to the Swedish Employer's Federation (SAF), the Swedish Federation of Industries, or the Swedish Export Council could acquire stacks of studies, reports, and analyses, all pointing to the benefits of integration for the Swedish economy. SAF launched a highly visible public campaign that attributed Denmark's economic revival to membership in the European Community.[80] The pro-EC social coalition, supported by Sweden's leading sector, captured the momentum of the campaign—in sharp contrast to the situation in Norway, where the government and pro-EC groups were put on the defensive.

One of Sweden's most important industries, forestry and paper manufacturers, exported more than 75 percent of its products to the European Community. Two Swedish forestry companies, Iggesund and SCA, acquired subsidiaries within the EC during 1987: Iggesund acquired Thames Board (U.K.), and SCA acquired French Peaudouce. Iggesund became Europe's largest producer of cartons. SCA will also become a European market leader. The Swedish forestry industry, along with other industries, supported closer cooperation between the government and the European Community in response to the internal market program.[81]

Thus, the internal market program had a profound effect on the behavior of corporate Sweden and influenced the government's strat-

[79] Per Magnus Wijkman, "To Be or Not to Be a Member: The Swedish Referendum Debate," working paper no. 8 (Stockholm: Industriförbundet, 1995), p. 5.

[80] Full-page advertisements appeared in the Swedish daily, *Svenska Dagbladet*, advocating the economic benefits of EC membership.

[81] Interviews at the Swedish Foreign Ministry, 1990–91.

egy. The prospect of remaining outside the EC became unthinkable to the Social Democratic government as more and more jobs moved from Sweden to the continent. Companies established subsidiaries in European member states, yet there was no comparable foreign direct investment in Sweden. As capital relocated to the EC, there were new pressures on the Swedish government to attract foreign capital to Sweden and to be at the table to protect the interests of leading sectors.[82] Since many of the products exported by Sweden (transport equipment, machinery, and paper products) are purchased by public authorities, firms had even more at stake in the integration process. The political contacts necessary for securing deals in the EC are critical to Swedish business.[83]

The political influence of business became increasingly important as the Social Democratic prime minister contemplated whether to apply for EC membership. The effects of capital flight were compounded by strong pressure from the most prominent business federation and influential industrialists. Swedish industrial leaders and the Federation of Swedish Industries actively supported a pro-EC policy. The CEO of Volvo, Pehr Gyllenhammar, and Peter Wallenberg of the Wallenberg group of companies, served on the government's secret advisory board on EC questions and contributed to the debate on EC membership in the Swedish press in the summer of 1990. Gyllenhammar and Wallenberg both advocated closer ties to Europe, including Swedish membership in the European Community.[84] In 1987, the Federation of Swedish Industries had initiated a series of studies on the consequences of European integration on the industrial development of Sweden. The conclusions were favorable: Swedish membership in the European Community would be beneficial for the competitive position of Swedish industry.[85] According to Karl-Erik Sahlberg, director of the Swedish Federation of Industries, "a precondition for Swedish industry to sup-

[82] For a discussion of the internationalization of the Swedish economy and the capital flight that undermined the assumptions of the Rehn-Meidner plan, see Jonas Pontusson, "At the End of the Third Road: Swedish Social Democracy in Crisis," *Politics and Society* 20 (September 1992), 321–324.

[83] Discussions with Bo Rothstein, 1995.

[84] See Pehr Gyllenhammar, "Ge upp neutraliteten," *Dagens Nyheter*, August 26, 1990, p. A4.

[85] See, for example, Lennart Ohlsson, *Industry and the EC: Consequences of the EC for the Swedish Manufacturing Industry* (Stockholm: Industriförbundets Förlag, May 1988).

port the EEA agreement is that EC membership will not be ruled out."[86] During the campaign, the SAF distributed a list of reasons for joining the EC:

The European Community secures peace and democracy.
Cooperation is better than isolation.
EC cooperation provides benefits: stronger companies, new jobs, increased competition, and lower prices.
We will have more influence.
More jobs will be available in Sweden.
The EEA is ineffective: no vote and less influence, fewer investors and fewer jobs, more expensive goods and services, and insecurity.

Source: Translated from "Sex Tunga Argument för EU-Medlemskap," Svenska Arbetsgivareföreningen (SAF), Stockholm, 1994.

The leader of Sweden's federation of small industries (Småföretagens Riksorganisation), Jan Krylborn, expressed concern that the government's EC proposals reflected a preoccupation with the competitive position of larger Swedish companies. Nonetheless, the organization supported the government's adherence to the EC's internal market program.[87]

Other interest groups also lined up in favor of accession. In June 1990, the Swedish farmers' organization (LRF) announced its support for government cooperation with the EC's internal market program. "We are positive to a connection with the EC. Farmers must follow developments in Europe," LRF spokesman Bo Dockered announced. "Swedish agriculture is internationally oriented, so we are not apprehensive about competing on equal terms."[88] Thus, in contrast to Norway, the farmers' organization supported the government's decision to adapt economic policies to the CAP and to pursue membership in the European Community.

The labor unions were less willing to discuss the prospects of EC membership but supported the government's strategy of adapting national policy to the EC's internal market program. In a visit to LO in 1989, I expected to find opposition to the internal market program—a partnership between business and governments. Instead, I found the labor unions concerned about maintaining the power to implement EC regulations that affected Swedish workers. Gudmund Larsson, an

[86] "Industrin varnar Carlsson," *Dagens Nyheter,* June 6, 1990, p. A4.
[87] See Thomas Lerner, "Småföretagare går samman inför EG," *Dagens Nyheter,* June 8, 1990, p. C6.
[88] "LRF stöder anslutning till EG," *Dagens Nyheter,* June 14, 1990, p. C4.

EC analyst for LO, and Håkån Arnelid, an economist from the Swedish Metalworkers' Union, explained, "It is impossible for a small country to manage its economic policy without consideration for developments in other countries. We must pay attention to our competitive position, or adversely affect the economic base for welfare and employment. Many environmental questions cannot be solved at the national level, and require international cooperation."[89] Compared to the Norwegian trade union confederation, this group articulated a more outward-looking approach and reflected the imperatives of international market integration in the manufacturing sector. LO initiated its own study in 1989 about the implications of EC directives for Swedish working life and what closer ties to the EC would mean for the "Swedish model." The Swedish trade union confederation supported closer ties to the EC because it anticipated benefits to the consumer in the form of lower prices and benefits to workers in terms of employment and pay: the pressures of the European economy would improve the competitive position of Swedish industry.

By spring 1990, labor union preferences had changed in favor of EC membership. Changes within EC institutions suggested that the Swedish model would not be incompatible with other European welfare states.[90] The macroeconomic benefits of participation and the importance of having a voice in European Community institutions were cited as the most important reasons for joining the EC. According to LO researcher Lars Nyberg, transferring decision-making capacity to EC institutions is the preferred method of managing internationalization of the Swedish economy.[91]

Sweden's public sector union, TCO, announced its support for EC membership in June 1990. "Sweden should seek full membership in the European Community," union leader Lars Hellman asserted. "Otherwise we risk losing influence and becoming isolated from cooperation among EC workers."[92] Another TCO leader, Björn Rosengren,

---

[89] "Olycklig EG-lösning," *Dagens Nyheter*, June 7, 1990, p. A4.

[90] The German welfare state provides benefits to its citizens comparable to—and in some cases better than—the Swedish *folkhem*, according to the LO study (interview with Lars Nyberg, 1991).

[91] In his discussion of the difficulty for national governments to stabilize the economy under conditions of economic interdependence, Nyberg argues that "the most effective solution to this situation is to allow a supranational authority to take responsibility." Lars Nyberg, *Den Europeiska Modellen* (Sweden: Tidens Forlag, 1991), p. 32.

[92] Malin Holmquist and Gunnar Jacobsson, "Tjänstemän tar ställning för EC," *Dagens Nyheter*, June 2, 1990, p. C2.

argued that "a Swedish membership in the EC will give Sweden possibilities to strengthen the forces in the Community that recognize that the EC should have a social dimension."[93]

By fall 1990, all the major interest organizations were in agreement: Sweden should join the European Community. Even the agricultural interest organizations, which had previously opposed Swedish integration because of the prospects of competition from abroad and liberalizations at home, reversed their position on the EC in favor of membership. The Swedish Farmers' Union preferred the EC's Common Agricultural Policy to the prospect of further liberalizations imposed by Stockholm.[94]

Opposition to the EC was surprisingly weak in Sweden during the early 1990s. Per Gharton, leader of Sweden's Green Party, did voice his opposition in the Parliament and to the press.[95] According to Gharton, the Swedish people have not been adequately informed about the consequences of adapting Swedish policies to the internal market, which will affect everything from "the sugar content in marmalade to social security."[96] Several leading Social Democrats came out against the government's decision to join, but these voices were a minority. Only after the Danes vetoed the Maastricht Treaty did we see growing skepticism among the Swedish population over European integration. Yet by this point, the government had already committed itself to enter the EC, and core policies had been adopted. In contrast to Norway, where the anti-EC social movement put the government on the defensive from the beginning of the campaign, the anti-EC organization in Sweden was smaller, and its appeal did not encompass the most important economic interests. The backbone of Swedish opposition to the EC could be found in the area most similar to Norway—the agricultural district of Jämtland, where farmers have remained resistant to integration.

In sum, capital flight from Sweden to the European Community (1985–90) contributed to a fundamental change in the preferences of the Swedish government. From 1985 to 1990, Swedish foreign direct investment in the EC increased by 500 percent. By the time the public voted to join the EC, the government had already substantially altered national policies to position the economy to compete in the new Eu-

---

[93] "TCO kan acceptera EG-medlemskap," *Dagens Nyheter*, June 7, 1990, p. C5.

[94] Interview with Swedish parliamentary representative and Conservative Party expert on Swedish-EC relations, Stockholm, 1991.

[95] See Per Gharton, *I stället för EG* (Stockholm: Ordfront, 1990).

[96] Magdalena Ribbing, "Svenskarna vet inte vad EG innebär," *Dagens Nyheter*, June 6, 1990, p. A8.

rope.[97] The transformation was remarkable in its speed and in the government's commitment to the European project.

The redirection of Swedish EC policy was remarkable for two reasons: first, the decision was made at the elite level without an extensive public debate, national referendum, or information campaign, and with a speed uncharacteristic of Swedish politics.[98] In 1988, Prime Minister Ingvar Carlsson convened a secret advisory council of Swedish industrial elites to advise the government on EC questions. It was not until an article appeared in the Swedish newspaper *Svenska Dagbladet* in June 1991 that the public was informed about the process. Carlsson's advisory committee members are listed in Table 6.7.

Although public opinion polls indicated that a majority of Swedes favored EC membership, the government applied to join the European Community without holding a national referendum. The referendum was held after negotiations between the Swedish government and the European Community were completed, and many national policies had already been changed to conform to EC policy regimes.

Most major policy reversals in Swedish politics require years of consultation and deliberation to mobilize consensus. This change in Swedish policy was introduced in a finance bill to the Parliament at the end of October 1990, and by July 1991 an application to join the European Community was submitted to Brussels. Much of the consensus-building took place behind the scenes within the Social Democratic Party.

Electoral pressures and the status of the Austrian application for EC membership also contributed to the speed of the decision. The Social Democrats reversed their position on the eve of an election. The Conservative Party had successfully monopolized the EC question, and the Social Democrats were faring poorly in the public opinion polls. The Austrian government defected from EFTA negotiations in 1991 and announced its intent to join the Community. According to Sweden's chief negotiator for the EC, Ulf Dinkelspiel, if the government promptly applied to become a full member of the EC, then the applications of the two neutral states could be negotiated simultaneously. The Swedish state, however, had already joined the EC, with all major interest

[97] These include reforms in Swedish company law, alcohol import regulations, and rules governing foreign direct investment and levels of support to agriculture.

[98] Discussion with Bo Rothstein at "Where Is Sweden Heading?" conference organized by the Swedish Information Service, New School for Social Research, New York City, October 1991.

Table 6.7. Ingvar Carlsson's advisory committee on the European Community

Government
   Prime minister, chairperson (Ingvar Carlsson)
   Foreign minister (Sten Andersson)
   Finance minister (Allan Larsson)
   Minister of industry (Rune Molin)
   Foreign trade minister (Anita Gradin)
Administration
   Chairman of Sweden's Central Bank (Bengt Dennis)
   University chancellor (Gunnar Brodin)
   Chairman of the Organization of Industry (Gunnar Johansson)
   Director of National Business Organization (Torbjörn Ek)
Economic Organizations
   Chairman of the Organization of Cooperatives (Leif Lewin)
   Chairman of Swedish Metall (Leif Blomberg)
   Chairman of LO (Bertil Jonsson)
   Chairman of TCO (Björn Rosengren)
   Chairman of the Swedish Employers' Federation (Karl Onnesjö)
Industry
   Director of Handelsbanken (Tom Hedelius)
   Director of Axel Johnson (Antonia Johnson)
   Director of Volvo (Pehr Gyllenhammar)
   Director of Wallenberg Companies (Peter Wallenberg)
   Director of Tekn (Curt Nicolin)

Source: "Hemligt råd styr Sverige mot EG," *Svenska Dagbladet,* June 30, 1991, p. 6.

groups and the representatives from leading sectors in the membership coalition.

The argument made by corporatist Sweden (the government, the representatives of the leading labor unions, and industrial federations) in response to the EC's internal market program was the following: the only means to protect Sweden from economic decline and stop the flight of capital to the EC is by joining the Community. While this voice began on the right, it spread to the center of Swedish politics and rapidly gained consensus. Even Stefan Edman, a representative from the left wing of the Social Democratic Party, became a proponent of EC membership. His reasons, however, were more ideological: "Swedish social democracy must urgently work out a vision, according to which the whole of Europe becomes an arena for its ideals of solidarity, internationalism, and environmental struggle."[99]

Thus, Swedish membership in the EC held the promise of improved

[99] Quoted in Aleksundra Ålund and Carl-Ulrik Schieup, *Paradoxes of Multiculturalism* (England: Avebury Publishing Group, 1991), p. 8.

competitiveness for national industries and the economy, yet it also offered the possibility for Swedes to influence the substance and direction of political change within the Community. Per Magnus Wijkman, chief economist at the Federation of Swedish Industries, recalled, "My assessment was that the EEA would involve appreciable costs compared with EC membership. Consequently, like 52% of the voters, I voted for membership. I did this even though I found the EC to have many unattractive features. . . . However, by becoming a member, Sweden would be in a position to improve the EC. A 'yes' vote would benefit Sweden and could change Europe for the better."[100]

The Swedish government, in contrast to that of Iceland or Norway, had the capacity to pursue a multilateral strategy. In Norway, the government also sought to join the EC, but the political constraints were entirely different. For Norwegians, European Community membership can wait. The political influence of leading sectors defined the capacity of governments in each state to pursue political integration. In Finland, however, the support for the EC was the strongest, as Finns viewed their economic future as synonymous with European integration. Finns followed a Swedish path to Europe, less out of tradition than out of necessity.

FINNISH RAW MATERIALS, MANUFACTURING, AND THE PULL OF EUROPEAN INTEGRATION

Finns proceeded cautiously toward integration with western Europe so as not to antagonize their Soviet neighbors. In 1961, Finland negotiated a special agreement with the EFTA countries, which they immediately extended in kind to the Soviet Union.[101] It was not until 1985 that Finland became a member of the EFTA. The Soviet market has always been more important to Finland than to the other Nordic states, and the Finnish economy secured long-term trade agreements for manufactured goods in exchange for relatively low-priced Soviet oil. The end of this arrangement in 1990 and the collapse of the Soviet market (which accounted for as much as one-quarter of total Finnish trade in the 1980s) devastated the Finnish economy. As Lars Svåsand argues,

[100] Wijkman, "To Be or Not to Be a Member," p. 6.

[101] For a discussion of the FIN-EFTA agreement and the pursuit of a balance between East and West in Finnish trade policy, see Riitta Hjerppe, "Finland's Foreign Trade and Trade Policy in the 20th Century," *Scandinavian Journal of History* 18 (1993), 57–76.

the Finnish motivations to join the EC were much stronger than else-where in northern Europe.[102] European integration became the means to revive an ailing Finnish economy, which recorded a record fall in GDP between 1989 and 1991 from 5 percent to −6.5 percent.[103] Un-employment soared to 18 percent, unheard of by Nordic standards. Finland could have avoided this pitfall if it were blessed with abundant petroleum resources like the Norwegians. Instead, the Finnish econ-omy depends on timber and manufactured goods as the primary sources of export income, with distinct political consequences.

Finland's leading sectors are a mix of raw material exporters (for-estry products and metals) and manufacturers (engineering and high-tech industries). Forestry has traditionally been the most important sec-tor. In 1993, forestry exports accounted for approximately half of total export revenues. The most important market for these products is west-ern Europe, the recipient of 80 percent of the Finnish forestry indus-try's exports.[104] To compete in that market and to adjust to the new imperatives of recycled wood products, Finnish forestry producers sup-ported European integration.

Finland's manufacturing sector is internationally oriented and re-sponded to the pull of European integration by relocating to the conti-nent and purchasing subsidiaries in the EC. Once the government announced its intent to join the EC, foreign direct investment substan-tially tapered off.[105] For Finnish industry, Europe has become even more important since the loss of its special trade agreement with Russia. EC integration offers the hope of future prosperity. European integration imposes liberalizations on the Finnish economy that prom-ise the revival of investment, economic growth, and employment. "EC membership alone will allow industry to compete on an equal footing in its main markets. It will provide opportunities for full-scale eco-nomic integration, which will in turn promote efficiency and structural

[102] Lars Svåsand, "From Autonomy to Integration," seminar at Department of Compara-tive Politics, University of Bergen, May 8, 1995.
[103] When Finland debated entry into the EC in 1994, GDP per capita was lower in Finland than the EC average. See Ministry of Foreign Affairs of Finland, *Fact Sheet: Fin-land* (Helsinki, 1996), p. 2.
[104] "Forest Industry Still the Cornerstone of the Finnish Economy," in *Finland 1994: Forests and Nature* (Helsinki: Finnish Government, 1994), p. 6.
[105] See Raimo Väyrynen, "Finland on the Way to the European Community," in *The Nordic Countries and the EC*, p. 70.

adjustment of all national resources."[106] Filip Hamro-Drotz, senior adviser at the Confederation of Finnish Industry and Employers, viewed the accession process as critical: "We regard membership as completely indispensable."[107] The process of reform is under way in Finland: "despite popular skepticism, the hegemonic project is to turn Finland into a fully fledged *European market economy.*"[108]

Finnish industry and government officials viewed EC membership as essential to attracting foreign direct investment to the country. Portraying Finland as the ideal gateway to investment in Russia and the Baltic states is one of the government's strategies for reviving the depressed economy. "Membership in the EC clearly affects the profile of our country" among investors, according to Filip Hamro-Drotz.[109] To stand outside the European market, for Finland, is to risk marginalization. For the Nordic state that shares the longest border with Russia, foreign direct investment plays an important stabilizing role.[110]

When Sweden announced its plan to join the EC, Finnish businesses expressed concern about investment diversion. Finnish industry, which relies heavily on the Swedish market, feared the prospect of remaining outside the EC if Sweden joined.[111] Finnish industrialists were among the most prominent supporters of entry into the European Community and sought to mobilize support for accession to the EC.[112] Raimo Väyrynen refers to the coalition of government and industry that formed in 1992 as a kind of elite bargain, with agreement on the EC orientation of Finnish economic policy.[113] In Finnish domestic politics, the social coalitions made up of the leading export sectors endorsed political integration, as we witnessed in Sweden.

The backbone of Finnish opposition to integration was similar to the situation in Norway. Finns, like Norwegians, have maintained high levels of subsidies to agriculture. "The desire to maintain settlements in

---

[106] Ibid.

[107] "Finnish Industry Fears Exclusion from European Union," *Reuters,* June 1, 1994.

[108] Jan Otto Andersson, Pekka Kosonen, and Juhana Vartiainen, *The Finnish Model of Economic and Social Policy: From Emulation to Crash* (Åbo: Åbo Akademis Tryckeri, 1993), p. 49.

[109] "Finnish Industry Fears Exclusion from European Union."

[110] See Ministry of Foreign Affairs, "Finnish Foreign Policy and EC Membership," *Finnish Features* (October 1992), 2.

[111] Wijkman, "To Be or Not to Be a Member," p. 10.

[112] "Finland redoatt betala för vår ställning," *Hufvudstadsbladet,* November 19, 1988.

[113] Raimo Väyrynen, "Finland and the European Community: Changing Elite Bargains," *Cooperation and Conflict* 28, no. 1 (1993), 44–45.

the sparsely populated northern provinces led to heavy subsidies for farmers in those regions."[114] Producer prices have been much higher in Finland than in EC member states, and Finnish farms are, on average, less productive.[115] Farmers, who depend on support from the state, were the most resistant to the European project. Finland's Center Party (the traditional agrarian party) officially endorsed EC membership, yet the party was internally divided precisely because of the consequences for farmers. In sharp contrast to Norway, where the Center Party directly opposed European integration, the Finnish Center Party brought the nation into the EC. Prime Minister Esko Aho and the minister of agriculture and forestry both came from the Center Party. In Sweden, on the other hand, the Center Party was marginally important in the EC debate and endorsed entry into the Community. The relative power of the Center Party in the three parliaments is indicated in Table 6.8.

In the negotiations with the EC, the Finns accommodated the concerns of the agricultural sector. The former head of the Finnish Farmers' Union, Foreign Minister Heikki Haavisto, was responsible for negotiating the details of agricultural trade with the EC. The agricultural agreement made between Finland and the EC permitted the retention of national subsidies and also committed the EC to pay for a substantial proportion of them.[116] In sharp contrast to the situation in Norway, the Center Party led the state into the EC instead of fighting the integration process at every step of the way.

The other opponents of European integration were found among members of the Christian People's Party, the Rural Party, and the former Communist Party. The opposition, however, failed to mobilize enough support to counter the strength of Finland's pro-EC social coalition. This became apparent when Finnish parliamentarians and voters were asked to voice their preferences on EC membership.

When Finland took its treaty to the Parliament for approval, the representatives approved the treaty with a clear majority (152 of the 200 members). When the government sought advice from the public on whether to join, the outcome was also positive. Of the Finns participat-

[114] Eric Solsten and Sandra Meditz, eds., *Finland: A Country Study* (Washington, D.C.: U.S. Government Printing Office, 1990), p. 164.
[115] Lauri Kettunen and Jyrki Niemi, *The EU Settlement of Finnish Agriculture and National Support* (Helsinki: Agricultural Economics Research Institute, 1994), pp. 9–13.
[116] Ibid.

Table 6.8. Representation in Parliament

Country	Number of Representatives
Norway (based on election results, 1993)	
Social Democratic Party	67
Center Party	32
Conservative Party	28
Socialist Left Party	13
Christian People's Party	13
Progress Party	10
Sweden (based on election results, 1994)	
Social Democratic Party	162
Conservative Party	80
Center Party	27
Liberal Party	26
Left Party	22
Green Party	18
Christian Democratic Party	14
Finland (based on election results, 1994)	
Center Party	55
Social Democratic Party	48
National Coalition Party	40
Left Alliance Party	19
Swedish People's Party	11
Green Party	10
Finnish Christian Union	8
Finnish Rural Party	7

Source: Economist Intelligence Unit, Norway, Sweden, Finland, 1994.

ing in the national referendum, 56.9 percent voted yes, and 43.1 percent voted against.[117]

It is no accident that Finns were in favor, since they had much more at stake than did oil-dependent Norway and fish-dependent Iceland. Since accession, the Finns have deepened cooperation with the European Community by linking the national currency (the markka) to the exchange rate mechanism of the European Monetary System on October 12, 1996. Finland, like Sweden, is a Nordic export-oriented pragmatist with European ambitions.

SECTORS AND THE STATE

The preceding discussion isolates the preferences of societal groups within each Nordic state. Sectors vary in the capacity to influence the

[117] "Finnish Parliament Approves EU Membership," *Reuters,* November 18, 1994.

government within each political economy, and each government is embedded in an entirely different array of political coalitions—some aligning in favor of European policy coordination and others against, depending on the separate markets that each state participates in (fishing, manufacturing, petroleum, forestry, and agriculture). The following discussion focuses on how particular economic interest groups participate in the political process of integration.

Leading sectors influence the political process in three ways: the mobility of factors of production, representation in the political party system, and participation in social movements. In the Nordic campaigns for EC membership, sectors played distinct political roles and varied in the capacity to exercise influence within the state.

Sector Mobility

In Sweden, manufacturers were mobile and were included in the meetings of cabinet officials advising the prime minister on EC strategy. Only by agreeing to join the EC could the government stem the tide of job losses and be assured of attracting foreign direct investment to Sweden. Capital mobility was also important in Finland's accession process, as more and more firms invested in EC member states after 1985.

In Norway, on the other hand, the relative immobility of the industrial structure, combined with a smaller group of industrialists, created the opposite political effect: there was no equivalent pressure on the state to join the EC, nor did the economy experience the negative consequences of capital flight. Instead, the citizens of Norway's petroleum-based political economy had the luxury of debating what kind of society they wished to live in. The imperative of European integration never exerted the same pull as it did in Sweden or Finland. In Norwegian society there was more to be lost than to be gained by integrating with the European Community.

Economic interest groups mobilized for or against membership in the European Community depending on the anticipated costs or benefits of accession. In Sweden and Denmark, the economic interest organizations representing the export-oriented agriculture and manufacturing sectors supported closer ties to the EC. Norwegian coastal fisheries, agriculture, and small manufacturers were, on the other hand, considerably more hostile to the EC because they anticipated greater costs, expected reductions in state support, and feared greater foreign competition. Peripheral socioeconomic interests mobilized against the government in a manner reminiscent of the early debate over accession in the 1970s.

Because of the differences in each state's dependence on international markets, northern European governments faced alternative constraints and opportunities after 1985. Some sectors, however, were more effective at mobilizing against integration than others were, depending on the representation of sectoral concerns in party politics and participation in social movements.

Sectors and Political Parties

Norway was the only government that experienced a political crisis in the accession process. The Center Party, representing the sheltered agricultural sector, rural industry, and coastal fisheries, emerged as the government's primary opposition to European collaboration and contested every effort of the Social Democrats and Conservatives to bring Norway into the European Community.

In Norway, a governmental crisis occurred as the society debated the merits of European integration. The Norwegian Center Party shared power in a coalition government with the Conservative Party and the Christian People's Party until October 1990. The government was forced to resign when the Center Party refused to participate in the "selling of Norway" during the EEA negotiations. The Center Party, founded as a farmers' party, maintains close ties to the agricultural sector in Norway, in contrast to the Center Party in Sweden, which is much less of a truly agrarian party.[118] The Swedish Center Party's constituency is more urban than rural, with predominantly workers, civil servants in both private and state companies, and entrepreneurs. Jan Dale, the political secretary of the Norwegian Center Party during the campaign, worked closely with leaders of the anti-EC social movement to inform the public about the negative consequences of EC membership. These included the deterioration of smaller communities, giving up the important role played by the state in the economy, speeding up the disintegration of the Nordic model, accepting a decline in living

[118] Approximately 40 percent of Center Party supporters in Norway are farmers, as opposed to only 19 percent in Sweden (1988–89). See Dag Arne Christensen, "Fornyinga av bondepartia i Noreg og Sverige."

standards, and higher levels of unemployment. According to Jan Dale, "big government will not be good for our people."[119]

When I interviewed the political secretary of the Swedish Center Party, however, and asked him to comment on Sweden's relationship to the EC, he said, "Everyone agrees that we should have closer contact."[120] A few disaffected members of the Social Democratic Party and Green Party leader Per Gharton protested the government's decision to join the EC during 1992.[121] In sum, four political parties maintained anti-EC platforms in Norway: the Center Party, the left wing of the Social Democratic Party, the Christian People's Party, and the Socialist Left Party. Norway's largest party, the Social Democrats, has been internally divided over the question of EC membership and has lost some of its support to the Socialist Left Party. Table 6.9 illustrates how support for the two anti-EC parties (Center and Socialist Left) has increased since 1987, when European unity was central to the domestic political debate. In contrast to the other Nordic states that sought entry in the 1990s, opposition among rural interests represented through the party system had the capacity to block a Norwegian application for EC membership.[122]

The strength of anti-EC parties became evident in the parliamentary debates over the EEA agreement. It required forty-two members of the *Storting* (Norwegian Parliament) to block approval of the EEA treaty, and prior to the vote as many as thirty or thirty-five of the 164-member parliament maintained an anti-EEA stance.[123] In contrast to Norway, all the major Danish parties maintain pro-EC platforms. In Sweden, only the smaller parties (the Green Party and the Communist Party) maintained anti-EC platforms. All the major parties in Sweden supported approval of the EEA agreement in the *Riksdag* (Swedish Parliament) and endorsed EC membership.

Sectors and Social Movements

Another important difference in Nordic political systems was the strength of pro- and anti-EC social movements. In economies in which

[119] Interview at Center Party headquarters, Oslo, August 6, 1990.

[121] Interview with Åke Pettersen, Center Party headquarters, Stockholm, 1990.

[121] The director of the Swedish Central Bureau of Statistics voiced his opposition in *Dagens Nyheter*, spring 1992.

[122] See Fredrik Vogt Lorentzen, "Valget og ja-siden," *Aftenposten*, July 9, 1992.

[123] Erik Ramberg and John Myhre, "AP må gå hvis EØS faller," *Aftenposten*, August 13, 1992.

Table 6.9. Public support for the political parties in Norway

Party	% of Electoral Support		
	1987	1991	1992
Center*	6.8	12.0	13.8
Socialist Left*	5.7	12.2	15.5
Social Democratic	35.9	30.4	25.7
Conservative	23.7	21.9	23.3
Progress	12.3	7.0	8.4
Radical Left	1.3	1.5	0.9
Christian People's	8.1	8.1	7.0
Left	3.3	3.5	3.2
Other	2.9	3.5	2.1

*Party platforms oppose the EEA and EC membership.
Source: Opinion A/S for Aftenposten, June 20, 1992.

Europe was more likely to be perceived as a threat (Norway), anti-EC movements had a broader base of support and often engaged in protests against the government. For example, the Norwegian anti-EC movement captured the momentum in the EC debate right from the start, and put the "yes to Europe" groups on the defensive.[124] Farmers, fishermen, and women in the public sector were prominent actors in the opposition in Norway. In Sweden, on the other hand, the anti-EC group, *Nej till EG*, was not as successful in mobilizing the population against the EC and was much less visible during the EC campaign. It was difficult to locate the offices of *Nej till EG*, in Stockholm, but one easily came in contact with representatives from the pro-EC organization, *Ja till Europa*.

The Norwegian anti-EC group, *Nei til EF*, recruited many of the same leaders who were responsible for mobilizing societal groups against EC membership in the 1970s. The organization was inactive from 1973 to 1989 but resumed its battle with renewed energy in the 1990s. The leader of the organization, Kristen Nygaard, has been outspoken and politically active. The organization's headquarters are in Oslo, but it maintains offices throughout Norway. Nei til EF has published and distributed its concerns about the consequences of EC membership for Norwegian society. In *Fakta og Meninger om Norge og EF*, the leaders of the organization suggest that the undesirable consequences of Norwegian policy adaptation to the EC's internal market include "the cen-

[124] Interview with Henry Valen following the November 28, 1994, referendum, Oslo.

tralization, rationalization, privatization and alteration of the family structure. . . . Accepting a large and increasing loss of jobs typical of most EC member-states, where mass unemployment has been the largest social problem. . . . More pronounced class differences between the rich and secure and a growing number of poor in the society."[125]

Under Norwegian leadership, a Nordic anti-EC women's movement was established. The officers were members of Norway's anti-EC Center Party, and they sought ties to other Euroskeptics in Nordic societies. The movement appealed to women employed in the public sector who anticipated downsizing in the public administration as a consequence of EC membership. Women in the Nordic states also registered concern over a southern-Europeanization of social democratic institutions and policies. Specifically, opponents of the EC anticipated cuts in policies that disproportionately affect women.[126]

Social movements endure, even beyond the accession debates. In Denmark, the anti-EC social movement, *Nej til EF*, has had an active membership since it was founded the 1960s. But representatives from the Danish organization have also been represented in European institutions. The organization has become a transnational actor, endorsing social democratic values within EC institutions. At a meeting of the Danish anti-EC organization held in Copenhagen during the spring of 1991, the arguments made against political and economic union included the following concerns: the EC was not a democratic organization, big business interests were overrepresented, small states had too little ability to voice their preferences, and the transfer of authority from Copenhagen to Brussels does not allow the people to have a say in decisions that directly affect their working lives.

The deepening of European policy cooperation initiated in 1985 created different constraints and opportunities for Nordic governments, depending on the mobility of factors of production, and in the relationship between sectors and the state. Leading sectors acted in different ways to exert their influence on the state: by exiting to the EC, through ties to political parties, and as participants in social move-

---

[125] Per Lund, Kristen Nygaard, and Birgit Wiig, eds., *Fakta og Meninger om Norge og EF* (Oslo: Opplysningsutvalget om Norge og EF, 1989), pp. 138–139.

[126] Kvinnor Kan, "Sverige och EG," meeting in Stockholm, spring 1991. In 1991, an anti-EC Nordic women's organization (Nordisk Kvinner Mot EF) was organized by Norwegian feminists to focus attention on the negative consequences of economic policy adaptation for the society, particularly for women.

ments. Some economic interest groups representing leading sectors encouraged and promoted a pro-EC position (Danish, Swedish, and Finnish manufacturers), while others sought to defend their sector against liberalization or increased competition represented by further integration with the EC (Norwegian petroleum, Icelandic fisheries). Economic interest groups representing leading sectors became politically important to each state as Nordic governments pursued closer cooperation with the European Community.

The Swedish government's position was influenced by the mobility of firms: how could the state resist European integration when jobs were moving south to the EC? The Norwegian government, on the other hand, faced an entirely separate challenge: how to convince particular economic interests in the society that integration would be of benefit to them.

As one Nordic analyst put it, "Although most Scandinavians will readily agree that together they constitute a group of peoples which is identifiable in the modern world by its high standard of living, they prefer to look at the economies which have produced such gratifying results as entirely separate national structures."[127] It is within these structures that the governments in our five political economies faced the challenge of European integration. Economic producers were adversely affected in some countries but not in others. Some economic interest groups were particularly effective at capturing the heart of the nation during the accession debates. Thus, the effects of European integration were not uniform in northern European politics.

Sweden's leading sector, internationally oriented manufacturing, exercised influence on the government by investing increasingly in the EC between 1985 and 1992 and by participating in a secret advisory council organized by Social Democratic prime minister Ingvar Carlsson. In Norway, sectoral interests influenced the decision-making process through the anti-EC political party represented in the government (the Center Party) and by mobilizing public opinion against the EC through participation in a grass-roots social movement. In sum, sectoral dependence facilitated or constrained the capacity of each government to pursue a strategy of regional governance. Governments in manufacturing-dependent states (Sweden and Finland) experienced

[127] T. K. Derry, *A History of Scandinavia* (Minneapolis: University of Minnesota Press, 1979), p. 367.

capital flight and had fewer domestic political groups opposing accession. Governments in resource-dependent states (Norway and Iceland) had no equivalent pull to integrate and far greater opposition to accession in domestic politics.

The analytical framework introduced in this chapter combines differences in the structural constraints on governments that emanate from sectoral dependence and spells out how economic interest organizations become politically important in the domestic political debates over European unity. In contrast to their actions during earlier periods of European integration, none of the northern European governments resisted some form of deeper integration with the EC after 1985. Even Iceland, the Nordic state most resistant to supranationalism, approved the extensive reforms required under the EEA agreement. Nevertheless, the capacity of governments to join the core or remain on the semiperiphery of European politics was heavily dependent on the anticipated effect of integration on particular sectors and, in turn, on the political influence of sectors in domestic politics.

The implications of the sectoral approach extend beyond the 1995 entry of Finland and Sweden into the EC and Norway's and Iceland's decisions to remain more aloof as signatories of the EEA agreement. Instead, the differences extend to the European level and are visible in European politics, as the Nordic states align with two competing visions of integration—British intergovernmentalism and German multilateralism. Before discussing these alternative roles in European politics, however, consider the role of Nordic publics as governments increasingly pursued multilateralism.

Chapter 7 discusses how the role of the public was secondary in importance to the relationship between Nordic governments and economic sectors in the accession process. National referenda were held throughout northern Europe after the treaties with the EC had been negotiated and economic interest groups had voiced their preferences. Nordic publics reacted to a political discourse already in progress and were asked to weigh in when many decisions about the substance and direction of policy had already been made by national governments in partnership with leading sectors.

PART IV

The Implications

CHAPTER SEVEN

Votes Count, Resources Decide

In the words of Norwegian political scientist Stein Rokkan, "Votes count, but resources decide the outcome in the end."[1] The pursuit of European integration was initiated by governments, with societal groups supporting or resisting the political process in each state. In the Nordic accession debates, interest groups articulated their preferences early and often. Although Iceland's dependence on fisheries and domestic resistance to cooperating with a European fisheries regime prevented an application for entry, the Swedish, Finnish, and Norwegian governments applied to join the European Community. In the final phase, after the negotiations with the EC and a joint agreement on the content of the accession treaty had been reached, the Nordic governments turned to their respective publics to ask for approval. At this point, however, the die had already been cast: leading economic sectors were insiders in the negotiations, and important redirections in national policy had already been made. Each government's role in the integration process was structured by a separate configuration of economic interest groups with distinct preferences for or against closer cooperation with the EC. As argued by Rokkan, "political systems vary extraordinarily in the ways the votes of mass electorates count in national decision-making. But however weighty the decisions of electoral majorities, nothing is likely to get settled without the consent and participation of corpo-

[1] Stein Rokkan, "Norway: Numerical Democracy and Corporate Pluralism," in Robert Dahl, ed., *Political Oppositions in Western Democracies* (New Haven: Yale University Press, 1966), p. 105.

rate groups in controlling key resources."[2] Citizens were consulted after governments, in cooperation with leading sectors, negotiated separate treaties with the EC.

In this chapter, I focus on the implications of the political process of accession for our understanding of Nordic foreign policy making. Not everyone was consulted, nor did all groups have an equal say in the process. By examining public opinion data, it is possible to identify patterns of groups that favored or resisted European integration within each state. The first section discusses when and how the public had a voice in the process. The second section discusses how public preferences correlated with economic dependence. The final section discusses how public opinion varied within the Nordic area as European integration deepened.

WHO DECIDES?

European integration was initiated by Nordic governments and legitimized by their respective publics. The public's approval was not constitutionally required, yet Scandinavian governments have sought domestic support for transferring authority to supranational institutions.[3] The political process of integration was, as I have argued throughout, decided by a partnership between governments and economic interest groups in which the public had a limited voice in the outcome. As Gerald Schneider and Lars-Erik Cederman argue, "governments had a considerable edge over citizens in access to information."[4]

The closed nature of the political process of the EC negotiations became a subject for criticism in each of the campaigns against membership. Even in Finland, where opposition was comparatively weak and the government has historically had a tradition of top-down foreign policy making, the integration process came under attack in the press in 1989. In an article in the Swedo-Finnish language paper *Hufvudstadsbladet*, "The People Have Nothing to Say about Finland

[2] Stein Rokkan, "Votes Count, Resources Decide," in *Makt og Motiv: Et Festskrift til Jens Arup Seip* (Oslo: Gyldendal Norsk Forlag, 1975), p. 217.
[3] For a discussion of the role of public opinion in foreign-policy making, see Torben Worre, "Danish Public Opinion and the European Community," *Scandinavian Journal of History*, 20, no. 3 (1995), 209–227.
[4] Gerald Schneider and Lars-Erik Cederman, "The Change of Tide in Political Cooperation: A Limited Information Model of European Integration," *International Organization* (Autumn 1994), 633–662.

and Europe," Heidi Avellan writes, "The decision about Finland's role in European integration is made in very small circles. The people's participation in the decision-making process is therefore likely to be extremely limited. What the average Finn thinks is of little importance. The bureaucrats responsible for responding to integration-related questions openly proclaim that it is too complicated a situation for amateurs. At the same time, they ask us to debate this."[5] This view was shared throughout the north among the Euroskeptics. When asked to vote on the EC, however, some important patterns were visible.

NORDIC EC PREFERENCES: COMPARING THE DATA

In a systematic study of Nordic referendum data, Jonathon Moses and Anders Todal Jenssen argue that variation across and within the Nordic countries can be accounted for by relying on a political economy approach. Differences in economic export structures and what Europe offers each state can explain why some states were more positive than others to European Community membership. Norway's opposition to EC membership is "best explained by its relative wealth and the nature of its export dependence on the EC. . . . Finland and Sweden are both heavily dependent on European markets (goods and capital), and are economies in search of recovery."[6]

Preferences for or against membership in the EC varied according to the type of employment in each political economy. In the words of Ulf Lindström, "all we can safely say is that the likelihood of finding an industrial worker employed by a company facing cut-throat competition in the European market is much higher in Finland and Sweden than in Denmark and, especially, Norway. Likewise, one is more likely to meet a peasant afraid of losing government subsidies (read: his livelihood) in Norway than elsewhere in Scandinavia."[7] Regional differences in employment by industry and attitudes toward European integration

[5] Heidi Avellan, "Folket har ingen talan om Finland och Europa," *Hufvudstadsbladet*, November 25, 1989.
[6] Jonathon Moses and Anders Todal Jenssen, "Nordic Accession: An Analysis of the EU Referendums," paper presented to the Conference on the Political Economy of European Integration: The Challenges Ahead, University of California, Berkeley, April 20–22, 1995, p. 18.
[7] Ulf Lindström, "Scandinavia and the European Union: The Referenda in Denmark, Finland, Norway and Sweden, 1992–1994" (Bergen: Department of Comparative Politics, 1995) (mimeo), p. 43.

confirm the importance of "where you stand depends on where you sit" in each political economy. While voting according to one's wallet was not the only consideration, the prominence of northern and coastal opposition in fisheries and agriculture in Norway can be contrasted to the support of manufacturers located predominantly in southern Sweden and Finland.

In the fall of 1995, three referenda were scheduled in northern Europe on EC membership. The governments of Sweden, Finland, and Norway actively sought membership in the European Community, yet to do so they needed legitimacy from their respective publics. To facilitate a domino effect in the north, the Swedish and Finnish governments agreed to a proposal put forward by the Brundtland government to schedule the Norwegian referendum after the Finnish and Swedish vote. Given the trends in public opinion, the Finns consistently favored European Community membership; the Swedes were also positive, while Norwegians remained the most skeptical. It was the Norwegian prime minister's intent to draw the nation into the European project by default: if all our Nordic neighbors are joining, why not follow the lead of Finland and Sweden? Yet the Norwegian Social Democratic leader underestimated the strength of the opposition and the unwillingness of Norwegians to be swayed by the Europreferences of Swedes and Finns.

In his analysis of the Norwegian decision to reject EC membership in the 1970s, Rokkan attributes the outcome to the power of organizations in the primary sector: "The leagues of the fishermen and of the farmers felt threatened by the prospect of entry and could not agree to the terms offered in Brussels."[8] If we examine the 1972 referendum data by the type of economic production in each district (commune), it is possible to identify patterns in sectoral preferences for or against membership. Fishermen and farmers were more likely to vote against entry than were members of the service or industrial sectors of society, as indicated in Table 7.1.

The issue of EC membership divided Norwegian society; and even though a referendum was not considered legally binding, the government resorted to a plebiscite. When 53.5 percent of the voters rejected EC membership, the Social Democratic government withdrew the ap-

[8] Rokkan, "Norway," p. 218.

Table 7.1. EC referendum vote: Regional differences, 1992 (economic activity in districts)

Economic Base	Yes	No	Refuse	Total
Agriculture	38	98		136
Agriculture/industry	52	113		165
Service/agricultural/industry	59	72	2	133
Fisheries	16	61		77
Fisheries/industry	38	55		93
Industrial	147	129		276
Service/industry	420	251	2	673
Total	959	1,020	4	1,983

Source: Norwegian Social Science Data Services.

plication. Yet in Denmark, the EC issue played out in exactly the opposite way. Societal interests were less divided than in Norway, and "the organizations in the primary economy were as eager to join as the business community and the trade unions."[9] As a consequence of these differences in economic interests, the periphery mobilized against the center in Norway—but not in Denmark. Differences in urban and rural voters are visible in Table 7.2.

Many of the same forces described by Rokkan were visible in the recent accession process in northern Europe. As if frozen in time by the effects of the oil economy, Norwegian preferences have remained largely unchanged since the 1972 referendum. An alliance of economic groups in peripheral Norway (farmers, fishermen, and small industry) were the backbone of Norway's anti-EC social movement. Urban Norwegians employed in the public sector aligned with peripheral groups to resist European integration.

A comparison of the outcome of the 1994 EC referenda in Norway, Sweden, and Finland reveals some interesting patterns that help to confirm the importance of economic dependence. In the industrial areas of southern Sweden and southern Finland, we find the strongest support for European integration. In the rural agricultural districts, however, opposition to European integration was much stronger. The Norwegian Social Science Data Services provided the maps on the fol-

[9] Ibid.

Table 7.2. Urban-rural cleavages in Norway's EC
referendum, 1972

	Yes	No	Refuse	Total
Urban	749	522	3	1274
Rural	210	498	1	709
Total	959	1,020	4	1,983

Note: Missing observations = 679.
Source: Norwegian Social Science Data Services, Bergen.

lowing pages that correlate the EC vote in the 1994 referenda by region and show the nature of each state's industrial structure. Northern
regions, dependent on raw materials or agriculture, were more likely to
vote against the EC than were areas of the country dependent on oil
extracting, manufacturing, finance, insurance, or business. As indicated in Map 1, northwestern Sweden voted overwhelmingly against
membership. In this area, farmers had more in common with the Norwegian concerns than with the Swedish government. By far the greatest
opposition, however, was to be found in Norway, where the stakes of
entry were even higher.

As demonstrated in Chapter 6, Norway's oil dependence was critical
to the societal debate over whether to join the Community. European
accession appeared to be less of a necessity for a majority of Norwegians. In the words of Ulf Lindström, "Petroleum, immobile and sal-
able at a decent price for the foreseeable future, is a sedative to Norway's public debate about the fundamental consequences of a global
economy. The internationalization of capital and manpower beyond
the reach of national legislation, market shares, R&D, and employment—topics that came to occupy a prominent position in the debate
about Europe in Finland and Sweden—do not breathe down the neck
of a body politic (or its MPs) lulled by the comfort of inexhaustible oil
wells."[10]

The Norwegian public was far more uncertain about the EC than
were citizens in neighboring Sweden and Finland. The trends and os-
cillations in public preferences had discernible patterns, from high
marks for the EC early in the accession debates in Finland and Sweden
to a cooling-off period following Denmark's rejection of the Maastricht

[10] Lindström, "Scandinavia and the European Union," p. 14.

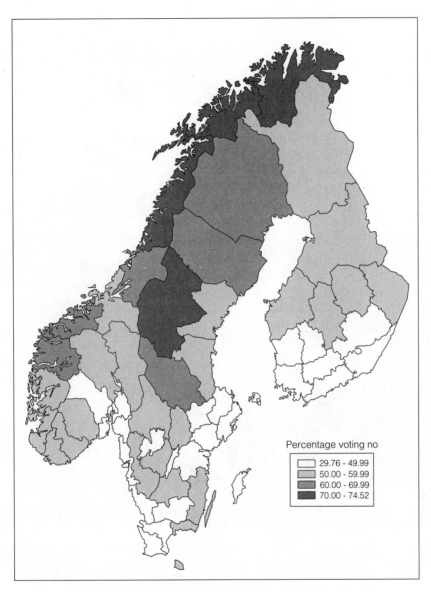

Map 7.1. Norway, Sweden, and Finland: EC referenda, 1994, no votes. Norwegian Social Science Data Services, Bergen.

Percentage voting no

	29.76 - 49.99
	50.00 - 59.99
	60.00 - 69.99
	70.00 - 74.52

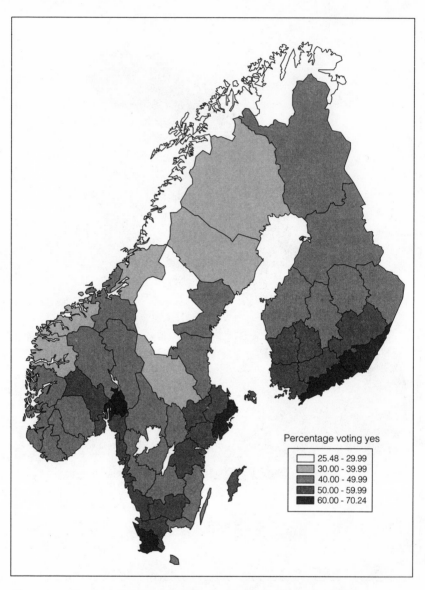

Percentage voting yes

	25.48 - 29.99
	30.00 - 39.99
	40.00 - 49.99
	50.00 - 59.99
	60.00 - 70.24

Map 7.2. Norway, Sweden, and Finland: EC referenda, 1994, yes votes.
Norwegian Social Science Data Services, Bergen.

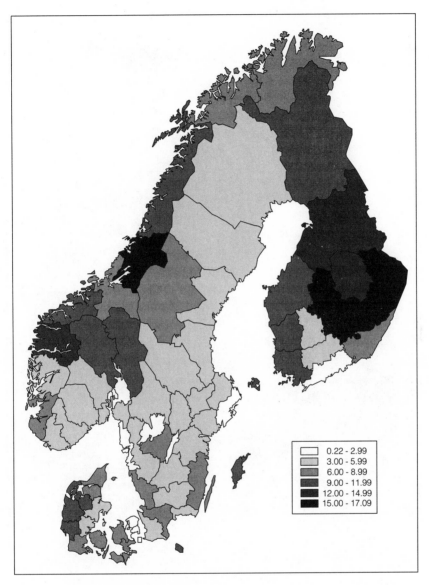

Map 7.3. Agriculture, fishing, and hunting, as percentage of industrial structure. Norwegian Social Science Data Services, Bergen.

Legend:
- 0.22 - 2.99
- 3.00 - 5.99
- 6.00 - 8.99
- 9.00 - 11.99
- 12.00 - 14.99
- 15.00 - 17.09

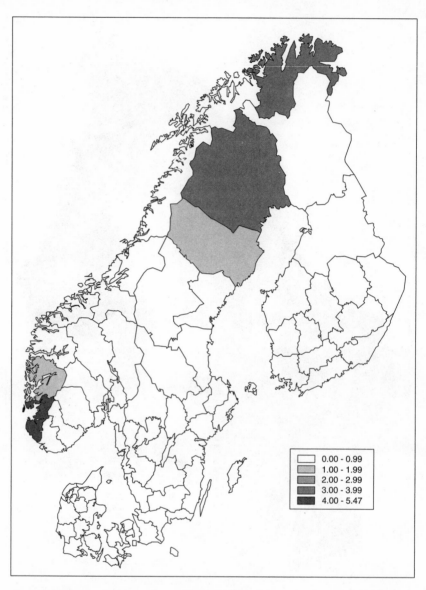

Map 7.4. Oil extracting, mining, and quarrying, as percentage of industrial structure. Norwegian Social Science Data Services, Bergen.

	0.00 - 0.99
	1.00 - 1.99
	2.00 - 2.99
	3.00 - 3.99
	4.00 - 5.47

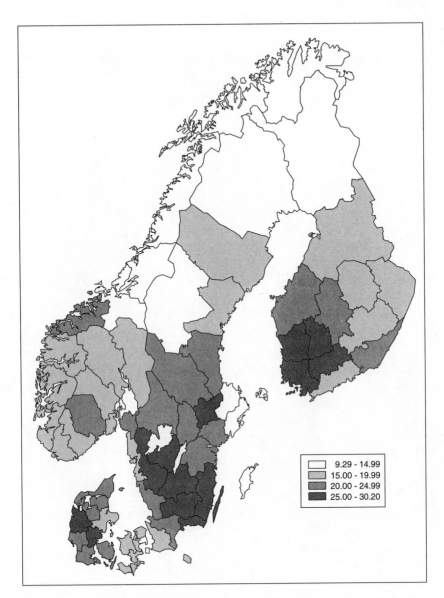

Map 7.5. Manufacturing, as percentage of industrial structure. Norwegian Social Science Data Services, Bergen.

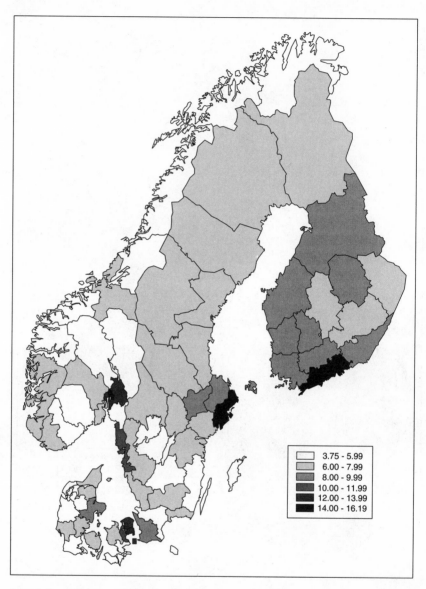

Map 7.6. Finance, insurance, and business, as percentage of industrial structure. Norwegian Social Science Data Services, Bergen.

Treaty. Norwegians, on the other hand, were deeply divided over the prospect of EC membership throughout the campaign.

NORDIC PUBLICS AND EC OPINION: TRENDS AND OSCILLATIONS

As Nordic governments negotiated seperate treaties with the EC and established the conditions for accession, the attitude of the public was closely monitored.[11] While opinions were volatile, it is possible to discern some trends in Norway, Sweden, and Finland. In a brilliant cooperative move among the Nordic governments, the timetable was set to allow the most pro-EC state to vote first (Finland), followed by the other state most likely to vote in favor of entry (Sweden), with the hopes that the outcome in these two states would bring the most reluctant applicant (Norway) on board. Nordic governments could deliver two out of the three, but even the most talented political strategist in the north, Prime Minister Gro Harlem Brundtland, could not overcome the forces of opposition in Norway.

Norway consistently maintained the strongest public opposition to the EC among the Nordic states in the 1987–94 period. As the referendum approached, the public became much more evenly divided—so much so that it became too close to predict an outcome even up to the moment. Norwegian support for European integration rarely exceeded 40 percent of the voters and was typically matched by an equal number of opponents.[12] Even the EEA agreement was viewed with skepticism. According to a public opinion poll conducted in August 1992, only 44 percent of Norwegians supported the European Economic Area agreement. Fifteen percent of those polled favored applying for Norwegian

[11] For public opinion data on the Nordics and the EC, see Katherine Moen, Irene Øyangen, and Anders Todal Jenssen, "The 1994 Nordic EU Referendums Study," University of Trondheim, November 1995; Tor Bjørklund, *Norway and the EU: The Development of Public Opinion up to 1994* (Oslo: Norwegian Ministry of Foreign Affairs, May 1994); Torben Worre, "Danish Public Opinion and the European Community"; Jan Bingen and Rutger Lindahl, *Nordiske skjebnevalg?* (Oslo: Europa-programmet, 1994]; Lindstrom, "Scandinavia and the European Union"; Per Arnt Pettersen, Anders Todal Jenssen, and Ola Listhaug, "The 1994 EU Referendum in Norway: Continuity and Change," paper presented at the Midwest Political Science Association, Chicago, April 6–8, 1995; B. Aardal and Henry Valen, *Konflikt og opinion* (Oslo: NKS Forlaget, 1995); and Jan Berg, *Swedish Public Opinion and the European Community* (Stockholm: Ministry of Foreign Affairs, 1992).

[12] See, for example, "Færre mot EF, flere usikre," *Arbeiderbladet*, December 18, 1989; EF-Gallup in *Nationen*, June 21, 1990, p. 10; and "Nei-siden har igjen overtaket," *Aftenposten*, June 14, 1991.

EC membership as soon as possible, 22 percent supported an EEA agreement and eventual EC membership, 22 percent supported an EEA agreement without applying to join the EC, and 16 percent indicated they opposed both the EEA agreement and EC membership.[13] While Norwegians remained deeply divided, their neighbors seemed more favorable to European integration.

Swedish and Finnish support for the EC was stronger than in Norway, with some polls indicating that well over 50 percent of the voters (and even above 60 percent) favored membership.[14] An important change occurred after the government applied to join and the treaty was under negotiation. During 1992, Swedish public support for the EC declined to less than 50 percent. Finnish support for EC membership also dropped from 56 percent in favor, 28 percent against, and 16 percent undecided in spring 1992 to 43 percent in favor, 41 percent against, and 16 percent undecided by fall 1992.[15] It seemed that the Danish no to the Maastricht Treaty's plans for economic and political union on June 1, 1992, had repercussions in the rest of northern Europe.

In Denmark, the public's rejection of the Maastricht Treaty on political and economic union came as a surprise to the government. According to Prime Minister Schlüter, "we are working for a new basis for the Maastricht Treaty that will make it possible for Denmark to approve the European cooperation agreement."[16] Although the public will have another chance to consider the treaty, the government will define the terms of the debate. Danish EC policy is typically made through a consultative process, in meetings between the prime minister and party leaders, between members of Denmark's EC parliamentary committee (*markedsudvalget*) and the foreign minister, and in special sessions of the EC parliamentary committee.[17] In comparison to the preferred position of sectoral interests, such as Danish agriculture and business, the public has been a relative outsider in the process of economic policy adaptation.

Danish public opinion polls indicate that the issue of EC member-

[13] Opinion A/S for *Aftenposten*. The poll was based on one thousand telephone interviews, August 17–19, 1992.

[14] For trends in Nordic-EU opinion, see Jon Bingen and Rutger Lindahl, *Nordiske skjebnevalg?*

[15] Finnish public opinion study by the Center for Business and Policy Studies, Helsinki, 1993, cited in Teija Tiilikainen and Ib Damgaard Petersen, eds., *The Nordic Countries and the EC* (Copenhagen: Copenhagen Political Studies Press, 1993), p. 77.

[16] Per Nordrum, "Schlüters EF-strategi er klar," *Aftenposten*, July 30, 1992.

[17] Ibid.

ship is no longer salient but that the course of European unity is a concern. Since entry into the EC, attitudes have become more positive. Nevertheless, the appropriate balance of power in EC institutions and the type of union that evolves are important to a majority of Danes, as indicated in Table 7.3 and Table 7.4.

GOVERNMENTS DECIDE

Public opinion waxes and wanes, but governments have ultimate authority in EC decision-making. For example, Swedish public opinion has shifted against membership since the government joined the EC on January 1, 1995. When Swedes were asked to vote for representatives to the European Parliament on September 17, 1995, the two parties opposing the EC, the Green Party and the Left Party, gained votes at the expense of the Social Democrats, who were associated with EC accession.[18] Almost half of the Swedish delegation may be EC skeptics, even though government authorities in Brussels are decidedly pro-integrationist. Attitudes toward integration may vary, and voters have the capacity to send delegates to the European Parliament, a relatively weak institution in EC politics. It is national governments, however, in partnership with coalitions of economic interest groups, that are the critical actors in the accession process.

Thus, Nordic publics have had an important role in legitimating the government-led integration process. Yet EC treaties also faced hurdles in the respective national parliaments of the applicant countries. Here, too, we saw much stronger opposition in Norway, for reasons I have identified in Chapter 6. Even if the Norwegian people had followed the goverment's lead, the accession process faced a tough fight in parliament. In Finland and Sweden, on the other hand, the legislature stood solidly behind the integration initiative.

Although Nordic leaders rely on national referenda for those agreements that require transferring power to supranational authorities, it is the government, constrained to a varying degree by coalitions of economic interest groups, that determines the timing of the vote and establishes the terms on which the public will be consulted. Even before the public went to the polls, it was possible (based on my leading sector

[18] Swedish Information Service, "Swedish Election to the European Parliament," September 20, 1995.

Table 7.3. Danish attitudes about the EC, 1987–93

Year	Yes	No	Don't Know	Number of polls
1987	44	45	11	1
1988	50	41	9	1
1989	49	34	17	1
1990	57	33	10	1
1991	60	22	18	2
1992	65	19	14	2
1993	70	16	14	1

Source: Gallup polls, average number of respondents one thousand per poll. Reprinted from "Danish Public Opinion and the European Community," by Torben Worre, *Scandinavian Journal of History*, 20, no. 3 (1995), 221, reprinted by permission of Scandinavian University Press.

approach) to predict that Norwegians had less to gain and more to lose by joining the EC.

In a public opinion study conducted in Norway after the November 1994 referendum, loss of sovereignty and independence were the two most frequently voiced objections to the EC. I maintain, however, that Norwegians would have pursued a different course if the political economy had been less dependent on petroleum and more dependent on manufacturing exports. Swedes and Finns were more committed to Europe and, to a much greater extent, sought to play a role in European institution building. When it leaked out in the European press that the EC got the one Nordic state it really wanted—Sweden—it became clear that the Community understood the differences among the northerners and their degree of commitment to integration.

Paradoxically, when Finland and Sweden joined the EC, the govern-

Table 7.4. Danish preferences for European unity (distribution of all voters, in %)

Preferences	1979	1986	1993
United States of Europe	6	5	6
Decisions should increasingly be left to the EC	8	6	7
EC member states should retain full sovereignty and veto rights	52	71	76
Denmark should leave the EC	34	18	12

Source: Election surveys. Reprinted from "Danish Public Opinion and the European Community," by Torben Worre, *Scandinavian Journal of History* 20, no. 3 (1995), 221, by permission of Scandinavian University Press.

ments agreed to accept more European cooperation than had any other Nordic state. Danes, on the other hand, retained a long list of exemptions to the Treaty on European Union, which prevented the government from deepening ties to the EC without further approval from the public. While Danes have a strong basis of public support for EC membership, they are more like the Icelanders and the Norwegians in their desire to stay out of the fray and avoid entanglement in supranational institutions. Consider how these differences matter at the European level, as the Nordic states embrace two competing visions of integration.

CHAPTER EIGHT

The Nordic States in European Politics

As Peter Gourevitch argues, politics is a struggle for the interpretation of interests.[1] The idea of European unity divided Nordic societies as interests were contested and groups sought to define who would win and who would lose in the European Community. The EC's internal market program had distinct political consequences in each of the Nordic societies. In manufacturing-dependent states (Sweden and Finland), businesses invested heavily in EC member states after 1985 and were influential partners in convincing the government to join the Community. As one Swede stated, "Industry in Sweden is moving to the EC. The rest of the country must follow, because we cannot survive on taxation and native language instruction."[2] In states dependent on natural resources (Norway and Iceland), EC policy regimes were viewed with skepticism, and social coalitions resisted European unity. In the 1980s, however, the political choices for Nordic governments narrowed as more and more governments aligned with European regimes (from the EEA to the EC). The EC, in contrast to the past, has become domestic politics in these states, even among nonmembers (Norway and Iceland).

Within northern Europe, governments align with two different visions of European unity—British intergovernmentalism and German multilateralism. On the one hand, the Danish, Norwegian, and Icelandic governments promote a British vision of Europe, where national

---

[1] Peter Gourevitch, "International Trade, Domestic Coalitions and Liberty," *Journal of Interdisciplinary History* (Autumn 1977), 281–313.
[2] "Vägen till Europa," *Dagens Nyheter*, June 16, 1991, p. A2.

authorities are vested with more power and Atlanticist solutions to security policy making are preferable to European solutions. On the other hand, Swedish and Finnish governments promote a German vision of Europe, where supranational authorities are vested with more power and European solutions to security policy making are preferable to Atlanticist solutions.

In this chapter, I discuss how the EC *is* domestic politics in the Nordic states. For the first time, Europe reaches deep into the internal affairs of governments, affecting policies that were once determined by national authorities. I then turn to a discussion of the implications of Nordic responses to European integration for the future development of European politics and the political influence of leading sectors in the Austrian and Swiss responses to European unity. I conclude with a summary of the implications of Nordic political choices.

THE EC *Is* DOMESTIC POLITICS

As my analysis demonstrates, all Nordic states have increasingly adopted EC priorities in national decision-making since 1985. European institutions are an anomaly in international relations because of the depth of changes required in domestic institutions, policies, and values.[3] The process of adapting to European integration is not an external shock, like the international oil crisis of 1973–74, but it requires deep changes within the territorial boundaries and identities of nation-states. The Nordic states have increasingly internalized European standards, regulations, and policies. Ideas originating outside the Nordic area have become a part of domestic politics, more contested in some states than in others.

In contrast to other types of internationalization, European policy coordination embeds national political economies and security policy making in a regional governance structure. Once a European strategy is adopted, European priorities become incorporated in domestic politics. For example, in Finland, EC macroeconomic convergence criteria for currency union have become national policy goals.[4] As Raimo

[3] See, for example, Miles Kahler, *International Institutions and the Political Economy of Integration* (Washington, D.C.: Brookings Institution, 1995), pp. 80–116.

[4] There are several conditions: the deficit on the public sector budget must not exceed 3 percent of GNP, public sector debt must not amount to more than 60 percent of GNP,

Väyrynen argues, "the convergence criteria of Maastricht have become the guidelines for the economic policy of the Finnish government."[5] Even in states outside the EC (Iceland and Norway), European solutions enter into the national debate. European security initiatives (such as the WEU) are discussed more frequently in Nordic parliaments now than during the cold war era of polarized politics.

As Nordic governments increasingly embed security and economic policies in the European Community's institutions, these states have, as I argued in Chapter 2, more to lose than do other states. When the southern European states entered the European Community in the 1980s, they anticipated the benefits of democratic institution-building and the promise of economic development. The central European and Baltic states seek European integration at the fastest possible speed, giving them little in common with the longheld Social Democratic institutions and policies of the Nordic states or the Nordic tradition of resisting supranationalism.

As other scholars have argued, the implications for Nordic societies are more than just economic. As these countries become a part of a political community of European states, this represents a shift in national identity. Being better off than the rest of Europe is a part of what it has meant to be Nordic.[6] Norwegian political scientist Truls Frogner argues, "Our new relationship with Europe is not only a question of economics and foreign policy. It is also a question of psychology, identity, and culture."[7] Accepting European solutions with increasing frequency has led to an identity crisis, particularly in Sweden, which has been held up as *the* model Nordic society.[8]

What is at stake in the process of integrating with Europe are the institutions and policies that have made the Nordic states model societies for those scholars who study war and peace, economic development, or comparative political economy. When the Nordic states choose European unity, it becomes more difficult to retain independent poli-

---

inflation should not exceed 1 to 1.5 percentage points higher than the lowest inflation rate in the group, and long-term bond interest rates may not be more than 1 to 1.5 percentage points higher than the rate in the country with the lowest long-term interest rate. See *Outlook on the Swedish Economy* (Stockholm: Nordbanken, November 1991), p. 1.

[5] Raimo Väyrynen, "Finland and the European Community: Changing Elite Bargains," *Cooperation and Conflict* 28, no. 1 (1993), 44.

[6] See Ole Wæver, "Nordic Nostalgia," *International Affairs* 68, no. 1 (1992), 77–102.

[7] Truls Frogner, *En lang marsj mot Europa? Politiske perspektiver på Norge og EF* (Oslo: Gyldendal Norsk Forlag, 1988), p. 98.

[8] Discussions with Göran Rosenberg and Ia Dubois, two Swedish observers.

cies, from neutrality to full employment. Policies that were once considered domestic become subject to EC regulations. Two LO economists lament changes in Sweden's Social Democratic full employment model: "Sweden has, until now, pursued a separate path from the European unemployment community. In the beginning of the 1970s, Denmark had a relatively low level of unemployment, but since entry into the EC and adjusting the krone to the D-mark, unemployment has risen to nine percent."[9] As these states join Europe, however, they bring with them the idea and the ambition to affect the course of European integration in a favorable, Nordic direction.

Although the Icelandic and Norwegian governments have been, to varying degrees, constrained by prominent economic interest groups resisting cooperation with plans for European unity, the Swedish and Finnish governments have actively pursued a new role in international relations as partners in European collaboration. British intergovernmentalism is a distinct role from German multilateralism in the forging of European bargains, yet both roles coexist in northern Europe.

BRITISH INTERGOVERNMENTALISM
AND GERMAN MULTILATERALISM

The responses of the Danish, Norwegian, and Icelandic governments to European foreign and economic policy coordination have much in common with the British government. For NATO's northernmost partners, the WEU and the CSCE are not viable alternatives to the Alliance. As the Danes demonstrated by vetoing the Maastricht Treaty, national governments should be granted more authority over economic and security policies, in accordance with the British interpretation of the principle of subsidiarity. The Danes are excluded from full participation in the so-called defense policy dimension that includes the Western European Union and the creation of a common currency or economic union. The Finns and Swedes, however, enter the European Community with ambitions to achieve domestic policy goals through multilateral cooperation and seek to reform the institution from within—preferably in a Nordic direction.

For Finland and Sweden, participation in European economic and

[9] Dan Andersson and P. O. Edin, "Säg nej till EG, Carlsson!" *Dagens Nyheter*, June 24, 1990, p. A4.

political union solves domestic economic problems and lessens post–cold war security risks. By embedding their political economies and security policies in European institutions, the Swedish and Finnish governments anticipate a revival of economic competitiveness, expect to play a political role in the development of Europe, and hope to receive assurance that, if events take a turn for the worse in Russia, military assistance from other European states will be provided.

With respect to security policy cooperation, Finland is behaving like "the best student in the class" of new entrants into the European Community.[10] After renouncing its treaty with the Soviet Union, Finland rapidly reoriented its policy in a European direction.[11] Max Jacobson argues that, "for Finland, applying for EC membership marks a sharp break with the past. Traditionally, the Finns have maintained their independence and national identity by exclusion."[12]

Sweden is as committed to pan-Europeanism as Finland is. The government no longer refers to Swedish neutrality policy as an obstacle to cooperation with other European states. This constitutes a major reversal in Swedish policy from the cold war era. According to former prime minister Carl Bildt, "the word neutrality no longer applies to the policies we intend to pursue. It was geared to the idea of us staying out of a European war, should it happen. And the only thing we know now is that the kind of war that was possible a few years ago is the war that is not possible in the future."[13] The Swedes intend to cooperate in the creation of common security institutions—a significant reversal of their historic isolationism. The government has expressed its willingness, to a much greater degree than the Nordic NATO member states, to engage in joint defense policy making with the WEU. As a neutral state, some exceptions may be made for engaging in out-of-area activities, but Sweden is willing to negotiate this as a member of the European Community. In the words of Nordic analyst Nils Morten Udgaard, "It is

[10] Pauli Järvenpää, visiting lecturer, University of Washington, Seattle, 1993.

[11] See Raimo Väyrynen, "Security of Small States in Europe: Finland," paper prepared for the Conference on Small State Security in Post–Cold War Europe, University of British Columbia, Vancouver, March 24–25, 1994; and Pauli Järvenpää, "Finland: Peace Treaty of 1947," in From Versailles to Baghdad: Post-War Armament Control of Defeated States, ed. Fred Tanner (Geneva: UNIDIR, 1992).

[12] Max Jacobson, "Finland Seeks Membership in the European Community," Finnish Features (Helsinki: Ministry of Foreign Affairs, 1992), p. 1.

[13] Interview with Swedish prime minister Bildt and Finnish prime minister Esko Aho by William Schmidt, "In a Post–Cold War Era, Scandinavia Rethinks Itself," New York Times, February 23, 1992, p. E3.

the ambition of the Swedish government as well as the Social Democratic opposition to bring Sweden into the very core of the EC, even if the European Community were to be split into an inner core and an outer ring."[14]

Sweden is vying for leadership within the European Community. As a former great power in the northern European region, Sweden is reclaiming its historic position and asserting itself in foreign affairs. In interviews conducted in Denmark, representatives from the Danish Foreign Ministry expressed alarm over Sweden's ambitions in Europe. Will Sweden be more European than we are? Since the signing of the Edinburgh Protocol, Denmark rejected elements of European unity that appear to be less problematic for the Swedes (or the Finns).

NORDIC ACCESSION AND POLITICAL COALITIONS IN THE EC

Nordic accession comes at a critical moment in the development of Europe. In the aftermath of Maastricht,

> the EC faces a clear-cut alternative: either it will become a several-speed or a multi-tier community, organized in a system of concentric circles, with a core group heading for a federal system (in the German, not the British sense of the word), or the EC with develop in the direction of the British vision (shared by countries like Denmark or Portugal), which means along the line of more intergovernmental cooperation, with less influence for community institutions like the EC Commission, the European Parliament, and the European Court of Justice.[15]

The accession of Nordic states affects the balance of these forces within the European Community. My analysis refutes the notion that the Nordic newcomers will vote as a bloc once they join the EC. As a consequence of fundamental differences in national political economies, the Nordic states are likely to play distinct roles in European politics.

Negotiations with the European Community create new forums for political bargaining. Policy networks have developed among officials with specialized knowledge, who are as familiar with lobbying in

---

[14] Werner Weidenfeld and Josef Janning, eds., *Europe in Global Change: Strategies and Options* (Gütersloh: Bertelsmann Foundation Publishers, 1993), p. 179.
[15] Ibid., p. 145.

Brussels as in their home states.[16] The transnational effects of European collaboration are not lost on a group of corporatist states with long traditions of interest intermediation and regular, informal consultation; however, this is more likely to be conducted in forums outside the Nordic region, in Strasbourg and Brussels.

The northern European states are exporting ideas, policies, and institutions to the continent. For example, Pehr Gyllenhammar convinced François Mitterrand of the importance of organizing business at the European level and was instrumental in founding a corporatist entity on the European level, the European Business Roundtable.[17] Labor, on the other hand, is comparatively weak institutionally at the European level, a phenomenon that Nordic labor unions hope to amend. Even prior to accession, Nordic trade unions were opening offices in Brussels and have begun to play a role in European politics. Lessons from the north are relevant among prominent Europeanists, who are consulting the best and the brightest for ideas on how to cope with differing conceptions of the public sector in the EC.[18] Northern European political parties are receivers and transmitters of ideas, serving as transnational links between states.[19] Social democratic parties had very few contacts with European parties and far greater contacts within the Nordic area in the 1970s. Yet in the 1990s, European contacts are as extensive as cooperation among the Nordic political party organizations.[20] Regularized meetings between EC and Nordic officials create an "epistemic community," as described by Peter Haas, where a close group of transnational experts are engaged in policymaking.

When a majority of Danes rejected the Maastricht Treaty on June 2, 1992, the decision temporarily slowed the pace of European integration. The Danes outlined a new position and effectively obtained an opt-out from the creation of a political and economic union in the

[16] This argument was made by Beate Kohler-Koch in the ECPR workshop "Transformation of Governance in the European Union," Oslo, March 29–April 3, 1996.

[17] See dissertation by Maria Green Cowles, American University, Washington, D.C., 1994.

[18] Swedish political scientist Bo Rothstein advised EC officials on the adaptation of public sector services, 1994.

[19] See Lars Svåsand, "Norwegian Political Parties and European Party Cooperation," paper prepared for the ICCR Conference "Is Harmonization Possible and Desirable?" Vienna, April 5–8, 1995; and Kristin Reichel Teigland, research project on transnationalism and political parties in Italy and Norway, Department of Comparative Politics, University of Bergen.

[20] Svåsand, "Norwegian Political Parties and European Party Cooperation," p. 8.

Edinburgh Protocol.[21] The government called for changes in EC decision making to make the process more democratic. It also called for more reliance on national governments, the adoption of a social charter specifying minimal standards to protect the rights of workers, and the establishment of EC guidelines for environmental standards.[22] Working within EC institutions is a Danish imperative, yet Denmark restrains the supranational ambitions of the EC.

In negotiating entry into the European Community, the Finnish and Swedish governments obtained an important concession from the EC in the form of structural funds. The Nordic states succeeded in convincing the EC to add another category to the existing criteria for funding underdeveloped regions of the Community. As a consequence of Nordic accession, regions with a population density lower than eight persons per square kilometer (characteristic of northern peripheries) are entitled to support from the EC's structural funds. Sweden and Finland received these monies upon entering the EC in 1995.[23]

Paradoxically, the weakening of social democratic institutions and policies and unique cold war solutions to security at home may be accompanied by a strengthening of Nordicism in European institutions and policy regimes. In Nordic social democracy in the 1990s, the ambitions are transnational: to influence the development and direction of European-wide programs. Sweden, for example, seeks to influence the future of European security, employment, welfare, and the environment *within* EC institutions.[24] The Swedish government endorses the enlargement, or widening, of the EC and a strengthening of cooperation in foreign, security, and commercial policies.[25] In the Swedish view, the current challenge for the government is to find support for its proposals among other EC member states.[26]

[21] The Edinburgh Protocol was approved in a second referendum held on May 18, 1993: 56.8 percent of the participants endorsed the agreement, while 43.2 percent voted against.

[22] *Danmark's tiltrædelse af Edinburgh-Afgørelsen og Maastricht-Traktaten* (Copenhagen: Foreign Ministry, 1993), pp. 5–6.

[23] See Bart Kerremans, "Enlarging the EU Market to the East: Mission Impossible?" paper presented at the Conference of Europeanists, Chicago, March 14–16, 1996, p. 9.

[24] Swedish Social Democratic Party, "Politisk Plattfom for 1990–talet," Fall 1990, p. 1.

[25] See report of the Swedish government on the position of Sweden in the IGC, November 30, 1995; and Statement of government policy presented by Prime Minister Goran Persson to the Swedish Parliament, March 22, 1996.

[26] Sven-Erik Svard, "The Social Democratic Model and the Future," paper presented at

THE IMPLICATIONS

Recognition that it is difficult, if not impossible, to achieve national ambitions has made multilateral cooperation more appealing for all Nordic governments. Since the cold war no longer divides the Nordic states between East and West, the capacity of governments to pursue European collaboration is dependent on which groups stand to win and which groups stand to lose within each society.

WHEN SECTORS MATTER

Since Charles Kindleberger's analysis of the role of economic interest groups in influencing the development of tariff policy, political scientists have disaggregated the state to examine who wins and who loses when international economic conditions change.[27] By rejecting the unitary, rational actor approach to the study of European integration, my analysis demonstrates how in some societies (Norway and Iceland) the balance of economic interest group preferences weighed against entry, while in other societies (Finland and Sweden) the balance was more favorable. The sectoral approach enables us to understand the different structural constraints facing the Norwegian government as an oil exporter compared to the Swedish government as a manufacturing-dependent state.

Sectors, as I have argued here, are also more or less well organized at the European level. The EC energy regime is weak, thereby imposing fewer transaction costs on Norway. In Sweden, on the other hand, cooperation among businesses is extensive and provided an incentive to be within the EC. Icelandic fisheries organizations resist European integration precisely because the European regime compromises national control over vital resources.

As Peter Lange argues, European integration has distributional consequences: "Some sectors, or firms within them, will reap substantial and relatively immediate benefits from less costly access to other European markets and are likely to respond well to exposure to international competition. Others can be expected to suffer, at least in the short run. There is also good reason to believe that these sectoral

---

the annual meeting of the Society for the Advancement of Scandinavian Study, Williamsburg, Virginia, May 4, 1996, p. 6.

[27] Charles Kindleberger, "Group Behavior and International Trade," *Journal of Political Economy* 13 (1951).

and firm effects will, at least in the beginning, benefit some regions of the European Community much more than others."[28] The distributional consequences of European integration are distinct for each state. Sectoral differences account for how much resistance governments face as regional collaboration becomes a more attractive solution.

The sectoral approach challenges some of the classic literature on how states respond to international change.[29] As argued by Herbert Kitschelt, "sweeping aggregate national patterns may hide considerable policy variance across industrial sectors within each country."[30] By disaggregating the state and focusing on the political influence of leading sectors, we obtain a better understanding of why some national governments pursued cooperation with the EC, while others have been more resistant. Nevertheless, sectoral analysis has thus far ignored another structural consideration—the breakup of a polarized system of military blocs that had prevented a generation of policymakers in Sweden and Finland from pursuing European cooperation. New security concerns emerged following the end of the cold war, and multilateralism became a more attractive option for all the Nordic governments—particularly the Nordic neutrals.

To what extent can the opening provided by the end of the cold war and the preferences of leading sectors account for government responses to European integration in other states? Two other small European states (Austria and Switzerland), long committed to a trading regime with the EC, also pursued distinct paths to European integration in the 1990s. As in the Nordic area, the end of cold war divisions in Europe enabled Austria and Switzerland to consider what was previously inconceivable: entry into the European Community. The obstacles were no longer concern about the credibility of neutrality policy but domestic political and economic reservations about the consequences of Europeanization for the state and society.

---

[28] Peter Lange, "The Politics of the Social Dimension," in *Europolitics*, ed. Alberta Sbragia (Washington, D.C.: Brookings Institute, 1992), p. 225.

[29] See, for example, Peter J. Katzenstein, ed., *Between Power and Plenty* (Madison: University of Wisconsin Press, 1978); Peter J. Katzenstein, *Small States in World Markets* (Ithaca: Cornell University Press, 1985); and John Zysman, *Governments, Markets and Growth* (Ithaca: Cornell University Press, 1983).

[30] Herbert Kitschelt, "Industrial Governance Structures, Innovation Strategies, and the Case of Japan: Sectoral or Cross-National Comparative Analysis?" *International Organization* 45 (Autumn 1991).

Swiss and Austrian Political Choices

The Austrian government actively pursued accession, while the Swiss government has been even more resistant to European political cooperation than the Norwegian or Icelandic governments. As in the Nordic states, the populations of both Alpine countries were internally divided over the prospect of pursuing closer cooperation with the European Community. Neutrality policy was rapidly redefined in Austria to be compatible with European collaboration, whereas in Switzerland it was viewed as a barrier to entry.[31] Swiss intransigence can best be understood by examining the socioeconomic groups for and against political cooperation with the EC.

Switzerland's economy has sizable reserves of capital and a business sector that is even more liberal and internationally oriented than the Swedish business sector. It also has a highly protected agriculture sector and a tradition of nationally determined policies that have more in common with Norway than with Sweden, Finland, or Denmark. When the EC initiated liberalizations in capital, this did not pose problems for Switzerland.[32] The leading sectors in Switzerland (international business and financial services) preferred economic interdependence to political integration.[33]

Numerous threats to Swiss society were associated with Europeanization, from the threat to domestic traditions of federalism and direct democracy to the expected changes in immigration and agricultural policy required by entry into the EC.[34] In December 1992, a majority of Swiss voters rejected the EEA agreement in a national referendum. The largest Swiss companies, however, were unaffected by the outcome, precisely because business and banking are so internationally oriented and already well integrated in European markets.[35] The Swiss anticipated fewer advantages to being at the table than did the neighboring Austrians, where the major economic interest groups representing leading sectors (machinery and manufacturers) were in favor of entry.

In Austria, the Association of Industrialists (Vereinigung österreich-

[31] Swiss neutrality policy is defined according to principles of international law, whereas Austria's neutrality policy is defined in the national constitution.

[32] René Schwok, *Switzerland and the European Common Market* (New York: Praeger, 1991), p. 82.

[33] James Bartholomew, "EC Membership Out, Money In," *Far Eastern Economic Review*, February 18, 1993, p. 44.

[34] René Schwok, "EC-1992 and the Swiss National Identity," *History of European Ideas* 15, no. 1 (1992), 241–247.

[35] See "Frozen Out: Switzerland and the EC," *Economist*, September 4, 1993, p. 68.

ischer Industrieller) strongly favored accession and played an influential role in the EC campaign.[36] The industrialists were supported by the largest trade unions, which also endorsed membership in the European Community. In contrast to the political situation in Switzerland and Norway, agricultural organizations did not become an obstacle to Community membership. The Agricultural Chamber of Commerce initially opposed political integration but changed its position to support of entry during the EC debate. Austrian agriculture is less subsidized than Switzerland's, and joining the CAP was viewed as a means of improving the competitiveness of Austrian farming.[37] As in Sweden, the major political parties (the Social Democrats and the Conservatives) endorsed accession, and only the environmental party (the Greens) and the Communist Party opposed EC membership. The anti-EC social movement had substantially less monetary or citizen support than did the pro-EC forces.[38] When Austrians held a national referendum on June 12, 1994, 66.6 percent voted in favor of EC membership and 33.4 percent against.

Divisions between the two Alpine states are reminiscent of the Nordic states—with the Austrian and Swedish governments deliberately pursuing European integration, supported by domestic coalitions, while the Swiss and Norwegian governments experienced no similar effects and faced far greater opposition to European cooperation among domestic economic interest groups. Only the Swiss remain firmly committed to economic interdependence and the institution of EFTA, while all other EFTA states have defected in favor of deeper participation in the European integration project.

THE END OF POLITICAL AUTONOMY

As I have argued, Nordic strategies have changed from the practice of retaining a critical distance from European institution-building to pursuing European political integration as a means of managing dependence on the international political economy. In the 1970s, Nordic governments could sign a free trade agreement with the EC and have access to European markets without compromising political autonomy.

---

[36] Schwok, *Switzerland and the European Common Market*, p. 52.
[37] Ibid., p. 55.
[38] Paul Luif, "How the Austrians Swung to Europe," *European Brief* (July/August 1994), 54.

In the 1990s, however, the choice is rather: which Europe and when shall we join? Collectively, the Nordic states have more to lose than do other regions in the process of integrating with the European core. Thus, it is stunning that because of changes in regional security and European politics these states trade economic interdependence for political integration.

The transformation of the international system from a tight, bipolar configuration of power to a multipolar system led to a parallel change in preferences throughout the Nordic area. The prominence of security policy concerns has substantially changed as Nordic defense planners no longer prepare for a great power war on the European continent. In addition, the relative importance of strategic and economic issues in national policymaking has been inverted.

It is those states that have been the most distant from Europe (Finland and Sweden) that have embraced the European project wholeheartedly. For these governments, cooperation with Europe is more than a functional necessity or a trade agreement: for the first time in the twentieth century these Nordic states are shaking off their status as neutral observers and playing a role in European power politics. This marks a dramatic change from the past, when these states were more likely to play the role of the conscience of the larger powers in international relations.

Since the Swedes and Finns have become EC members, their fate has been closely monitored by Norwegians and Icelanders, who have opted for another mode of political integration. As long as Iceland continues to defend its fisheries sector from EC policy regimes, the government will remain an observer in European politics. Until the oil and gas reserves are depleted and the interest groups lined up against membership lose their hold on national politics, the Norwegians will continue to resist further integration. The threats of isolation on the periphery made by the Social Democratic government prior to the November 1994 referendum seemed unwarranted when the Norwegian economy recorded a healthy recovery in the mid-1990s.

The political consequences of the petroleum economy have not been lost on neighboring Swedes. Sweden's ambassador in Oslo, Kjell Anneling, sees more than sectoral differences at work: "Since the Olympics, God has decided to be Norwegian the whole time."[39] There may be a tinge of resentment here as the Swedes pursue economic

[39] Hugh Carnegy and Karen Fossli, "Northern Delights: Norway's Rejection of the EU Has Not Harmed Its Economy," *Financial Times*, May 26, 1995, p. 12.

recovery strategies suited to a manufacturing economy, while Norwegians pump more oil and gas from the North Sea and free ride on a favorable international oil price. Yet one thing is certain: if Sweden and Finland shared the economic dependence on fisheries typical of the Icelandic economy or could count on petroleum like the Norwegians, the political implications of European unity would be quite different, as would the development of European politics.

Interviews in Scandinavia

Denmark (1990–91, 1995)

S. Bornholdt Andersen, major, head of section, NATO Division, Ministry of Defense

Peter Bogason, professor, Department of Political Science, University of Copenhagen

Sune Bøgh, information officer, Danish Federation of Trade Unions

Michael Borg-Hansen, head of section, Ministry of Defense

Svend Aage Christensen, research director, Danish Commission on Security and Disarmament (SNU)

Michael Clemmensen, lieutenant colonel and director of strategic studies, Royal Danish Defense College

Mary Dau, foreign policy advisor, Danish government

C. Robert Dickerman, counselor for public affairs, U.S. Embassy in Copenhagen

Ib Faurby, journalist and foreign policy analyst, *Politiken*

Jens Frobenius, program coordinator, Denmark's Radio

Troels Frøling, chairman, Danish-Atlantic Committee

Hans Garde, vice admiral, chief of defense staff

Henning Gottlieb, director, Danish Commission on Security and Disarmament (SNU)

Jørn Damgaard Hansen, information officer, European Parliament Office in Denmark

Carsten Pape, research scholar, Danish International Studies Program

Klaus Carsten Pedersen, director, Danish Foreign Policy Institute

Ole Karup Pedersen, professor of political science, University of Copenhagen

Ralph Pittelkow, international advisor, Social Democratic party

Anders Urshkov, director, Danish International Studies Program

Ole Wæver, research scholar, Center for Peace and Conflict Research

K. H. Winter, commander, head of long-term plans and policy, chief of
defense

NORWAY (1990–91, 1994, 1995)

Svein Andersen, professor, Norwegian School of Management (BI)

Maja Arnestad, energy policy analyst, Norwegian School of Management (BI)

F. Brenne Bachmann, economic counselor, American Embassy in Oslo

Jan Braathu, energy policy analyst, Ministry of Foreign Affairs

Arne Olav Brundtland, research scholar, Norwegian Institute of International Affairs

Jan Dale, general secretary, Center Party

Odd Fosseidbråten, political analyst/EFTA-EC, Ministry of Foreign Affairs

Johan Jørgen Holst, director, Norwegian Institute of International Affairs

Aneurin Rhys Hughes, ambassador, head of the delegation of the Commission of the European Communities

Tønne Huitfeldt, lieutenant general and editor of Norwegian military journal

Olav Knudsen, research scholar, Norwegian Institute of International Affairs

Stein Kuhnle, director, Institute of Comparative Politics, University of Bergen

Ole Lundby, political analyst/EFTA-EC, Ministry of Foreign Affairs

Janne Haaland Matlary, energy policy analyst, Center for Advanced Research on the Europeanization of the Nation-State (ARENA), University of Oslo

Svein Melby, research scholar, Norwegian Institute of International Affairs

Atle Midttun, associate professor, Norwegian School of Management (BI)

Iver Neumann, research scholar, Norwegian Institute of International Affairs

Eva Nordlund, political secretary, Center Party

Øystein Noreng, professor, Norwegian School of Management (BI)

Kristen Nygaard, leader, Nei til EF

Terje Osmundsen, director, Norwegian Federation of Industries (NHO)

Willy Ostreng, director, Fridtjof Nansen Institute

Arve Paulsen, information officer, International Peace Research Institute, Oslo (PRIO)

Bjørn Rogstad, member of working group on the free movement of capital, Norwegian Ministry of Finance

Martin Sæter, research scholar, Norwegian Institute of International Affairs

Fred-Olav Sørensen, head of working group on free movement of persons in the EC, Norwegian Ministry of Local Government and Labor

Rolf Tamnes, defense policy analyst, Norwegian Defense Research Institute

Carsten Tank-Nielsen, Marketing Division, Norsk Hydro

Kim Traavik, political analyst/CSCE, Ministry of Foreign Affairs

Ola Tunander, research fellow, International Peace Research Institute, Oslo (PRIO)

Henry Valen, professor, Institute for Social Research (ISF)

Bjørn Vatne, research fellow, Central Bureau of Statistics

Morten Wetland, head of working group on legal affairs, Norwegian Foreign Ministry

SWEDEN (1989, 1990–91, 1993)

Carl Johan Åberg, chairman of Swedish Defense Commission

Nils Andrén, research scholar, Swedish Institute of International Affairs

Christer Asp, policy analyst, Ministry of Foreign Affairs

Sverker Åström, defense policy expert, advisor to Swedish government

Svante Blomqvist, vice president, European Market Service, Swedish Trade Council

Fredrik Branconier, foreign editor, *Svenska Dagbladet*

Lars Christiansson, senior vice president, head of Information Department, Federation of Swedish Industries

Mona Saint Cyr, member of Parliament

Robert Dalsjö, defense policy analyst, National Defense Research Establishment (FOA)

Ulf Dinkelspiel, head of Swedish-EC negotiations, Ministry of Foreign Affairs

Ingemar Dörfer, defense policy expert, National Defense Research Establishment (FOA)

Per-Ove Engelbrecht, head of department, Ministry of Industry

Kjell Goldmann, professor of political science, Stockholm University

Nils Gyldén, assistant undersecretary of defense for security policy and long-term planning, Ministry of Defense

Jonas Hafström, advisor to Carl Bildt, Conservative Party

Tom Hansen, Swedish military analyst, American Embassy in Stockholm

Per Holmstrand, legal adviser, Banking Division, Ministry of Finance

Bo Hugemark, instructor, Swedish Military Academy

Bo Huldt, director, Swedish Institute of International Affairs

Hans Jørn Holm, information officer, EC Commission in Sweden

Per Kjellson, Economic Division/EFTA, Ministry of Finance

Leif Leifland, foreign policy advisor to Swedish government

Hans Lindblad, member of Swedish Parliament, Liberal party

Jan Mörtberg, major, Planning Division, Swedish military

Lars Nyberg, Research Division/EC, Landsorganisationen (LO)

Svante Nycander, editor, *Dagens Nyheter*

Lars Oxelheim, professor, Industrial Institute for Economic and Social Research

Åke Pettersson, general secretary, Center Party

Sven Eric Söder, policy analyst, Ministry of Defense

Bengt Sundelius, professor of international relations, Stockholm University

Johan Tunberger, security policy research analyst, National Defense Research Establishment (FOA)

Margareta af Ugglas, member of Swedish Parliament, EC expert, Conservative Party

Krister Wahlbäck, policy analyst, Ministry of Foreign Affairs

Ingemar Wahlberg, policy analyst, Ministry of Defense

Hans Zettermark, research analyst, National Defense Research Establishment (FOA)

INTERVIEWS

CONTACTS IN FINLAND AND ICELAND

Finland

Pauli Järvenpää, Finnish defense advisor, Ministry of Defense, Helsinki

Tomas Ries, Finnish defense expert, Institute of International Studies, Geneva, Switzerland

Raimo Väyrynen, professor of international relations, University of Helsinki

Iceland

Pora Gylfadottir, head librarian, Statistics Iceland

Office of Jón Baldvin Hannibalsson, minister of foreign affairs and external trade

Appendix

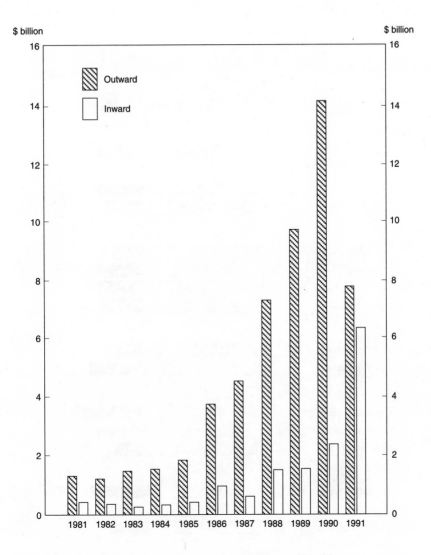

International direct investment from and to Sweden, 1981–91

Note: Balance-of-payments figures converted to dollars at average daily exchange rate
Source: OECD/DAF.

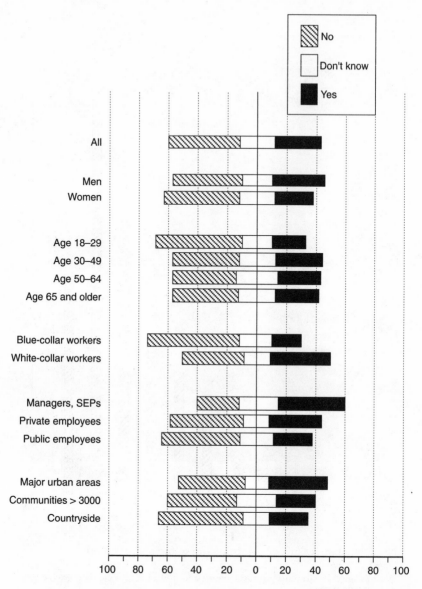

Public opinion, Sweden-EC, October 1993. If the referendum on Swedish EC membership were to take place today, would you vote yes or no?

Source: SIFO.

The Single European Act

In 1985, the Commission prepared a white paper outlining all the measures required for the completion of the internal market and established a timetable for implementation (by the end of 1992). At the European Council meeting in Luxembourg held in December 1985, the Single European Act (SEA) was approved by EC heads of state. The SEA was ratified by the member states in 1987.

The SEA specifies the conditions necessary to create a common market, or "unified economic territory," among the member states of the EC. The ambitions of the SEA include the reduction of trade barriers, the harmonization of member state activities (legislation, administration, and taxation), and the extension of cooperation in monetary affairs. The SEA revises the treaties establishing the European Community in the following manner:

The creation of an internal market for the free movement of goods, services, persons, and capital by January 1, 1993

The establishment of one common institutional and legal framework

Source: Office for Official Publications of the European Communities, *Treaties Establishing the European Communities: Treaties Amending These Treaties, Single European Act Resolutions-Declarations* (Luxembourg, 1987), pp. 1005–1058; Office for Official Publications of the European Communities, *European Unification: The Origins and Growth of the European Community* (Luxembourg, 1987), pp. 31–38.

207

The Maastricht Treaty

The Treaty on European Union (TEU) was negotiated by the member states in December 1991 at Maastricht in the Netherlands. The TEU significantly expands the depth of European political and economic cooperation among the members of the European Community in three areas: economic and monetary policy, common foreign and security policy, and justice and home affairs. The provisions of the treaty include the establishment of the following:

A European Union or EU

Specific criteria and stages of implementation for the creation of a common economic policy (convergence of inflation rates, government debt, and interest rates), central banking institutions (a European Monetary Institute and European system of central banks), and a single currency by the year 1999

A common European foreign and security policy, with intent to deepen cooperation in defense and strengthen the Western European Union (WEU)

A common legal basis for European citizenship and special rights

Cooperation in asylum, immigration, measures to combat drug trafficking, organized crime and fraud, and the creation of a European-wide police information-exchange system (Europol)

Other areas of European-wide collaboration included in the treaty are common rules on competition and taxation; common tariff and external commercial policies; social, educational, and environmental policy;

consumer protection; research and technological cooperation; and economic development goals for the member states and external regions.

Britain received an opt-out from the social dimension and monetary union. The British, however, remain involved in all subsequent negotiations regarding the implementation of the treaty.

Source: Treaty on European Union (Luxembourg, 1992), pp. 7–61; Edward McMillan-Scott, *Maastricht Card* (Yorkshire, U.K., 1997).

The Edinburgh Protocol

Danish rejection of the Maastricht Treaty on June 2, 1992, led to the negotiation of the Edinburgh Protocol between Denmark and the eleven members of the European Community on December 11–12, 1992. The Edinburgh Protocol exempts Denmark from participation in the following dimensions of European cooperation:

Currency union
A common foreign and security policy
Regulations for common citizenship

The Edinburgh Protocol is based on a document submitted by the Danish government to the EC outlining the reservations with the direction and substance of European supranationality. Full participation in the Maastricht Treaty is conditional upon public approval under Danish law.

Source: Danish Foreign Ministry, *Danmarks tiltrædelse af Edinburgh-Afgørelsen og Maastricht-Traktaten* (Copenhagen, 1993), pp. 4–6, 15–19.

The European Economic Area Agreement

The European Economic Area agreement (EEA) was negotiated between the six members of the European Free Trade Area agreement (Switzerland, Austria, Sweden, Finland, Norway, and Iceland) and the European Community. The agreement was signed in Oporto on May 2, 1992. According to the conditions of the treaty, the signatories of the EEA become part of a "homogeneous European economic area," the internal market for the free movement of goods, persons, services, and capital. The objectives of the EEA agreement include fair competition and closer cooperation in research and development, the environment, education, and social policy. Institutional and legal mechanisms established under the treaty (EEA Council, EEA Joint Parliamentary Committee, EEA Joint Committee, EFTA Surveillance Authority, and EFTA Court) are intended to ensure compliance by the contracting parties.

With the accession of Sweden, Austria, and Finland to the European Community on January 1, 1995, the EEA members are Norway and Iceland. The Swiss people vetoed the EEA agreement, and Switzerland is not a contracting party to the treaty.

Source: Agreement on the European Economic Area (Luxembourg: Office of the Official Publications of the European Communities, 1992), pp. 13–63.

Index

Cornell Studies in Political Economy

A SERIES EDITED BY PETER J. KATZENSTEIN